SATCHMO
BLOWS UP
THE WORLD

SATCHMO
BLOWS UP
THE WORLD

Jazz Ambassadors Play the Cold War

PENNY M. VON ESCHEN

Harvard University Press
Cambridge, Massachusetts
London, England
2004

Excerpts from *The Real Ambassadors,* by Dave and Iola Brubeck,
copyright © 1962, 1963 (renewed) Derry Music Company,
all rights reserved, used by permission.

Library of Congress Cataloging-in-Publication Data
Von Eschen, Penny M. (Penny Marie)
Satchmo blows up the world : jazz ambassadors
play the Cold War / Penny M. Von Eschen.
p.   cm.
Includes index.
ISBN 0-674-01501-0 (alk. paper)
1. Music and state—United States.   2. Cold War—Music and the war.
3. United States—Foreign relations—1945–1989.
4. Jazz musicians—Travel.   I. Title.
ML3795.V63   2004
781.65'092'273—dc22   2004047483

For Kevin and Maceo

Contents

Illustrations

SATCHMO
BLOWS UP
THE WORLD

CHAPTER 1

Ike Gets Dizzy

President Dwight D. Eisenhower got Dizzy in 1956—famed bebop trumpeter John Birks "Dizzy" Gillespie, that is—when Gillespie's integrated band embarked on the first government-sponsored jazz tour of the Middle East with the aid of the President's Emergency Fund.[1] Perhaps the only thing this diplomatic odd couple had in common was that they were both transplanted Southerners. Gillespie had been born on October 21, 1917, in the sleepy backwater of Cheraw, South Carolina. The young John Birks' South was noted for its African American Sanctified Church and its traveling jazz bands. He'd grown up in a house filled with instruments, getting his first trumpet from school and listening to national jazz broadcasts on a neighbor's radio. But Gillespie's South was also the South of ubiquitous white violence, the petty restrictions of Jim Crow segregation, and the crippling economic constraints that had led his family to relocate to Philadelphia in 1935. Gillespie would emerge from such humble beginnings as one of the most beloved and innovative musical geniuses of the twentieth century. A highly spiritual humanist who expressed his vision of world peace through adherence to the Baha'i faith, Gillespie was also a rebel who boldly challenged white America's appropriation of black music by creating a new style of music that couldn't, the musicians hoped, be easily copied. When Eisenhower got Dizzy, he certainly knew nothing of Gillespie's reputation as the hip and militant bebop artist who, in the mid-1940s, had teamed up with Charlie Parker and others to create the bebop revolution. The critic Whitney Balliett described Gillespie's style in the 1940s:

1

Few trumpeters have ever been blessed with so much technique. Gillespie never merely started a solo; he erupted into it. . . . [He] would hurl himself into the break, after a split-second pause with a couple of hundred notes that cork-screwed through several octaves, sometimes in triple time, and were carried in one breath, past the end of the break and well into the solo itself. . . . Gillespie's style at the time gave the impression—with its sharp, slightly acid tone, its cleavered phrase endings, its efflorescence of notes, and its brandishings about in the upper register—of being constantly on the verge of flying apart. However, his playing was held together by his extraordinary rhythmic sense.[2]

If the phrase "constantly on the verge of flying apart" captures the sound and sensibility of Gillespie's trumpet, it is also an apt description of Dwight Eisenhower's South as the first jazz tours began. Eisenhower had been born in Texas in 1890 to a Southern mother. Raised in Abilene, Kansas, "he was six years old when the Supreme Court established in *Plessy v. Ferguson* the 'separate but equal' doctrine of racial segregation as the law of the land."[3] As a boy, Eisenhower had often vacationed on a plantation with horse-drawn carriages driven by black servants. During an administration characterized by what the historian Thomas Borstelmann has described as the last hurrah of the old color line, Eisenhower was "troubled" that the Supreme Court, in its 1954 *Brown v. Board of Education* decision, showed concern for the feelings of black school-children rather than those of white Southern youngsters. He also resented the way the Court's decision strained his relationship with white Southerners, and declared at a 1958 news conference that "from babyhood I was raised to respect the word 'Confederate.'" Moreover, Eisenhower felt uneasy in the presence of black people "in any but subordinate positions," and during his administration the relatively easy access to the White House that prominent black Americans had enjoyed during the Truman years evaporated.[4] If Eisenhower's world was turned upside-down by the *Brown* decision, in December 1955, the same month that the Gillespie tour

1. *Dizzy Gillespie at Birdland,* New York City, 1955 or 1956. Courtesy of the Institute for Jazz Studies, Rutgers University.

was approved, the beginning of the Montgomery bus boycott, led by the young minister Martin Luther King Jr., inaugurated a new phase of the black freedom movement, ensuring that the jazz tours and the modern civil rights movement would be forever joined.

This unexpected joining of fates as Gillespie assumed the role of goodwill ambassador was doubly ironic. For with the stroke of a pen, this hitherto disreputable music—routinely associated in the mass media with drugs and crime—suddenly became America's music. Why did American policymakers feel for the first time in history that the country should be represented by jazz?

With America in the throes of a political and cultural revolution that had put the black freedom struggle at the center of American and international politics, the prominence of African American jazz artists was critical to the music's potential as a Cold War weapon. In the high-profile tours by Gillespie, Louis Armstrong,

Duke Ellington, and many others, U.S. officials pursued a self-conscious campaign against worldwide criticism of U.S. racism, striving to build cordial relations with new African and Asian states.[5] The glaring contradiction in this strategy was that the U.S. promoted black artists as goodwill ambassadors—symbols of the triumph of American democracy—when America was still a Jim Crow nation. Indeed, the primary contradiction of promoting African American artists as symbols of a racial equality yet to be achieved would fundamentally shape the organization and ideologies of the tours, as well as the ways in which the tours were contested by artists. And that U.S. officials would simultaneously insist on the universal, race-transcending quality of jazz while depending on the blackness of musicians to legitimize America's global agendas was an abiding paradox of the tours. Intended to promote a vision of color-blind American democracy, the tours foregrounded the importance of African American culture during the Cold War, with blackness and race operating culturally to project an image of American nationhood that was more inclusive than the reality.

When President Eisenhower requested special appropriations in "cultural and artistic fields" from the Senate in August 1954, he cited the "fabulous success of *Porgy and Bess,* playing to capacity houses in the extended tour of the free countries of Europe."[6] It is hardly surprising that Eisenhower supported cultural programs. He resented Europeans' depiction of the country as "a race of materialists" and was distressed that "our successes are described in terms of automobiles and not in terms of worthwhile culture of any kind."[7] But the fact that Eisenhower, resistant to change when it came to American race relations, named *Porgy and Bess* as an example of the importance of American culture abroad is telling. The Eisenhower administration had tried to counter Soviet charges of American racism through its financing of the four-year Cold War tour of *Porgy and Bess.* Performed throughout the United States, Europe, South America, and the Middle East, the production was directed by Robert Breed and featured Cab Calloway, opera star William Warfield as Porgy, and future opera star Leontyne Price as Bess. The rhetoric and tensions surrounding the *Porgy* tour foreshadowed the way struggles over artistic control and representations of race would intersect with shifting civil rights and Cold War politics throughout the period of the jazz tours.[8] Thus, despite the government's complacency on domestic race relations, even Eisenhower was profoundly affected by the widely shared sense that race was America's Achilles heel internationally.[9]

This insight shaped the government's cultural-presentation programs and resulted in the relative prominence of black American artists in the tours and the premium placed on integrated performance groups in all areas of the arts. It also produced the sense of urgency that would animate the tours. Cultural-presentation programs reflected the confidence that American leaders and diplomats felt in their ability to solve any problem and shape any situation to their liking. Writing to Secretary of State John Foster Dulles, Eisenhower described the initial $5 million budget as "funds to be used at my discretion to meet extraordinary or unusual circumstances arising in the international field" and requested that Dulles maintain "close personal contact with the program."[10] Indeed, in what might be described as a "can-do" foreign-policy culture, which extended across Democratic as well as Republican administrations, policymakers exhibited extraordinary confidence in America's ability to shape the world in its image with whatever tools it had, be they covert operations, carpet bombing, or jazz musicians. Indeed, given Eisenhower and Dulles' preference for covert action over conventional warfare (covert techniques were elevated to a cult of counterinsurgency by the time of the Kennedy administration), it is not surprising that many of the jazz tours appear to have moved in tandem with CIA operations.[11] As exemplified in Eisenhower's response to *Porgy and Bess* and his acceptance of the jazz tours, his well-honed sense of expediency superseded his well-documented condescension toward African Americans and "the race question."

Cold War foreign policy, the black American freedom movement, and sweeping changes in American cultural life converged to produce the dynamic synergy that animated the programs. Special appropriations designated for the President's Emergency Fund in the fall of 1954 were extended and formalized by the 84th Congress on August 1, 1956, as the President's Special International Program.[12] Initially supervised by the State Department in conjunction with the American National Theatre and Academy (ANTA), the programs involved an expansive notion of culture and a wide array of the arts. Yet very quickly jazz became the pet project of the State Department, the ideological heart and soul of the tours. Unlike classical music, theater, or ballet, jazz could be embraced by U.S. officials as a uniquely American art form.[13] Government officials and supporters of the arts hoped to offset what they perceived as European and Soviet superiority in classical music and ballet, while at the same time shielding America's Achilles heel by demonstrating racial equality in action.

Yet this compelling propaganda ploy was hardly the idea of the State Department. The idea of promoting jazz musicians as cultural ambassadors was the brainchild of an alliance of musicians, civil rights proponents, and cultural entrepreneurs and critics. The precise mechanics of how Ike got Dizzy as the first official jazz ambassador may never be clear. Since the Gillespie tour, and the early cultural-presentation programs in general, emerged in a highly opportunistic and haphazard fashion, records of the protean institutional life remain spotty. But it is clear that Adam Clayton Powell Jr., the controversial Democratic congressman from Harlem and long-time civil rights advocate, was instrumental in setting up the Gillespie gig. A figure steeped in the world of Harlem, who was then married to jazz singer, pianist, and organist Hazel Scott, Powell served as a crucial mediator between the jazz world and the government. According to a November 1955 *New York Times* report quoting Powell, the State Department had told him "that it would go along with his proposal to send fewer ballets and symphonies abroad and put more emphasis on what he called real Americana."[14] Wielding the new diplomatic authority he had gained earlier that year at the Asian-African Conference of Nonaligned Nations in

Bandung, Indonesia (he had defied the State Department by attending but then emerged as an unabashed defender of the West), Powell sketched a vision in which band leaders such as Gillespie, Armstrong and Count Basie and their bands would be sent "into countries where communism has a foothold."[15]

But if the mechanics of Eisenhower's getting Gillespie as the first jazz ambassador are obscure, much has been revealed about the broader contours of how Ike and his generational counterparts got dizzy as their world was irrevocably altered by a global rebellion against white supremacy.[16] The near-simultaneity of the Bandung Conference with the outset of the tours, and the convergence of Powell's roles as pro-Western diplomat, civil rights activist, and champion of jazz, were no accident. Indeed, for all the talk of Cold War with the Soviets, Powell's sense—deeply shared with Eisenhower and Dulles—that the conflict would be played out in the nonaligned and newly independent emerging nations of the Middle East, Asia, and Africa provided the blueprint for the early tours.[17] Between the end of World War II and 1960, as the United States consolidated its new position as the dominant global power, forty countries revolted against colonialism and won their independence.[18] Henry Luce's vision of the "American Century" had attempted to legitimize U.S. power with the claim that it served the interests of all by promoting economic expansion, national sovereignty, global peace, and security. But in practice these goals often collided with the global movement against white supremacy and colonialism. All too often, U.S. policymakers found themselves in what Nikhil Singh has described as the self-interested role of "patron of older imperialisms and an agent of specifically capitalist freedoms."[19] Indeed, the story of the tours disrupts a bipolar view of the Cold War and takes us into a far more tangled, and far more violent, jockeying for power and control of global resources than that glimpsed through the lens of U.S.-Soviet conflict.

Aiming to spread jazz globally in order to win converts to "the American way of life," proponents of the tours cited the popularity of jazz in Europe to make their case. African American soldiers who remained in Europe after World War I and World War II created the first European and international audiences for jazz. Many members of the Harlem Hellfighters—volunteers in New York's 15th Heavy Foot Infantry Regiment during World War I—chose to remain in France after they were demobilized. An African American community formed on the Right Bank in Paris, drawn by better employment opportunities, freedom from the discrimination faced in the States, and a high demand for black musicians. In clubs such as Le Grand Duc—run by Eugène Jacques Bullard, the first black combat pilot who had flown for France during the war—African Americans transformed the Montmartre area and contributed to the development of Paris as a crucial site for black performance and interaction in the period.[20] Buoyed by the energy of the expatriates, the jazz scene of Paris and other European cities received a boost from the steady increase in the circulation of jazz records and in the number of concert and club tours by American jazz groups. By the time of the State Department jazz tours, band leaders including Louis Armstrong, Duke Ellington, and Dizzy Gillespie had been touring Europe for years, often finding the tours more lucrative and the audiences more appreciative than those in the States. Ironically, the official State Department cultural-presentation programs in Western Europe did not include jazz, precisely because jazz was considered already established, popular, and commercially viable.[21] To U.S. officials in the late 1950s, that battle for hearts and minds in Western Europe had already been won. The new battles focused on the loyalties of those in the nations currently emerging from decades of colonialism.

Leonard Feather, the British-born jazz critic and host of the first Voice of America jazz program (*Jazz Club USA,* which hit the airwaves in 1952), stumbled onto this expatriate jazz world during what he described as a rebellion against his suburban Hampstead upper-middle-class Jewish upbringing. Feather was "hooked" the first time he heard Louis Armstrong's "West-End Blues," when a friend took him to a record shop on lunch break from school. After graduating from high school in the early 1930s, Feather spent six months in Berlin and several months in Paris, discovering in each an enthusiasm for jazz that had "elements in common with membership in a resistance movement."[22] Indeed, Armstrong was later banned in Nazi-occupied Europe and "came to symbolize the freedoms associated with Allied culture [as] his recordings were clandestinely distributed and imitated in live performances by attaching 'coded' titles to the songs."[23] Rushing back from Paris when he learned that Armstrong was to play at the London Palladium, Feather was transfixed by Armstrong's opener "Sleepy Time Down South" and profoundly moved when he was able to talk with Armstrong and his future wife, Alpha: "That they were not merely approachable but affable and treated me like an equal was almost more than I could comprehend."[24] The next year, Feather heard Duke Ellington on his "maiden voyage" to Europe, and although he could never have imagined that he would be working for Ellington a decade later, he had embarked on his life's work of producing records and concerts and lecturing on music. As Feather followed his obsession with jazz, he also learned that the triumphant European tours of the music's black pioneers were "greeted with total silence" in America (with the exception of the black press). For Feather, the encounter with jazz in its role as an antifascist music of resistance, and the discovery of what he termed the "white curtain which hung over an Afro-American art form lest someone on home ground become aware of its importance," would forever shape his sense of jazz as the music of African Americans and a music intimately bound up with the struggle for social justice.[25]

As illustrated by Feather's first meeting with Armstrong, the emergence of the trumpeter as "Ambassador Satch" prior to the inauguration of the official tours demonstrates the ways in which musicians and critics brought jazz to the center of the international stage. The sobriquet "Ambassador Satch" was coined by Columbia record producer George Avakian. But the inspiration was Armstrong's international stature. Indeed, where the tours were concerned, Armstrong led the way and the State Department followed.

Armstrong had made his first European trip in 1932. Twenty-three years later, his celebrated swing through Europe began in Stockholm on October 2 and included a three-week stand at Paris' Olympic Theater and concerts in Barcelona, before ending in Frankfurt on December 29, fueling the excitement that led to the government tours.[26] In November 1955, just three weeks before the approval of the first government-sponsored jazz tours, Felix Belair, Stockholm correspondent for the *New York Times,* proclaimed that "America's secret weapon is a blue note in a minor key" and named Louis "Satchmo" Armstrong as "its most effective ambassador." Belair had been in Geneva covering the decidedly unsuccessful East-West conference of November 1955 when Armstrong passed through Switzerland on this triumphant tour, which would be commemorated on the Columbia album *Ambassador Satch,* produced by Avakian. "What many thoughtful Europeans cannot understand," wrote Belair, "is why the United States Government, with all the money it spends for so-called propaganda to promote democracy, does not use more of it to subsidize the continental travels of jazz bands. . . . American jazz has now become a universal language. It knows no national boundaries, but everyone knows where it comes from and where to look for more."[27] Reading jazz as part of a heroic Cold War struggle for democracy, Belair argued: "Men have actually risked their lives to smuggle recordings of it behind the Iron Curtain and by methods that the profit motive cannot explain."[28] If, as Belair suggested, the U.S. government was a bit slow to catch on to the political value of jazz, the State Department would soon take up Belair's suggestion with a missionary zeal.

Despite Belair's celebration of Armstrong's role, other coverage of Armstrong's tour underscores the difficulties faced by musicians and black artists in particular, as critics and diplomats alike began to recognize the international appeal of jazz. A *Newsweek* critic explained that "the simple emotional impact of jazz cuts through all manner of linguistic and ideological barriers, and Louis Armstrong becomes an extraordinary kind of roving American ambassador of goodwill."[29] That this *Newsweek* critic could glibly claim that jazz worked through "simple emotional impact" while lionizing Armstrong as an ambassador suggests the writer's lack of appreciation for Armstrong's extraordinary skills. The *Newsweek* article was typical: often, Armstrong was not credited or appreciated as a disciplined artist and innovative musical genius, but viewed as a natural purveyor of something simple and uncomplicated. Indeed, when establishment and mainstream writers equated jazz with the central Cold War trope of freedom, they were depending, in part, on what musicologist Ingrid Monson has argued was a deeply problematic assumption that what was fundamental to jazz was "spontaneity," not discipline, rhythm, or the nuanced musical conversations entailed in improvisation.[30]

Adding insult to injury, the *Newsweek* writer condescendingly characterized Armstrong's assessment of the tours as "extremely uncomplicated." According to the article, Armstrong had commented: "When I played Berlin, a lot of them Russian cats jumped the Iron Fence to hear Satchmo, which goes to prove that music is stronger than nations."[31] *Newsweek*'s patronizing tone obscured Armstrong's fundamental role not simply in the State Department tours, but also in the effort to provide an alternative image of America to foreign audiences impatient with what they saw as American hypocrisy. In fact, Armstrong's views of the tours were quite complex.

Bassist Arvell Shaw, who traveled with Armstrong on the 1955 European trip and his later State Department tour of Africa, declared: "No boundary was closed to Louis."[32] And indeed Armstrong, raised in poverty in Jim Crow America, knew a lot more about crossing boundaries than most Americans. Shaw captured the stature and charisma of Ambassador Satch in action on a later gig in East Berlin.

We opened in East Berlin, and after a couple of nights there was nothing to do. When we got off, the streets were dark. No restaurants—we were lucky to get a roll and coffee. West Berlin was swinging, and Louis said: "Let's go to West Berlin." Can't do that with papers from Russians in East Berlin and from the U.S. Louis said, "Let's go anyway." So we got on the bus—Checkpoint Charlie—to go through the Berlin Wall. We got to the East German side, and the Russian soldiers and East German police had their guns out. One of the guards looked at us and said "Louis Armstrong." He called out all the guards, got Louis' autograph and waved us all on. And when we got to the American side, a six-foot-seven sergeant from Texas—oh, he was fierce!—said, "How'd you get through here? Where are your papers?" And he got out handcuffs. Sergeant looks and says, "Satchmo—this is Satchmo!" He called the guards and they got autographs and waved us on. Every night we went back and forth. When the American ambassador heard, he said: "How'd you do that? I can't do that!"[33]

From 1955 on, Armstrong was greeted enthusiastically by foreign audiences wherever he went. Whether on official State Department tours such as his 1960–1961 African trip, or on unofficial journeys such as those to Ghana in 1956, Latin America in 1957, and East Berlin, Armstrong was Ambassador Satch.[34]

As suggested by Armstrong's insight that music transcends national boundaries—and as Armstrong himself would soon demonstrate on his unofficial tour to Ghana only a few months later—the tours would not only take musicians across national borders, but would open an avenue for pursuing civil rights, solidarity, and musical exchange in a transnational arena. Armstrong, along with other African American musicians, would also bring an expansive sense of democracy and utopian politics—rooted in African American traditions—to their friendships with those behind the Iron Curtain, as well as a new embrace of Afro-diasporic connections and a deep interest in African independence. Paradoxically, as tours allowed the expression of certain kinds of pan-African or universalist sentiments, the appeals and interventions made by musicians were pointed and adamant precisely because they understood their unique position as representatives of a globally ascendant nation.[35]

"This is a diplomatic mission of the utmost delicacy. The question is, who's the best man for it—John Foster Dulles or Satchmo?"

2. *Cartoon* by Mischa Richter, *New Yorker,* April 19, 1958. Copyright © by the *New Yorker.*

The Voice of America (VOA) radio broadcasts by Leonard Feather and Willis Conover helped to lay the groundwork for the emergence of the jazz ambassadors. Following Feather's short-lived *Jazz Club USA* (1952), Conover's jazz show, *Music USA,* began in 1955 and continued for more than three decades. It is tempting—and not altogether inaccurate—to claim that Conover was a figure of unparalleled importance in the spread of jazz and in its relationship to Cold War foreign policy. Indeed, when Conover died in 1996, his *New York Times* obituary not only proclaimed him the most widely known and loved American in the world; it further suggested that Conover had played a major role in bringing about the collapse of Communism—a claim that Conover himself had proudly embraced.[36] When the thirty-five year old Buffalo-born disc jockey was selected in a Voice of America audition, his qualifications included mellifluous, precise speech readily "understood by foreigners with little English," and an intimate knowledge of jazz. The show was launched over short-wave radio on January 6, 1955. Conover was paid fifty dollars per week. According to *Look* magazine, "powerful VOA relay stations in Tangier and later Munich beamed the pilot program toward the jazz-happy Scandinavian countries, only to receive a flood of letters from points east as far as Iran." Indeed, mail came in from all over Europe, Africa, and Asia, including countries behind the Iron Curtain. In response to listeners' complaints that *Music USA* was aired at the "craziest hours," VOA responded by broadcasting the show all over the world each evening at peak listening hours, at slots just before and after the evening news. In 1955 it reached an estimated 30 million people in eighty countries—a number that would more than triple, to 100 million, over the next decade. Drawing on Conover's own collection of 40,000 records, the shows were recorded on tape in Washington and broadcast from VOA stations a month later. One typical show from 1956 included Count Basie's swinging "Straight Life," Joe Newman's "Midgets," Charlie Parker's "Air Conditioning," the Modern Jazz Quartet's "Django," oldtime New Orleans trumpeter Papa Celestin's "When the Saints Go Marching In," cornetist Bix Beiderbecke's "Singin' the Blues," and a rousing number called "I'm All Bound 'Round with the Mason Dixon Line" by the day's interviewee, Dixieland trumpeter Jimmy McPartland.[37] Tapes of VOA jazz broadcasts sold for as much as forty rubles (forty-four dollars) on the Moscow black market in 1962. The Egyptian weekly *Al Zaa* declared that "Conover's daily program has won the United States more friends than any other daily activity."[38] By November 1955, after just ten months, *Music USA* had prompted more than ten thousand letters from fans in places ranging from "Tangiers to Tahiti."[39] The show's opening theme was the Duke Ellington Orchestra's signature piece— "Take the A Train," by Billy Strayhorn—which was followed by Conover's salutation,

3. *Louis Armstrong and Willis Conover at the VOA microphone,* Washington, D.C., June 28, 1955. Courtesy of the Louis Armstrong House and Archives, Queens College, New York City.

"Time for jazz!" Broadcasting for one hour, seven days a week, fifty-two weeks a year, Conover had enormous influence on how audiences throughout the globe listened to what *Time* magazine called this "valuable exportable U.S. commodity, jazz."[40]

Yet Conover's rise to fame depended not only on the prior presence of African American jazz musicians abroad, but also on the infrastructure of America's emerging global dominance. In promoting jazz and American consumer culture, U.S. officials appeared unwilling to abide by their own counsel to developing nations—namely, to trust in "people's capitalism." Too impatient to wait for the market to work its magic, the United States Information Agency (USIA) accelerated the process by distributing thousands—perhaps hundreds of thousands—of transistor radios throughout Asia, Africa, and the Middle East so that people could tune in to defenses of U.S. foreign policy, along with such radio broadcasts as Conover's *Music USA*. This USIA decision was critical in producing the enormous audience for Conover's jazz programs.[41]

U.S. officials quickly caught on to the fact that jazz was more valuable than didactic programming. Through informal polls taken at exhibitions, State Department and USIA officials learned that Soviet citizens tended to resent what they regarded as the heavy-handed propaganda of Radio Free Europe (RFE). In contrast, they welcomed VOA's cultural programming, and Conover's jazz programs ranked as the most popular. Conover himself was adamant about avoiding "overt pro-American or anti-Communist propaganda." For Conover and the VOA staff, "jazz is its own propaganda." Radio Free Europe appeared to take heed of its relative weakness when it set up "a pidgin foreign language school for U.S. jazz musicians." Musicians—including Earl Hines, Chet Baker, Cal Tjader, Woody Herman, Dave Brubeck, Duke Ellington, Roy Eldridge, Lionel Hampton, Stan Getz, Dizzy Gillespie, and Oscar Peterson—were taught words and phrases in Czech, Polish, Romanian, Bulgarian, and Hungarian, phrases which they used in taped interviews with RFE's Czech disc jockey Eva Stanlova. The interviews were then aired along with records by the featured jazz artists.[42]

While Conover shunned overt propaganda, he believed deeply in the political importance and potential of jazz. He described jazz as "structurally parallel to the American political system" and saw its structure as embodying American freedom: "Jazz musicians agree in advance on what the harmonic progression is going to be, in what key, how fast and how long, and within that agreement they are free to play anything they want." For people behind the Iron Curtain, "jazz represents something that is entirely different from their traditions."[43] Conover believed that people who were denied freedom in their political culture could detect a sense of freedom in jazz. Riffing on the popular governmental distinctions of the day, he declared: "Jazz is a cross between total discipline and total anarchy. The musicians agree on tempo, key and chord structure but beyond this everyone is free to express himself. This is jazz. And this is America. That's what gives this music validity. It's a musical reflection of the way things happen in America. We're not apt to recognize this over here, but people in other countries can feel this element of freedom. They love jazz because they love freedom."[44]

Such arguments linking jazz to freedom paralleled arguments that were being made about abstract expressionism.[45] Many Cold War intellectuals shared with Alfred Barr, director of the Museum of Modern Art, the view that "modern artists' nonconformity and love of freedom cannot be tolerated within a monolithic tyranny." For Barr, "abstract art was synonymous with democracy" and was on "our side" in the Cold War struggle.[46] Yet jazz could speak to America's Achilles heel of racism in way that a painting by Mark Rothko or Jackson Pollock could not. For Conover, jazz helps people "to identify themselves with America" and "corrects the fiction that America is racist."[47] Jazz artists likewise reflected on the relationships between jazz, freedom, democracy, and racism, but often with views that were subtly and not so subtly different from those held by Conover. For many of these artists, the democratic ideals of American society were something to aspire to, not something achieved. Jazz, democracy, freedom, and civil rights were evolving entities and their relationships had not yet been resolved.

Even as artists and critics were promoting jazz's status as America's "classical" music (Duke Ellington's term) and its diplomatic value, its newfound utility as a Cold War weapon was aiding its rehabilitation in mainstream popular culture. Writing in *Billboard,* which called itself "the amusement industry's leading newsweekly," Burt Korall noted jazz's "recently acquired vestments of legitimacy and respectability." This formerly "forbidden fruit" had not only gained acceptance in the media, including film, clubs, records, concerts, and books in its "native perimeter of the U.S.," but had extended its "shadow forward to the world through the medium of the radio." For Korall, "the Voice of America, Radio Free Europe, and the Armed Forces Radio Network have exposed much of Europe, Asia, and Africa to the Sounds of Jazz. . . . Jazz has succeeded where American diplomats have floundered. It has created a meeting ground, been something that made for a deeper understanding of the American way of life, for to be interested in jazz is to be interested in things American."[48] Indeed, by the mid-1950s jazz was widely celebrated in establishment and middlebrow circles alike as a pivotal cultural weapon of the Cold War—in newspapers and magazines ranging from the *New York Times* and *Newsweek* to the *Reader's Digest* and *Variety*.

In a period when big bands were breaking up and jazz record sales were declining as a result of the ascendancy of rock and roll and rhythm and blues, critics and musicians were defending their own status and that of jazz against widespread associations with criminality, drugs, and behavior regarded as deviant. Jazz critics successfully promoted the view, later embraced by the State Department, that jazz held a culture-transcending, universal appeal. Critics John Wilson and Marshall Stearns served on the State Department's music-selection committees. Wilson reviewed jazz for the *New York Times;* Stearns was president of the Institute of Jazz Studies (Rutgers University) and taught courses on jazz appreciation at Hunter College in New York City. Wilson, Stearns, and other critics who selected artists for State Department tours embraced modernism as a way of distinguishing American art from classical Soviet and European forms. Jazz, they claimed, was the most original product of American modernism.

The meaning, contours, and value of modernism would remain contested throughout the tours. But critics promoted art forms such as modern dance and jazz not only for their purported relationship to democracy, but for their clear differences from classical music and ballet—forms in which Russian and European artists traditionally dominated.[49] In a world of fierce ideological competition, political supporters of the cultural-presentation programs, as well as jazz and dance critics and patrons of the arts who served on the selection committees, saw the United States as lagging behind the Soviet Union in terms of funding for the arts. Speaking before a House Appropriations hearing in 1956, Representative Frank Thompson Jr., Democrat from New Jersey, described U.S. cultural programs as a "counter-offensive" against the highly effective Soviet program. According to Thompson, the United States was "behind the Communists in our cultural appeal. Throughout the world, they were (and still are) denouncing us as materialistic, uncultured barbarians, soulless. They spoke sneeringly of our 'gadget' civilization."[50] Defending the integrity of American art against such slights, many critics on the selection committees promoted American modernism as an effective counter to Soviet promotion of folk art and classical ballet productions. Adamant about distinguishing between art and entertainment, they emphasized art forms in which Americans were undisputed leaders and innovators. For these critics, modernism was the most effective way of advocating art forms that could be seen as uniquely American.[51]

In the quest by musicians and critics to have jazz recognized as legitimate art, the subsequent canonization of jazz as high modernism proved to be a double-edged sword. On the one hand, it countered the perceptions exemplified in *Newsweek*'s condescending view that jazz was a simple folk form. On the other hand, it abstracted jazz from its origins in African American working-class culture, which would also have linked it to what was consistently disparaged as "mere entertainment." Indeed, given the widespread adherence to a color-blind liberalism that assumed "black" and "modern" were incompatible, many critics could only elevate jazz to modernism by dissociating it from black culture.[52] But downplaying the African American cultural and social origins of jazz and insisting on the separation of art from entertainment led to myriad contradictions. For example, to suggest that Armstrong was not an entertainer is as implausible as the claim that he was not an artist. As critics met in private to debate the selection of artists, U.S. officials in the field confronted local audiences with their own tastes and sets of expectations. There was constant tension between the view of jazz as high modernist art and the view of jazz as popular culture meant to appeal to the masses.

The claim on the part of critics, and later the State Department, that jazz embodied a unique American freedom transcending race collided with many musicians' experiences of jazz as deeply embedded in African American history and cultural practices. Black artists jumped into the fray in these debates, invoking what Paul Gilroy has called a black counterculture of modernity.[53] In the era of modernism and the multifaceted American state-sponsored projects of global modernization, many black artists had their own deep investment in the notion of modernity.[54] For those whose lives and professional careers had been molded amid the quotidian terror and humiliating constraints of segregation—and this is true of virtually all the black artists, since the tours began a full nine years prior to the formal dismantling of Jim Crow—the "modern" connoted mobility and freedom, a cosmopolitan future where the tremendous constrictions of race in America would be transcended. Yet if black artists and writers embraced modernity, it was a "counterculture" of modernity, as musicians continued to confront such products of modernity as a racial, social, economic, and political order crafted from the vestiges of slavery. Moreover, artists such as Gillespie, Duke Ellington, and many others engaged in a complex debate, albeit often indirectly, with proponents of artistic modernism as they resisted in myriad ways the construction of a hierarchical and exclusionary modernist canon that had no place for the hybrid sensibility characterizing black diasporic forms.[55]

Yet the reading of jazz as high modernism remained compelling to critics on the selection committees, as they tried to reconcile its appeal abroad with their insistence that America promote its best and most unique (distinguishable from European and Soviet) modern art. Seeking a distinctly American alternative to Soviet and European dominance in the arts, the program committees became venues for debating what was considered "modern" and "uniquely American" in dance, art, and music.

Women were at a distinct disadvantage in this postwar modernism. This was evident in the critics' rejection of the jazz composer and pianist Mary Lou Williams and the choreographer Katherine

Dunham. Suggesting again the paradoxical image of jazz both as high modernism and an alluring "forbidden fruit," those responsible for choosing artists appeared to be concerned first and foremost with improprieties linked to sex and drugs. When politics did enter the picture, the experiences of men were interpreted differently from those of women. Dizzy Gillespie had been a card-carrying member of the Communist Party because it enabled him to get gigs in CP halls. Later, in the 1970s, Charles Mingus, long known for his outspokenness, was accused of attempting to disseminate his pro–civil rights and antiwar politics through his song titles while on a State Department–sponsored Newport Jazz Festival tour of Eastern Europe. Yet rather than challenging Mingus, much less punishing him, officials simply altered the titles for the playbills.[56] Officials as well as the critics responsible for choosing the artists seemed to delight in what they saw as the eccentricities of male artists. The behavior and political views of women artists were not viewed so indulgently. When Mary Lou Williams was rejected by the music committee in 1958, she was a deeply respected, much admired, and beloved member of New York City's jazz world. She hosted a jazz salon in her Harlem apartment where colleagues Dizzy Gillespie, Bud Powell, Art Tatum, Thelonious Monk, and others would exchange ideas with their hostess, an acknowledged master of composition and arranging.[57] Dizzy Gillespie's Big Band for example, performed pieces of what would become Williams' *Zodiac Suite* in the 1940s. Later, Williams joined the Gillespie Band for a performance of the suite at the 1957 Newport Jazz Festival. Duke Ellington described Williams as "perpetually contemporary. Her writing and performing are and always have been just a little ahead. . . . She is like soul on soul."[58] Jazz critics John Wilson and Marshall Stearns, however, regarded Williams as too "unstable" for a State Department tour, citing her "religious fanaticism" and her recent withdrawal from public performances.[59] The construction of Williams as unstable contrasts sharply with views of such male musicians as Sonny Rollins and John Coltrane, who also went through a period of spiritual withdrawal from public life in the

1950s, beginning in Paris in 1953. To many jazz writers, Rollins and Coltrane were on a heroic journey of self-discovery, developing and enriching their art. Williams, on the hand, was just "crazy."[60] The dancer and choreographer Katherine Dunham was repeatedly rejected for the State Department tours that were much coveted by dancers. The critics' debate over the worthiness of Dunham's art and their ultimate unwillingness to support her hinged precisely on the issue of whether she was producing art or "catering to popular taste and producing cheap entertainment." One panelist said that "the last time he saw her she had become theatrical in the cheapest sense." Dunham however, felt that her lack of support from the international exchange program and the State Department was a response to her piece *Southland,* a confrontational ballet about lynching.[61]

If music critics fastened onto jazz as America's "secret weapon," a unique American art form with which the Soviets could not compete, dance critics continued to reference a European-centered canon and were unable to recognize Dunham's brilliance as an anthropologist and choreographer in her interpretations of African diasporic dance. Moreover, Mingus' song titles notwithstanding, instrumental jazz and much of modern dance were embraced by some as nonrepresentational, paralleling the government support of such abstract painters as Mark Rothko and Jackson Pollock from the 1940s onward. However innovative its aesthetic form, the overt political content of *Southland* violated these modernist standards. Although jazz lent itself to more ambiguous readings, on jazz tours all over the world the question of art-versus-entertainment remained a matter of contention.

State Department cultural policy was often as improvised (though not as skillfully) as the solos of jazz artists. Compared to other nations, including Mexico and the countries of Europe, the United States has been relatively indifferent to culture and cultural policy.[62] Instead, government policy has often promoted the idea that the market itself is the highest cultural value, leaving Hollywood and the music industry to implement what Reinhold Wagnleitner has termed the Marilyn Monroe Doctrine and the policy of Rock 'n' Roll-back.[63] When the government did support the arts, as in such New Deal programs as the Federal Theatre Project and the Federal Writers' Project or its support of abstract expressionist painting in the 1940s, such efforts met with sharp opposition.[64] Though arguments linking freedom and modernist art helped to establish the Museum of Modern Art and led to the display of Jackson Pollock canvases in U.S. embassies throughout Eastern Europe, government funding of abstract art was "vigorously contested in Congress," where conservatives denounced it as subversive and "un-American."[65] As Frances Stonor Saunders has demonstrated, such criticism of government sponsorship of the arts led to more covert efforts by the Central Intelligence Agency. During the Cold War, the agency provided clandestine support for many purportedly independent artistic and intellectual projects throughout the world.[66]

Far from covert, the jazz tours were highly visible and celebrated in the media. But like the earlier support of abstract painting, state sponsorship of jazz was under constant attack from conservatives. And in a dynamic more suggestive of the USIA, whose propaganda was for export only, prohibited by law from distribution within the United States, State Department officials frequently tried to shield the integrationist and modernist imagery of the tours from crucial audiences at home. Perhaps, in some minds, the tour evoked the cultural radicalism of an earlier popular-front culture.[67] Duke Ellington for example, had been active in an integrationist popular-front culture. His production *Black, Brown and Beige* had challenged racial hierarchies in the 1940s, and he had collaborated with librettist John LaTouche on the musical *Beggar's Holiday,* which made its debut as a fundraiser for the Council on African Affairs, a radical anticolonial organization.[68] Performing-arts tours even made occasional use of groups such as the Golden Gate Quartet, who were championed by leftist audiences. Yet to see New Deal–era programs as antecedents for the jazz tours implies an institutional memory among policymakers that simply didn't exist. The tours were a contingent product of a fluid and indeed chaotic transformation within American culture and in global power relations. Accordingly, it was an "emergency" fund that Eisenhower approved when he launched the tours.

It was precisely the absence of a coherent cultural policy that created a space for a unique alliance of artists, supporters of the arts, and liberals within the State Department to project a jazz vision of America throughout the globe. Indeed, following from the haphazard and accidental ways in which the jazz tours emerged, the tours suggest the open-ended and unpredictable nature of cultural exchange. If policymakers grasped the possibility of appealing to emerging nations and the Eastern bloc through jazz, they never dreamed that the musicians would bring their own agendas. Nor did they anticipate that artists and audiences would interact, generating multiple meanings and effects unanticipated by the State Department.

The positioning of jazz musicians as ambassadors in the State Department tours was both peculiar and enabling. Summoned from the margins of their society to represent the nation, their status calls to mind the anonymous narrator of Ralph Ellison's 1952 classic *Invisible Man,* for whom jazz provided aural evidence of "invisibility," the condition of being black in postwar America. The musicians were paradoxically highly visible as goodwill ambassadors, but also in crucial ways invisible, as actors with social concerns and political viewpoints that were ignored by State Department bureaucracy. For the narrator of *Invisible Man,* invisibility "gives one a slightly different sense of time, you're never quite on the beat. Sometimes you're ahead and sometimes behind. . . . And you slip into the breaks and look around." Invoking Louis Armstrong, the narrator continues: "That's what you hear vaguely in Louis' music."[69] Here, to be invisible is not simply to be unacknowledged or dismissed. Instead, one sees better, or more, because of the way one is positioned. Tracing the steps of Armstrong and the other jazz musicians who toured for the State Department during the Cold War offers an alternative position from which to view post-1945 international dynamics, and a way of slipping between multiple sets of official archives and areas of study (music, diplomacy, civil rights). The tours allowed the musicians to "slip into the breaks," to see around the corners of the neat story most Americans were told by their government with regard to Cold War foreign policy. The narrator of *Invisible Man* also suggests a methodology for understanding the musicians' approach to the world and the way they made sense of their surroundings. Jazz musicians didn't simply accept the way they were deployed by the State Department. Whether fostering informal musical connections after hours or backstage, pursuing romantic liaisons, or expressing political opinions in interviews and on stage, musicians slipped into the breaks and looked around, intervening in official narratives and playing their own changes on Cold War perspectives. Following the narrator's suggestion that there is a parallel between this particular stance toward the world and the aesthetics of jazz, one might "vaguely" suggest, as the narrator puts its, that jazz offers an alternative approach to the arena of politics, and specifically to international diplomacy. Indeed, the language of diplomacy, like jazz, is about time—but in the case of diplomacy, language is premised on assumptions about modernity and backwardness, the developed and underdeveloped. Furthermore, diplomacy is concerned with the necessity of doing what has to be done at a particular moment.[70] Approaching diplomacy from the stance of the musicians, the jazz approach suggested by *Invisible Man* finds the "breaks," the discontinuities and unevenness in diplomacy's attempts to manage historical time. Following Armstrong, Gillespie, and other jazz musicians into the interstices between the official stories reveals a unique glimpse into the magnitude and hubris of the multifaceted American projects of global expansion in the post–World War II world, exposing troubling questions about the character of American global power in the decades that spanned the collapse of formal European colonialism.

When Ike got Dizzy, he got a lot more than he bargained for. The State Department tours illuminated connections and collisions between domestic and foreign policies, and between race, nation, and modernism. The immediate success of the tours testified to the newfound importance of jazz, but vociferous opposition to the tours indicated deep fissures within the nation. In April 1956, with the Gillespie tour under way and four months into the Montgomery bus boycott, the White Citizens Council of Alabama, formed to resist desegregation, announced its opposition to jazz, which it called a "plot to mongrelize America" engineered by the National Association for the Advancement of Colored People (NAACP). According to *Newsweek,* Asa E. Carter, leader of the North Alabama Citizens Council, had said that "be-bop, 'Rock and Roll,' and all Negro Music" were designed to force "Negro culture" on the South.[71] Indeed, for Eisenhower and his conservative and Southern segregationist allies, to have bebop trumpeter Dizzy Gillespie representing the nation portended the end of the world as they knew it.[72]

CHAPTER 2

Swinging into Action

Jazz to the Rescue

The haphazard and improvised beginning of the jazz tours created a space for musicians to assert their own vision of cultural exchange and democracy. But particularly in the early tours, it left the musicians vulnerable to logistical chaos and the consequences of diplomatic bravado, as well as setting them up as targets for American conservatives. The first major jazz tours—Dizzy Gillespie to the Middle East in 1956, Benny Goodman to South East Asia in 1957, and Dave Brubeck to Poland and the Middle East in 1958—sent the musicians straight into the middle of Cold War hotspots and global crises. Indeed, the tours were intimately linked to U.S. responses to such crises, and exposed a freewheeling, bold willingness on the part of policymakers to wield covert and overt military and diplomatic muscle to serve their immediate strategic and economic interests. Why did policymakers send jazz to the rescue in foreign-policy crises? What was the Cold War "common sense" that made sending musicians into the preludes and aftermaths of coups d'état seem normal to policymakers, journalists, supporters of the arts, and artists?

The early jazz tours take us into the world of the expansive internationalism of the postwar period, as well as popular reveling in the boisterous one-upmanship of the Cold War and the masculinist adventurism that over the course of the 1950s elevated covert action into a cult of counterinsurgency.[1] On the one hand, jazz tours embodied what Christina Klein has described as an outward-looking, open, popular internationalism. Reflected in such government programs as People-to-People as well as in middle-brow media ranging from magazines to movies and novels, this emphasis on positive global connections versus the ominous connotations of containment was critical in forging domestic support for the ambitious global agendas of the American Century.[2] On the other hand, not only was jazz consistently represented as a stealth weapon, but many State Department jazz tours moved in a world of spies, espionage, and counterinsurgency, challenging us to account for the juxtaposition of belligerence and the connective bonds forged through the languages of modernization, modernism, and egalitarianism.

In a sense, the musicians ended up in close proximity to coups and wars simply because there were so many such crises. As European colonial regimes collapsed in the aftermath of World War II, U.S. policymakers did not seek to take over European forms of colonialism. Rather, asserting the legitimate right of the United States to lead the "free world," they pursued a project of global economic integration through modernization and development. Those American policymakers committed to making sure that the West had access to the world's markets, industrial infrastructure, and raw materials preferred to see the project of global economic integration as "benevolent supremacy."[3] But in the face of persistent attempts on the part of formerly colonized peoples to regain control of their resources, U.S. policymakers made repeated use of (often covert) military force, making the term "Cold War" a misnomer for the peoples of Asia, Africa, Latin America, and the Middle East.[4] The CIA was so involved in behind-the-scenes Middle East scheming that an officer in Beirut wondered if "we'd soon be out of key politicians for CIA personnel to recruit. These included the so-called million-dollar agents who steadily received six-figure subsidies."[5] By the time the jazz tours began, the CIA had already carried out covert actions in the Middle East, Southeast Asia, and Latin America.[6] Certainly many policymakers viewed these actions as a necessary evil. The "common sense" of covert action depended on a worldview in which the Soviet Union was a dangerous enemy that fundamentally threatened the "American way of life." But in seeing a ubiquitous Soviet threat, American policymakers repeat-

edly confused nationalism and Communism. Moreover, participation in the ouster of leaders throughout the Middle East, Africa,
Asia, and Latin America depended on ethnocentric assumptions
about non-Western leaders that prohibited American policymakers from imaging them as independent thinking political agents.
Rather, U.S. policymakers tended to see leaders in those regions as
pawns or potential pawns of the Soviets.[7] Despite the enormous in-
tricacy of America's senses of global connection and interdepen-
dence, with control of global resources at stake, American policymakers rarely tolerated ambiguity or complexity when it came to
assessing the allegiances of national leaders.

But what "common sense" made visiting global hotspots seem
normal to musicians? In part, musicians and journalists alike reflected the widely shared patriotism of the Eisenhower and Kennedy years. The vast majority of musicians, especially in the first
decade of the tour, expressed pride at representing the nation and
helping their country in what most Americans believed was a
global battle for freedom. Moreover, the edgy, competitive mascu-
linity of Cold War America was hardly foreign to jazz culture.[8]
Musicians, like other Americans, could be tempted by the intrigue
of adventure, especially in the form of a gig that allowed them to
keep struggling bands together.[9] Moreover, for those who had long
been denied artistic recognition and fundamental rights as citizens, the tours represented a critical victory in civil rights. The
Gillespie tour began as the five-month-old Montgomery bus boycott brought unprecedented national and international attention to
American racism and the Southern civil rights struggle. As the
hitherto unparalleled visibility of the civil rights movement imbued the tour with optimism and purpose, for many musicians the
common sense of patriotism and democratic struggle went hand in
hand. Indeed, this irresistible combination of a chance to work,
support a big band (no mean feat, since rock and roll was dominating popular music), serve one's country, meet musicians abroad, and
contribute to the civil rights cause made State Department tours
highly prized gigs. Finally, the inherently secretive nature of covert

action meant that U.S. policies were highly opaque. Neither musicians nor the State Department personnel directly involved in the tours were aware of the broader objectives or actions surrounding the tours. Indeed, the full extent of the era's covert activity would not be known for decades, long after such actions had succeeded in undermining the broader liberal internationalist agendas of which it was a part. The romance of Cold War adventurism depended on the illusion that the "war" was "cold," with just enough spy intrigue for excitement, but ultimately effective at containing hostilities that would claim a great many human lives.

While musicians repeatedly stated that they felt honored to have been chosen to represent their country, difficulties on the tours as well as vociferous opposition by congressional conservatives quickly made it clear that the tours exacerbated rather than resolved conflict within the country over civil rights and government funding of the arts. Jazz musicians were not necessarily welcomed with open arms by U.S. foreign-service personnel abroad. With government involvement in the arts anathema to many Americans, and violent white resistance to the civil rights movement, musicians sometimes encountered the foreign-service counterparts of the segregationists in American posts abroad, only to return home to be attacked by conservatives. Musicians also wondered about and were sometimes unnerved by the political tensions they sensed and the high levels of military security they often witnessed. Thus, what musicians and policymakers had in common in their sense of the Cold War could and did fracture along multiple lines.

Yet out of the chaos and bravado that at times put musicians in physical danger, and out of the nation's exported political and cultural fissures, there emerged in those early tours the outlines of an alliance of artists and liberal internationalists within the State Department that would flourish over the following decade. In addition to racist foreign-service personnel contemptuous of culture and black Americans, the musicians also encountered allies who seized upon the power of jazz in their efforts to rescue the image of America and promote a liberal internationalist vision of America in an egalitarian world. Just as the State Department had followed the lead of Louis Armstrong—Ambassador Satch—in conceiving the tours, many in the State Department followed the lead of musicians such as Dizzy Gillespie, who exported a more egalitarian vision of America's relationship to other nations than the officials had ever imagined. And in this international version of what the historian Casey Nelson Blake has called the modernist moment in American art, musicians joined with critics and State Department personnel, to forcefully promote the importance of art in American culture and American foreign policy.[10] As different as each of the principal band leaders (Gillespie, Goodman, and Brubeck) were in musical style and personality, each emerged from his tour as a passionate advocate of government support of jazz and the arts.

All the broad features of U.S. global economic, political, and military ambition, as well as the export of America's deepest political conflicts, were abundantly evident in the first jazz tour by the Dizzy Gillespie Band. Alto saxophonist Phil Woods remembered that the band arrived in Abadan, Iran, to "the smell of crude oil and the sound of gunfire from nearby Iraq." While giving three performances in the Taj Theatre beginning on March 27, 1956, the musicians, Woods explained, lived in the oil workers' barracks "as the upper-echelon workers did."[11] It was no accident that the first State Department jazz performance of the hundreds that would occur over the next two decades took place at the heart of the former British Empire, in a country rich in that coveted Cold War commodity, oil. Three years earlier, Iran had been the site of the first CIA-backed coup of that decade—a coup that ousted the nationalist government of Prime Minister Muhammad Musaddiq and installed the shah. As a result, American firms gained entry into the Iranian oil industry and acquired a share of profits from selling Iranian crude and refined products on the world market.[12] Over the next decade, musicians would return to Iran and its oil-rich neighbors numerous times. The Dave Brubeck Quartet and the Duke Ellington Orchestra would even find themselves in the middle of Iraqi coups in 1958 and 1963 respectively. Looking at the itinerary of Gillespie's tour, one can trace America's increasing assumption of the former role of the British in assuring Western access to the region's oil—a policy that had begun with the 1947 Truman Doctrine commitment to take over British funding of anti-Communist forces in Greece and Turkey. Beginning in Iran, the tour culminated in Turkey, Yugoslavia, and Greece, with stops along the way in Syria and U.S. military allies such as Pakistan and Lebanon.[13] Indeed, the Gillespie tour, like Dave Brubeck's trip two years later, moved through the Eisenhower administration's conception of a "perimeter defense" against the Soviet Union "along the Northern Tier," extending from Turkey to Pakistan. In 1955, this U.S. proposal was concretized in the Baghdad Pact, an anti-Soviet mutual defense treaty signed first by Turkey and Iraq and later by Pakistan and Iran.[14]

In the itinerary, one can also read American policymakers' anxieties about the coming Suez crisis. As the twenty-two-piece Dizzy Gillespie Band rehearsed in New York City in March 1956 for its State Department tour—crafting a program that "illustrated the history of jazz as well as the latest experimental music"—the coordinated British, French, and Israeli attack on Egypt in the Suez War of 1956 was more than six months away.[15] But President Eisenhower and Secretary of State Dulles were already deeply preoccupied with tensions in the Middle East. They were suspicious of the nonaligned politics of Egyptian president Gamal Abdel Nasser, and feared he was falling under Soviet influence.[16] Indeed, Dulles had demonstrated his contempt for nonaligned positions at the time of the Bandung Conference in 1955, and declared in June 1956 that neutrality "has increasingly become an obsolete conception, . . . immoral and shortsighted."[17] But if Eisenhower and Dulles could wield their diplomatic muscle to attack neutralist positions in the more vulnerable emerging states, such sentiments were held in check by the fact that they "did not want to antagonize nationalist sentiment in the Middle East, Asia, and Africa" and did not want to be associated with British or French colonialism in the region.[18] It was such sentiments that led to America's defiance of its European allies when the war broke out.[19] Diplomatically, the tour sought to shore up the support of allies and persuade those on the fence by distinguishing the United States from European colonial powers. U.S. officials also sought to rebut charges by nonaligned leaders (specifically, Nasser and India's Jawaharlal Nehru) that America's racism and imperial ambitions made a mockery of its claims to lead the free world.[20]

For leaders anxious to distinguish the policies of the United States from those of the British and French, the integrated jazz band of bebop trumpeter Dizzy Gillespie, which featured the trombonist Melba Liston at a time when female jazz instrumentalists were rare, was a dream come true.[21] With his spell-binding virtuosity, arresting solos, and egalitarian sensibility buoyed by playful humor, Gillespie won over a wide variety of audiences—from sophisticated fans in Beirut, to habitués of the underground jazz scene in Yugoslavia, to people in Dacca, East Pakistan, who probably had never before heard jazz. "The language of diplomacy," argued a Pakistani editorial, "ought to be translated into the score for a bop trumpet."[22] Observing the popular success of Gillespie's band in Yugoslavia, the U.S. ambassador wired Washington that "Gillespie's band has made our job much easier."[23] The *New York Times* reported from Beirut that the reception of the band was "beyond expectations" and that U.S. diplomats there "hope the noise stays in the walls for a long time to come."[24]

Marshall Stearns, one of the jazz critics on the cultural-presentations music selection committee, was appointed by the State Department as a special consultant to the tour, serving, in effect, as the escort officer. Extremely well respected among musicians, Stearns was among the first scholars to connect African music with jazz and had founded the first jazz education program in the country, the Institute of Jazz Studies.[25] Stearns exemplified the alliance of musicians and critics that nurtured the tours, and in his dual role as music committee member and State Department escort, he was critical in cementing the State Department's relationship with the jazz world. As John Gennari has argued, Stearns had "foreshadowed his role as a consultant for the State Department tours" in a 1954 program for the Newport Jazz Festival."[26] Stearns had attributed the global popularity of jazz to an anti-totalitarian ethos "that transcend[s] rules and regulations" and "offers a common ground on which the conflicting claims of the individual and the group may be resolved."[27] For Stearns, "the acid test of jazz as an ambassador of goodwill came in Athens." Gillespie's band flew in to play a matinee for students following the stoning of the U.S. Information Service office by students angered by U.S. support of Greece's right-wing dictatorship. "We arrived just after the rioting," Stearns recalled, "and the anti-American feeling was real and intense." Gillespie later described playing to "a seething audience of anti-American students. . . . They loved us so much that when we finished playing they tossed their jackets into the air and carried me on their shoulders through the streets of the city." The headline in the local paper the next day ran: "Students Drop Rocks and Roll with Dizzy."[28] Gillespie, not missing a chance to promote the importance of jazz, wired Eisenhower: "Our trip through the Middle East proved conclusively that our interracial group was powerfully effective against Red propaganda. Jazz is our own American folk music that communicates with all peoples regardless of language or social barriers."[29] In the eyes of many newly converted diplomats, Gillespie was the "jam-bassador" the State Department needed.[30]

While State Department officials hoped that sending jazz musicians abroad would demonstrate American democracy in action, with Gillespie they got a lot more democracy and a lot more action than they could have imagined. If officials had already come to appreciate the failure of didactic propagandists, Gillespie's candor must have been refreshing. Gillespie later recalled that "I sort of liked the idea of representing America, but I wasn't going to apologize for the racist policies of America." He managed to avoid his official State Department briefing, noting that "I've got three hundred years of briefing. I know what they've done to us and I'm not going to make any excuses."[31] Gillespie and his band members quickly realized that their own desires to play music and meet local musicians, as well as their own agenda of bringing jazz to new audiences, conflicted with the State Department's focus on indigenous elites as target audiences in fraught political circumstances. Deeply aware of the politics of the tours, Gillespie didn't hesitate to defy State Department and local convention, promoting his own vision of America, which was considerably more democratic than that of the State Department. He later recalled that the tour skipped India because that country was nonaligned. Instead, his band played in Karachi, Pakistan, where the United States was supplying arms. Gillespie refused to play until the gates were opened to the "raga-muffin" children, because "they priced the tickets so high the people we were trying to gain friendship with couldn't make it."[32] In Ankara, Turkey, Gillespie likewise opened the gates, declaring: "I came here to play for *all* the people."[33]

Dizzy Gillespie's big band had broken up in the lean years of the early 1950s, when many band leaders found it impossible to get enough work to keep their organizations together.[34] For Gillespie and his musicians, then, assembling a twenty-two-member band for a State Department trip meant a chance to work. And the tour meant not only a great gig, but long-overdue recognition from a society that had previously failed to acknowledge its greatest music. For trombonist Al Grey, it meant "that they finally saw merit, after all these years."[35]

Such recognition, coming in 1956, was not without rough edges. The noted jazz arranger Quincy Jones, who had directed the band's rehearsals in New York before Gillespie joined them in Rome en route to the Middle East, was shocked by the arrogance and conde-scension of the American National Theatre and Academy repre-sentative who briefed the band. For Jones, the band "was a serious crew" with a deep understanding of what they were doing: "This was a chance to take jazz to places in the world where it had never been before and to represent our country." But after being told by the ANTA representative to "indulge in your various idiosyncrasies discreetly," Jones recalled, "we couldn't believe it. If the New York Philharmonic were about to tour Europe for the State Department, would he feel obliged to say the same thing?"[36] "We were pissed off," Jones said, "but like the black soldiers of World War II, we kept keepin on."[37]

Once overseas, the band continued to encounter patronizing ignorance on the part of some officials. In Beirut, the USIS "thought Dizzy was Dizzy Dean, the old baseball pitcher." The irony, for Jones, was "that when we got overseas, the people doing the freaky-deaky were the State Department emissaries themselves." In contrast to the "highly educated, skilled, and dignified" jazz musicians, Jones saw some of the officials they encountered as stuck in "hardship posts" with "the guys the State Department wanted to sweep under the rug. They were the alcoholics . . . who rode around in air-conditioned limousines which were almost too big for the dirt roads, with the young boys wearing tunics, sandals, exotic musk, and little else."[38] One of the worst insults came in Greece, where Washington, delighted with the anti-American students' response to Gillespie, wired $4,000 for a party. But, Jones recalled, the cultural attaché in Athens "advised his staff not to mingle with us" and "informed his female staff that in the United States, respectable girls did not mix with black jazz musicians."[39]

Despite his anger at hypocritical officials, Jones enthusiastically embraced the intertwined civil rights and foreign-policy agendas. However obnoxious, racist American officials could not derail Gillespie and Jones's civil rights agenda: "A lot of the people we played for in Europe and the Far East thought that Negro musicians had no opportunities, and never mingled with white musicians. When they saw the Gillespie band was mixed and quite happy about it, they realized what they had been hearing was a little off the track."[40] And like Gillespie, Jones took the diplomatic mission to heart, even as the band encountered disconcerting unrest that they had not been briefed on and "knew nothing about." "We thought we were high-minded diplomats," Jones recalled, "'til we hit our fourth city, Beirut, which was a shock." As the band arrived at the airport with 3,000 people to greet them, an Air Force One plane en route to Israel swooped in and Secretary of State Dulles got out and stretched his legs. Not apprised of the mounting tensions between Israel and Egypt, or where Beirut stood on the matter, the musicians could only wonder about the presence of the Secretary of State. What was clear to them was that the atmosphere was "hot, funky, and tense," and "when it came time to play the concert, there was no one who could say outright that we'd be safe onstage, but Dizzy wouldn't hear of canceling it."[41]

Many musicians were struck by the sheer novelty of what they were doing. The tours took them to places that would simply not have been possible—not commercially viable, or politically or logistically negotiable—without government sponsorship. Phil Woods described "without a doubt the most fascinating and interesting trip I will ever take. Twenty-nine hours to another world by plane."[42] Typically playing three concerts a week, plus an additional two benefits for children through UNICEF or local agencies, the musicians found time to meet local musicians. In Ankara, Turkey, tenor saxophonist Billy Mitchell and trombonist Rod Leavitt sat in and played with Turkey's top trumpeter, Muvaffak Falay, at a local hotspot called the Intime Casino. At the next night's concert, Gillespie presented Falay with an engraved cigarette case "in token of the brotherhood of jazz."[43] Also in Ankara, Quincy Jones met Arif Mardin, an "elegant young gentleman in a white silk scarf and black tuxedo." Mardin handed Jones a score that was so good that back in the States, Jones used his arrangements with an "all-star band" on Voice of America and obtained a scholarship for Mardin at Berklee College of Music. Mardin later co-produced with Jerry Wexler, arranged for the Young Rascals, Aretha Franklin, the Bee Gees, and Bette Midler, and eventually became a vice president at Atlantic Records.[44] Arriving in Damascus after a drive from Beirut in six cars and a truck for instruments, the musicians gave an afternoon jam session at the Semiramis Hotel and then a concert that night. They learned the national anthem by listening to children singing it. Melba Liston "worked in her room all afternoon" hastily scoring a version "which went over big."[45] The USIS officer, Dan Snooke, had been skeptical about a jazz band but was floored by the audiences' reaction: "I've never seen these people let themselves go like this."[46]

The rare acknowledgment of Melba Liston was an exception that proves the rule, underscoring the equation of creativity and maleness and the stark marginalization of women that the jazz world of this era shared with mainstream America. Liston had met with deep hostility and skepticism when she joined the Gillespie big band in 1947. Male musicians questioned Gillespie's judgment in sending "all the way to California for a bitch" (as one of them put it).[47] Liston would later recall that while Gillespie tried to protect her, she faced constant sexual harassment from fellow musicians while touring with the band.[48] This may have been softened on the State Department tour by the presence of other women such as Gillespie's wife, Lorraine. But with racial hierarchies in motion nationally and internationally, gender roles had "changed little in a bebop community that venerated male creativity."[49] Both musicians and critics reflected on the tours in the language of male bonding. Though a few of the musicians unfamiliar with Stearns's reputation in jazz circles suspected that the State Department "had sent him along as the great white father to make sure the brothers didn't get out of control," they eventually decided that "he was a great dude and he bonded with us immediately."[50]

Early cultural-presentation programs attempted to highlight government partnerships with free enterprise as a way of distinguishing America from state-controlled Soviet organization. For Stearns, "the idea was simply to make new friends for the United States, especially those in critical nations which Russia, at enormous expense, is flooding with free but strictly supervised talent." Stearns emphasized that the very organization of the tours distinguished the "American approach" to cultural affairs from that of the Soviets. Attempting to turn the chaos of the tours into an asset, Stearns argued that in sharp distinction to the government-organized Soviet tours, the American versions were "a sort of do-it-yourself plan with emphasis upon free enterprise." Stearns explained the logistics of this public-private partnership: "The band did its own booking, with the help of the American embassies and the United States Information Service, and the government more or less guaranteed it against loss. The band was paid a reasonable minimum, no matter how financially successful the concerts might be. It was a sparkling new idea for the jazz world, and it worked out beautifully."[51]

The emphasis on free enterprise was later modified when officials determined that audiences often failed to understand the connection between the U.S. State Department and Pepsi-Cola or between the USIA and the Iranian Oil Refinery Company, and were therefore frequently confused about the sponsorship of events. James Magdanz, head of the cultural-presentations staff in 1957, explained to the music committee: "It is harder to explain arts under a free-enterprise system than under government." Moreover, with impresarios doing the booking, the emphasis was too often on getting the most revenue, instead of booking "areas which were most desirable from a strategic viewpoint." Corporate cosponsorship was not abandoned and was viewed as necessary for financing the tours, but henceforth the State Department determined the locations of bookings and made its sponsorship clear.[52]

Yet if the early tours attempted to mark their difference in organization from Soviet cultural efforts, for Stearns the deepest value of the Gillespie tour was that "jazz was born and grew up in the United States and nowhere else." "It has never dawned upon Americans," continued Stearns, "that many people in foreign lands consider jazz a new and impressive contribution to culture." Emphasizing that "the stereotypical notion that jazz is lowbrow never got in the way" of audiences' enjoyment of Gillespie, Stearns ended his *Saturday Review* piece "Is Jazz Good Propaganda?" by quoting a European composer: "Jazz is one of America's best-loved *artistic* exports."[53] For Stearns, Gillespie had not only won friends for the United States; he had succeeded in elevating the art of jazz.

If Gillespie and his band brilliantly distinguished themselves—and by association America—from European colonialists, they also managed to distinguish themselves from many Americans. The cultural attaché in Athens was not the only one unprepared to appreciate Gillespie's achievements. Despite their enthusiastic reception, early jazz tours were targeted by congressional critics and beset by political controversy and threatened cutbacks in funding. Representative John Rooney, a New York Democrat, led the attack, supported by Southern segregationists such as Senator Allen J. Ellender of Louisiana.[54] Suggesting that jazz tickets had been given free to journalists to bribe them into writing positive articles, yet also cynically asking why free tickets were necessary if jazz was as popular as advocates claimed, Rooney questioned every item of expense connected with the tours.[55] Ellender complained: "I never heard so much noise in all my life. . . . To send such jazz as Mr. Gillespie, I can assure you that instead of doing good it will do harm and the people will really believe we are barbarians."[56] In July 1956, as Gillespie began his State Department tour of Brazil, the Senate Appropriations Committee added a stipulation to the appropriations bill that no more funds could be used to send abroad "jazz bands, ballet companies, and similar activities." Senator Ellender, who authored the restriction, suggested "choral groups and miscellaneous sports projects" as alternatives.[57]

In the midst of these congressional discussions, Gillespie and his band embarked on a trip to South America. In Brazil, they found "a lot of brothers, Africans—and their music is African."[58] Gillespie had long been interested in Afro-Cuban jazz and had developed extensive ties with Latin jazz musicians. For him, the opportunity to encounter Afro-Brazilian culture and drumming, and play with samba musicians, was an extension of this long-standing interest. In a club in Buenos Aires, Gillespie and Jones met a young jazz pianist, Lalo Schifrin, who hooked them up with Astor Piazzola, "a visionary composer and bandoneon player who created the modern city tango and later did a record with Dizzy."[59] Lalo also told the musicians about the bossa nova movement in Brazil. While in Rio, Gillespie sat in with the house samba combo at the Gloria Hotel on Copacabana Beach. João and Astrud Gilberto and Antonio Carlos Jobim—teenagers at the time, and the creators of bossa nova—were in the audience. When "Dizzy threw his be-bop trumpet into the mix," recalled Jones, "that was the first time any of us had heard the fusion of jazz 'n' samba. In fact, the song 'Desafinado,' by Jobim, feels just like a Dizzy solo." Eight months later, prominent Brazilian musicians were invited to play in a midnight concert at Carnegie Hall. In Jones's assessment, "Dizzy had a great hand in cooking the jazz 'n' samba gumbo. He put his fingerprints all over it."[60]

But such connections did not sit well with congressional critics of jazz. In his attempt to end government funding of jazz, Representative Rooney seized on State Department reports that the band had been interested in meeting Brazilian musicians at the expense of attending the proper official functions.[61] While the stipulation prohibiting the funding of jazz and ballet companies had been excised from the final version of the bill passed in September, these criticisms affected the content of the programs, leading in the early 1960s to the inclusion of amateur musicians, including high school and college marching bands.[62] Just as USIA and Voice of America programs were officially "for export only," making their distribution within the United States illegal, the State Department cultural programs often tried to shield the integrationist agenda of the tours—their core diplomatic message—from conservative audiences at home.

Of the many art forms represented in the tours, the political and aesthetic issues surrounding modern dance most closely paralleled those of jazz. The inclusion of modern dance reflected critics' concern for promoting unique forms of American modernism and distinguishing art from mass entertainment; and by the late 1950s, important dance companies such as Martha Graham's had been integrated. Indeed, participation by Martha Graham was especially valued in the early years. A diplomat par excellence, Graham once startled her dancers by telling them that "what we are doing transcends art."[63] The dancer Stuart Hodes recalled, "We always thought it was the other way around."[64] Yet Graham elicited considerable conservative opposition, exposing deep fissures in American culture over what constituted acceptable art. After Representative Edna F. Kelly of Brooklyn saw Graham's State Department–sponsored production of *Phaedras* in Germany, Kelly and Peter Frelinghuysen of New Jersey called Graham's adaptations of Greek drama and mythology, containing depictions of overt sexuality and incest, "un-American." Graham's *Phaedras,* they charged, was not a proper cultural export. Frelinghuysen explained in a letter to his constituents that "the dance was shocking, portraying a mother who lusts after her stepson." Without pretending to any critical expertise, Frelinghuysen knew what he was seeing: "They use couches, and there are a lot of men running around in loincloth. It is very confusing but the meaning is clear enough."[65] He found it incredible that taxpayers' dollars were sending this production overseas as an example of American culture. Despite such opposition from conservative congressional members, Graham's company prospered as a result of the tours.[66]

For Gillespie, the contradictions of 1950s liberalism were experienced as the sharp contrast between wildly enthusiastic crowds abroad and the venomous animosity of Southern segregationists—and Dizzy came out swinging. In his *Esquire* article of June 1957, controversially entitled "Jazz Is Too Good for Americans," Gillespie lamented that "jazz, the music I play most often, has never really been accepted as an art form by the people of my own country." Gillespie charged that "the great mass of the American people still consider jazz as lowbrow music. They believe . . . people hear jazz through their feet and not their brains. To them, jazz is music for kids and dope addicts. . . . Not serious music. Not concert-hall music. Not music to study. Not music to enjoy purely for its listening kicks."[67]

Citing his overwhelmingly positive reception on his State Department tour and what he described as a "steadily growing exodus of our U.S. jazzmen abroad," Gillespie explained that "this lionizing of American jazzmen overseas has had a great effect on our morale."[68] But it had also caused musicians to turn a more critical eye on the United States. "As an American," wrote Gillespie, "I'm deeply sorry that they [foreign countries] have beat us to the punch in exploiting so fully a music we originally created. Most of all— and this is the really great irony—I'm disappointed that the enormous upswing in jazz enthusiasm abroad has been accompanied by a decline in several major areas of jazz interest here at home."

To combat the lack of respect for jazz in America, Gillespie advocated national jazz education "taught to school children at all levels of their education," and the formation of a National Jazz Institute. Radio broadcasters had a critical role to play in America's recognition of the music. Distressed that "nowadays, an American traveling overseas can get better jazz from the disc jockeys of any country in the Western world than he can get from the deejays in the USA," Gillespie insisted that disc jockeys "exercise a bit more taste and discretion in the records they select for the public."[69]

Having won the distinction of becoming the first official jazz ambassador *and* the target of conservative ire, after a second trip to Brazil in 1956, Gillespie would not perform again for the State Department for fourteen years (he would tour Eastern Europe with the Giants of Jazz, through the Newport Jazz Festival). And it would be eighteen years before he was invited to represent the United States again in an individual billing (as jazz ambassador to the 1973 independence anniversary celebrations in Kenya). In the meantime, the advocate of civil rights and social justice would turn his newfound diplomatic capital to his advocacy of jazz, and to a campaign for world peace, disarmament, and the black American civil rights struggle through his 1963–1964 "Dizzy for President" campaign.[70]

Given the highly focused conservative attacks on Gillespie, it was no accident that the State Department turned to the opposite spectrum of the jazz world, in style and substance, for the next jazz tour later that year. On December 7, 1956, Benny Goodman and his orchestra embarked on a seven-week tour of Thailand, Singapore, Malaya, Cambodia, Burma, Hong Kong, South Korea, and Japan.[71] Goodman had been a key figure during the swing era, as his orchestra first traveled, then broadcasted, cross-country, bringing

Fletcher Henderson arrangements to enthusiastic, jitterbugging fans. As the featured performer at the first jazz concert at Carnegie Hall in 1938, Goodman was widely credited with helping jazz to be taken seriously. Born in Chicago on May 30, 1909, to Russian-Jewish parents, and the first white band leader to hire black musicians, Goodman was widely hailed for his role in integrating jazz.[72] Like Gillespie, he was a crusader in the cultural battle to gain recognition for jazz as a legitimate music. In 1947, long before the Voice of America began regular jazz programming, he was named by the State Department as the Consulting Director of Popular Music Programs on Russian Language Broadcasts.[73] Within weeks of being appointed, Goodman was fighting for the survival of the programs through a campaign of letters to Congress, since the programs faced suspension for lack of funds.[74] But whereas for Gillespie the fight to have jazz taken seriously was part and parcel of a fight for the recognition of the cultural and artistic achievements of black America, Goodman held firmly to the view that jazz was a race-transcending music. Calling jazz "a completely democratic music," Goodman wrote that "neither a difference of race, creed, or color has ever been of the slightest importance among the best of the jazz bands."[75] While Goodman's statement illustrates the heartfelt convictions that animated his role in the integration of jazz, it was also a view that would be hotly contested by many African American musicians, who experienced on a daily basis the way racial discrimination limited their access to venues (such as Carnegie Hall), their control over recording productions, and their share of the profits from their labors. Goodman carried his self-absorbed social analysis—claiming that since he had been playing in an integrated band for twenty-five years, discrimination no longer existed in America—into his State Department tours. After returning home, Goodman explained: "I was constantly asked by the press over there about the colored people here. They were quite concerned. I guess they had been fed a lot of Communist propaganda. . . . I really didn't have anything particular to say, other than that we've had colored musicians in the band for twenty-five years.

That was probably more than enough to offset what they'd been hearing from the other side."[76] Thus, from the beginning of his goodwill ambassador tours in 1956, Goodman's was a voice declaring that the victory over racism in America had already been achieved—a position markedly different from those black musicians, who saw the tours as a way to advance the struggle for equality.

When Goodman's band began playing for two weeks at a U.S. exhibit at the Constitution Fair, in Bangkok, most Americans' ideas about Thailand—and the region—derived from the Rodgers and Hammerstein musical *The King and I,* which had opened on Broadway in 1951, and from the popular film adaptation released in 1956.[77] Yet the Eisenhower administration was already providing $85 million per year to the neighboring South Vietnamese army, along with many other forms of aid to South Vietnam.[78] And in a story still unknown to most Americans, the administration, driven by Eisenhower and Dulles' fierce opposition to neutralism and fear that the region would go the way of Communist China, was already engaged in extensive covert operations in the region, throughout Indonesia, Burma, Cambodia, and Laos.[79] Thailand, the closest American ally in the region, was for these officials a pro-Western voice and an essential strategic bulwark against the spread of communism. Thailand's King Bhumibol Adulyadej had been born in 1927 in Cambridge, Massachusetts, where his father studied medicine. Though he had his own ambivalence toward the West—sharing his compatriots' abhorrence of *The King and I,* which was banned in Thailand—he not only loved jazz, but happened to be an accomplished jazz saxophonist, clarinetist, and trumpeter who held all-night jam sessions at the royal palace every Friday night.[80]

Seizing this unique opportunity for diplomacy by jamming with King Adulyadej at every opportunity, Goodman was a brilliant ambassador, charming audiences and musicians alike with his obvious delight in their cultures and musical traditions, as well as in their shared appreciation of jazz. Goodman's fifteen-man orchestra arrived in Bangkok on the afternoon of December 6 after three straight days of travel, and immediately launched into "Bugle Call Rag" for King Adulyadej and Queen Sirkit in the Theatre Room of the ancient Amporn palace.[81] Under the front-page headline "Kings of Swing and Thailand Jive," the *New York Times* reported that, following the band's performance, Goodman and the king "teamed up for about an hour of Dixieland and boogie-woogie. . . . The two Kings, improvising before an audience of a hundred or so, seemed to be having the time of their lives as they went through such jazz classics as 'Muskrat Ramble,' 'Honeysuckle Rose,' and 'On the Sunny Side of the Street.'"[82] Following up their auspicious opening set, the band played the palace three times in ten days, in addition to appearing at the fair in Lumpini Park, where they drew more than 10,000 people in each of their twice-nightly concerts. "'Playing for the Palace' will have a new meaning in jazz lore," quipped the *Saturday Review*.[83] According to the *Times,* the king called the band back to his palace for four jam sessions, and "his intimates said they had 'never seen him so happy.'" Beyond adding saxophonist Budd Johnson's arrangement of a popular Thai song to the band's repertoire, and bringing down the house with Dottie Reid's vocal rendition of a popular Thai ballad, Goodman and his band established the "closest bonds of understanding" by making "a circuit of the nightclubs and dancehalls, jamming with the local musicians."[84] The warmth shown by Goodman and his band in embracing the music and cultures of the nations they visited was reciprocated with decorations and honorary titles. In Phnom Penh, Cambodia's King Norodom Sumamarit decorated Goodman with the order of the Chevalier de Monisaraphon. Goodman was further granted the award of honorary fire chief of Singapore, honorary governor of Kuala Lumpur, and honorary mayor, traffic commissioner, and police chief of Bangkok. In Rangoon, Burma, the Burmese adopted the Goodman band's rendition of the Burmese national anthem as the official version.[85]

For Robert Schnitzer of ANTA, Goodman's tour "counteracted the propaganda that jazz is a degenerate art form." Praising the "boys in the band" as a "credit offstage and on," Schnitzer argued that the "tour strengthened the impression that America is not only great in modern plumbing and fancy cars, but in things of the spirit and the arts."[86] And in the words of the *Christian Century*, reporting on the Goodman tour, "music hath charms such as Mr. Dulles hath not."[87]

The friendship between King Adulyadej and the King of Swing was further cemented in the Thai ruler's visit to Washington, D.C., and New York City in 1960. Eisenhower's vision of cultural diplomacy was somewhat square. Despite the demonstrable value of jazz in this case, he "personally invited Guy Lombardo and his Royal Canadians to play for the King." The king's hosts in New York were a bit more tuned in. Governor Nelson Rockefeller, a fan of Thelonious Monk and Miles Davis, whisked the king to his estate to jam with the Goodman sextet. The king and Goodman later performed at a New York City party in honor of the king, hosted by Goodman, who was joined by drummer Gene Krupa, pianist Teddy Wilson, and nine other musicians. In the words of the *New York Times* reporter McCandlish Phillips, the musicians proved "their devotion to the policy of amity-by-pandemonium."[88]

Jazz devotees would surely have taken issue with the characterization of a jam session as "pandemonium," but the confusion that word implies would certainly characterize the organization of some of the jazz tours. Nothing better exemplifies the infusion of diplomatic bravado into the early tours than the highly chaotic tour of the Dave Brubeck Quartet in 1958. Touring without a State Department escort officer, Brubeck was first sent across the Iron Curtain into East Germany without a visa; then to Poland, Turkey, Afghanistan, Pakistan, India, and Ceylon; then straight into the Middle East crisis of 1958 and a coup in Iraq.[89]

Dave Brubeck had been born on December 6, 1920, in Concord, California, where he grew up working on his father's ranch and absorbing his mother's passion for music. As a boy, he had listened to the records and broadcasts of Teddy Wilson, the Billy Kyle Trio, Fats Waller, Art Tatum, Duke Ellington, and countless others. Beginning to play as a teenager in local venues, he had studied music at the College of the Pacific in Stockton, California, where he put together his first bands before going overseas with the army in World War II. A replacement in Patton's Third Army, 140th Regiment, A Company, Brubeck had been the leader of the Jazz Band of the Third Army Replacement Depot, nicknamed the Wolf-pack.[90] After the war, Brubeck had remained apart from the bebop revolution, pursuing a different path of innovation through his exploration of harmonic and rhythmic complexities from Europe, Africa, and Asia and his use of polytonality and polyrhythms.[91] To alleviate the grueling schedule of travel that kept him away from his growing family, his wife, Iola Brubeck, had set up a wildly successful tour of the college circuit, the basis of the 1954 Columbia album *Jazz Goes to College*. In November 1954, Brubeck was selected for the cover of *Time* magazine.[92] Always an adamant supporter of integration in jazz and civil rights, Brubeck was embarrassed at receiving high-profile recognition when, to his mind, more worthy black musicians had been overlooked. Brubeck later recalled Duke Ellington's showing him the *Time* cover, and called it "one of the worst moments of my life—Ellington deserved that, not me."[93] This incident, along with the confrontations with Southern colleges and universities that wanted to ban his integrated quartet (leading Brubeck to cancel twenty-three out of twenty-five engagements on one southern tour), increased his resolve to support civil rights, a resolve that would be reflected in the 1962 musical he recorded with Louis Armstrong, *The Real Ambassadors*.[94]

The Brubeck tour began uneventfully, but haphazard organizing and an apparent strategic resolve by U.S. policymakers to use jazz musicians as diplomatic tools in Poland and the Middle East, quickly complicated things. Always strapped for resources, the administration's cultural-presentation programs would frequently "pick up" a group which was already performing abroad, extending its tour into countries identified by the State Department as strategic priorities. In such a "pickup," the Brubeck quartet began their 1958 tour with a commercial leg in Europe, playing Great Britain, Germany, Holland, Belgium, Sweden, and Denmark. In Brubeck's

"Classic Quartet," he was joined by alto saxophonist Paul Desmond, drummer Joe Morello, and bassist Eugene Wright. Brubeck's wife, Iola, and their two oldest children, Darius (eleven) and Michael (ten), accompanied the quartet. The State Department expected the family to go home after performing in Sweden, and refused to assist them in obtaining visas that would allow them to continue on to Poland. The Brubecks, however, were determined to bring the family along, and Iola Brubeck later said she spent "every spare moment [trying] to get a visa to go to Poland."[95] The Brubecks explained their dilemma to a Swedish journalist, and later the same day they received a message to go to the Polish Embassy. They arrived at the embassy and the family had visas within an hour—to the annoyance of the American officials, who told Brubeck, "No more tricks."

But it was lack of planning on the part of the State Department rather then the family's acquisition of visas that would create the first dangerous logistical snag for the musicians. While at the airport, the Brubecks heard announcements for direct flights leaving Stockholm for Warsaw. As they were routed through Berlin, Brubeck remembered: "We were puzzled: Why weren't we flying to Warsaw?" Once in Berlin, to their great surprise, the Brubecks were confronted with a dilemma: they now all had visas for Poland, but no transit visas through East Germany. This struck the Brubecks as sheer bad planning on the part of the State Department, since they could have been booked on a direct flight to Warsaw. And the absence of transit visas created more than a mere minor inconvenience. When tensions over spying between the United States and the Eastern bloc were at their height, and when people with questionable documentation were known to simply disappear into East German prisons for months on end, Brubeck was told that the visas could only be acquired in East Berlin and "we have to sneak you into East Berlin." Brubeck recalled: "I was supposed to get into the trunk of a car and go through the Brandenburg Gate." Although the moment inspired his composition "Brandenburg Gate," written in Berlin, and an album by the same name, it was a harrowing experience. Brubeck said: "I'm not getting in the trunk. I'll get in the back seat, and if I'm questioned I'll tell the truth." After slipping through, Brubeck sat for hours in a barren police station. "Then this guy came in and sat next to me, and asked: 'Are you Mr. Kulu?' He got out a 'cool jazz' piece from a [Polish] newspaper that had a picture of me, Mr. Kulu." It was an article announcing Brubeck's arrival in Warsaw. The official had all of the papers and visas Brubeck needed in order to travel within the Eastern bloc. Brubeck sneaked back to pick up his family and his quartet, but his adventures had only begun. With proper papers finally in hand, the group was ill-prepared for the journey. "We had no help from the State Department," Brubeck remembered. The first obstacle was simply getting a train to Frankfurt (where they would get further conveyance to Warsaw). "We couldn't speak the language," Brubeck recalled, and they had no idea how to answer the question of whether they were going to Frankfurt-am-Main or Frankfurt-an-der-Oder. On one occasion Brubeck took a wild guess at Oder, and the children's tickets were marked with a different destination from the adults'.[96]

When they arrived in Warsaw, shock at the dilapidated conditions of the railway station and buses gave way to warm feelings of solidarity for "the wonderful Polish people." From March 6 to 19, the group played twelve concerts in small auditoriums, on every night but two. In addition to Warsaw, the quartet played in Stettin, Danzig, Rostlow, Krakow, Lodz, and Poznan.[97] A "small entourage of young jazz buffs" followed the quartet from city to city and became friends with whom they would remain in touch for decades.[98] The Brubecks attributed the ease of their trip through Poland also to the fact that people took great interest in Darius and Michael. In Settin, the promoter decided to take advantage of the musical family and sent the boys onstage to play, although they had never performed publicly with their father. Michael was behind the drums with Morello. Darius, at the piano, began to improvise right away, until Brubeck whispered, "Play the melody, stupid!" "The next day, a German paper opened with a good-humored headline quoting Brubeck: "Spiel die Melodie, Dummkopf!"[99]

The Brubecks developed an affinity for the Polish fans. After their return to the States, they worked hard to get jazz recordings into U.S. consulates and USIS offices and to stay in touch with Polish musicians. Iola Brubeck told jazz critic Ralph Gleason: "Jazz in Poland was underground until after the Polish October Revolution of 1956 and the emergence of the Gomulka government as quasi-independent. Prior to that time, no assembly of more than three persons was allowed, and Polish jazz fans and musicians had to meet illegally in cellars to hear the music they liked."[100] And the Polish jazz musicians were "very very good." Talking to Gleason, Dave Brubeck observed that "whenever there was a dictatorship in Europe, jazz was outlawed. And whenever freedom returned to those countries, the playing of jazz inevitably accompanied it." Brubeck often spoke at his performances, and drew tremendous applause when he said: "No dictatorship can tolerate jazz. It is the first sign of a return to freedom."[101]

Brubeck recalled that the word "'freedom'. . . was in the mouths of everybody we had anything to do with." For the last concert in Poland, in Poznan, on the train trip from Lodz, Brubeck wrote a song called, "Dziekuje," Polish for "Thank you." In recognition of the reverence for Chopin in Poland, Brubeck wrote a "Chopinesque introduction" for the song. The quartet played the piece as their final encore. After a moment of silence during which Brubeck was afraid he had offended the audience, people burst into applause. A Polish government worker asked Brubeck backstage: "Why don't the artists rule the world?" There were tears in his eyes, and Brubeck almost wept.[102]

Indeed, for the Brubecks, as for Gillespie, the tours both underscored the power of the arts and further sensitized them to the scarce resources allotted for cultural exchange, especially when compared to the U.S. defense budget. When Brubeck asked John Wiggin, the senior officer in the USIS in Madras, whether he thought they were doing any good, Wiggin said: "In all of Russia, there is no one who can come here and play the drums like Joe Morello. You reach people on a personal level. It's that simple." Brubeck ended his *New York Times Magazine* reflections on the tour with the story of meeting Al Riedel, an ex-policeman from Berkeley, California, in Kabul, Afghanistan. There to help organize Afghanistan's security forces, Riedel pointed out a wall at the top of the huge mountain surrounding Kabul. Noting 5,000 years of fighting over the wall, Riedel argued that "if a small fraction of what they spent went into education instead of defense, that wall would have come down long ago. At best, defense is a temporary thing." At the time, lying in the compound where he was staying, and listening to the flutes of nomadic shepherds, Brubeck was moved by music that had survived for 5,000 years. "How many things that were fought for over the wall on that mountain had?"[103] Years later, he would look back and wonder at the paltry resources committed to music—much less than "the tip of the wing of a fighter plane. How can an intelligent people—and we are intelligent—be so stupid?"[104]

The reverence Brubeck and his quartet felt for the non-Western musics they encountered could be heard in their own evolving style.[105] Always interested in harmonic complexity and polyrhythms, he relished the opportunity to learn new musics. In Bombay, Brubeck had "tried to play piano behind Abdul Jaffar Khan," a nationally known sitar player. "His influence," Brubeck wrote, "made me play in a different way. Although Hindu scales, melodies, and harmonies are so different, we *understood* each other. I feel that in a few more meetings we would have been playing jazz together. The folk origins of music aren't too far apart anywhere in the world." Despite the differences in the musics, Brubeck was most struck by the intricate rhythms and the shared practice of improvisation. Brubeck tried to capture some of India's sounds in "Calcutta Blues," "using Indian rhythms that were adaptable to the Blues" and using the piano "as a strictly melodic instrument such as the sitar or harmonium."[106] As the quartet arrived in Istanbul, they were greeted by a Turkish band composed of a bass player and two trumpeters, who serenaded them with the quartet's own arrangement of "Tea for Two." In Ankara, they invited Turkish bass, French horn, and drum players, along with an Italian guitarist, to join them

4. *Brubeck with Indian musicians, April 1958.* Copyright © by Dave
Brubeck. Courtesy of the Dave Brubeck Collection, Holt-Atherton Special
Collections, University of the Pacific Libraries, Stockton, California.

onstage, and they "jammed fifteen choruses of 'All the Things You
Are.'" As with his tribute to Chopin and the people of Poland,
"Dziekuje," Brubeck built many of the pieces that eventually appeared on the quartet's *Jazz Impressions of Eurasia* album, on the
theme of thanks. "Choc Teshejjur Ederim" is "Thank you very
much" in Turkish. Brubeck explained that "spoken very rapidly it
becomes the rhythmic pattern of the theme of 'Golden Horn,'" a
piece named for the narrow inlet of the Bosporus that divides Istanbul. Brubeck sought to evoke the bridge between Europe and
Asia "by using a modal-like theme characteristic of the music of
Turkey, along with Western harmony."[107] Other compositions on
the album were "Nomad," inspired by the music of Afghanistan,
"The Brandenburg Gate," commemorating the dramatic trip across
the Iron Curtain, and "Marble Arch."

Iola and the children had returned home after Istanbul, but Iola's absence didn't detract from her insights into the politics of the tour. The tour was a "circle of Russia," a classic attempt at containment. The quartet played in Afghanistan, and "far more Russians came to the concert than Afghanis." Despite their delight at meeting musicians and audiences, as the hectic pace accelerated and the group became more and more fatigued, they were overwhelmed by the physical challenges of no-frills travel and political tensions. Ill-prepared for the weather, the quartet flew from the mountains of Afghanistan to East Pakistan. Brubeck explained, "It was so cold, there was ice on the windows inside the plane. When we landed, it was 120 degrees. The day before we left, we were given three shots for cholera, yellow fever, and typhus. We were so swollen! We had been traveling and had had no sleep. We had been given pills to put in the water, but we were so thirsty we couldn't wait. And then we played in an air-conditioned palace with wonderful acoustics."[108] In India, the quartet stayed at the heavily guarded home of an American official, and anxiously wondered why such extreme measures were necessary.[109]

These tensions were minor, compared to what lay ahead. With the trip scheduled to end in April, Secretary of State Dulles unilaterally canceled their engagements in the United States and extended the tour to Iran, then to Iraq and straight into tensions leading to the Middle East crisis of July 1958. Dulles ordered the quartet "to keep playing way longer than we had planned," Brubeck remembered. "They just kept us moving." In Iran, they played before local and expatriate elites in performances co-sponsored by the Iranian Oil Refinery Company and the USIS.[110] Although the State Department had not briefed them on national and regional politics, to Brubeck and his band, things seemed dangerously amiss when they arrived in Baghdad, Iraq. Deliriously ill with dysentery and ordered by a British physician not to travel, Brubeck nonetheless found a flight out through Istanbul. On July 14, only weeks after their departure, General 'Abd al-Karim Qassim led a nationalist revolt which overthrew the Iraqi monarchy and established a regime friendly to the United Arab Republic (UAR), threatening the delicately constructed Baghdad Pact and challenging U.S. oil

5. *Brubeck signing albums at a record store in Baghdad, May 1958.* Copyright © by Dave Brubeck. Courtesy of the Dave Brubeck Collection, Holt-Atherton Special Collections, University of the Pacific Libraries, Stockton, California.

interests. As Qassim's troops rolled into Baghdad, clearing out the swank New Baghdad Hotel Brubeck had only recently left, Lebanese president Camille Chamoun responded to the coup with an urgent request for military assistance from the United States.[111] Alto saxophonist Paul Desmond had left the group as they went to Iraq and had headed to Beirut for what he thought would be a peaceful vacation on the beach. Instead, Desmond woke up to 14,000 American marines wading ashore amid the sunbathers, to quell the threat of civil war in Lebanon and warn the new Iraqi regime that any threat to Western-controlled oil resources in the area would not be tolerated.[112]

On the one hand, the Eisenhower administration appears to have been caught off guard by the coup in Iraq. Alone among the Arab states to join the Baghdad Pact (the U.S.-backed regional defense organization) and to challenge Nasser's radical nationalism, Iraq was seen by top U.S. officials as "an island in a sea of instability."[113] Yet earlier that year, State Department officials had worried that the

Iraqi regime lacked popular support and had sought ways to shore up its autocratic rule. Given Dulles' extension of the tour into Iraq, it is clear that jazz was a part of the Eisenhower administration's hope of working behind the scenes for "peaceful change" and "a more broadly moderate government."[114] And given that the consequences for the quartet, however unanticipated, simply capped an arduous and chaotic tour, it would be an understatement to suggest that U.S. personnel often seemed insensitive to the musicians' needs. As was typical of the tours, the Brubeck quartet followed a grueling schedule of appearances, with traveling considered an "off day." In every country, from Poland on, each post "would use us to the full. Performances, meetings—it was just exhausting." Brubeck, who described himself as "doing this out of love for [my] country, to be corny about it," said: "We did feel deserted at times. Our health wasn't taken care of." Yet he emphasized that while "we complain about the State Department tours, . . . it was one of the great events in my life." Brubeck would eventually tour many more times for the department and would become a champion of government support of the arts.

In the Gillespie, Goodman, and Brubeck tours, despite logistical chaos and the surrounding international and domestic political conflicts, jazz musicians exceeded expectations as ambassadors. They charmed audiences, journalists, and State Department personnel. For State Department converts, the irreverence, egalitarianism and creative brilliance of the musicians achieved far more in winning friends for America than any sanctimonious pronouncement of American superiority. For the musicians, the tours brought international cultural capital as artists and civil rights emissaries, and solidified their commitment to public advocacy for jazz and the arts. The Brubecks would bring their experiences in the tours— their insights into domestic politics and foreign policy, their joy at meeting so many different musicians and fans, and their often nerve-racking logistical trials—to the creation of the musical *The Real Ambassadors* in 1961. But to understand that tale, we must turn to the story of their collaborator in that venture, Louis Armstrong,

Ambassador Satch himself. Since many liberal internationalists in the State Department were fast recognizing their dependence on the vitality of jazz and black American culture, as seen in the multiple dramas building up to Armstrong's first official State Department tour in 1960, the ongoing resistance to the civil rights movement ensured that this wasn't going to be an easy relationship.

CHAPTER 3

The Real Ambassador

The first and only official State Department tour by
Louis Armstrong, the creative genius whose inimitable élan had inspired the very idea of the jazz ambassador, almost never took place.
The State Department had approved Armstrong for a tour in November of 1955, the moment of its "sudden discovery" of jazz.[1] But
Armstrong, like many Americans, was inspired by the growing national prominence of the southern civil rights movement. Indeed,
the heightened awareness of civil rights across the nation, as activists organized boycotts and staged sit-ins and freedom rides, per-
vaded the jazz world.[2] As boundary-crossing ambassador par excellence, Armstrong was acutely conscious of the irony inherent in a
black man's representing a still-segregated America. Infuriated by
the refusal of the Eisenhower administration to enforce court-or-
dered desegregation in Little Rock, Arkansas, in 1957, Armstrong
shunned the mantle of ambassador. While Armstrong would tour
for the State Department three years later—with many stops across
the African continent in 1960 and 1961—the era's tangled international and civil rights politics are revealed in the long road taken by
the State Department to actually engaging Armstrong for an official tour. Thorny questions plagued musicians as well as State Department personnel. What would happen when tours symbolizing
freedom clashed with white violence at home? What would happen when tours symbolizing cultural exchange unfolded in the
context of America's political and economic rivalries—as in fact
they did with such African leaders as Patrice Lumumba in the
Congo? If such tragic encounters shadowed and undermined tri-

umphant renderings of the tours, at times embarrassing U.S. officials, these contradictions also took their toll on Armstrong.

From his 1955 designation as "Ambassador Satch," the next milestone in Armstrong's career as ambassador and on the path to his 1960–1961 tour was his unofficial trip to the British Gold Coast Colony, soon to become the independent nation of Ghana. Coming in May 1956, just as Dizzy Gillespie's band returned from the Middle East and in the midst of the congressional attacks on jazz, the trip was an unexpected boost for the jazz ambassadors. Coinciding with Ghana's preparation for its independence ceremonies in March of the following year, and occurring seven months into the Montgomery bus boycott—the first large nonviolent direct action with national and international visibility—the trip made a profound statement about ties between black Americans and Africans. The trip was arranged by Edward R. Murrow, producer of the CBS television series *See It Now* as a way of collecting footage for his film *The Saga of Satchmo.* Murrow had financed Armstrong's 1955 tour of Europe and had made, independently, a film on Africa that same year with a segment on the Gold Coast. He then brought these projects together when he decided to "send Armstrong to Africa, the land of his ancestors, and to film the result."[3] Prior to their arrival in Accra, Armstrong and his group, the All Stars, had been playing for four weeks in Europe—a different European city every day. After flying from London all afternoon and all night, Armstrong stepped off the plane to find thirteen African bands perched atop trucks playing and singing "All for You, Louis, All for You!" Joined by his band, which included singer Velma Middleton and trombonist Trummy Young, Armstrong raised his trumpet and joined in. The Australian journalist Robert Raymond observed that a dozen trumpet players fell in behind Armstrong. As the animated mass of players and singing people moved across the tarmac, gathering strength and impetus, "the noise and the clamour rose to the skies in the greatest paean of welcome Accra had ever known."[4]

Kwame Nkrumah, the prime minister of Ghana, who knew Armstrong's music from his years as a student in the United States, invited Armstrong and his wife, Lucille, to lunch. While this delighted Armstrong, it horrified the local CBS film crew, who were jealously guarding their limited time with Armstrong. It also annoyed U.S. officials who had set up a public relations luncheon with the local press, though they were forced to acknowledge that the tour had been arranged as a private venture rather than through the U.S. government. As the Armstrongs lunched with Nkrumah, Trummy Young broke off from the press luncheon and, before a group of delighted local musicians, demonstrated how to control one's breathing with the diaphragm while playing the trombone. He was eventually joined by clarinetist Edmund Hall for a jam session.[5]

The outdoor afternoon concert was at the Old Polo Ground, a structure the size of three football stadiums. Despite the size of the venue, local authorities panicked when roughly 100,000 people showed up to hear Armstrong. With no experience managing such crowds, they expected a riot. And in fact tensions were high in the packed stadium when Armstrong finally arrived in Nkrumah's car. Waving his trumpet, Armstrong walked to the front of the platform and called out, "Greetings all you cats!" before launching into "When It's Sleepy Time Down South." Under the headline "Satchmo Is a Smash on the Gold Coast," *Life* magazine reported that "hot blasts from a horn heard round the world came close to setting off a riot in the sweltering tropical town of Accra last week."[6]

Throughout his stay in Ghana, Armstrong was overwhelmed by his feelings of connection and kinship with the Ghanaian people. At an event arranged by the Gold Coast Arts Council, Armstrong and his All Stars were greeted by dancers, musicians, and drummers from every region of the country. Raymond described the moment:

> Groups from each region, accompanied by their own drummers and musicians, came into the arena and danced in front of the visitors. There were white-robed dancers from the north, spinning and leaping in the stick dance, while their drummers squeezed and pounded

the twanging under-arm drums. . . . There were crouching Ewe fishermen, advancing and retreating in unison, swinging cutlasses to the insistent rhythms of the bead-covered gourds. There were gorgeously robed Ashanti dancers, moving to the relentless pouncing of the Ashanti talking drums. The Americans watched, entranced. It was a great and moving tribute to a black man from beyond the seas.[7]

Beattie Casely-Hayford, the son of Archie Casely-Hayford, a minister in the Convention Peoples' Party and an organizer with the Arts Council, introduced Armstrong, saying, "Mr. Armstrong, the great American musician, who is black like all of us, is going to play. . . . We have been dancing for him all afternoon, and now he wants anyone who feels like it to dance to his music too."[8] Led by Lucille Armstrong, who danced with an elderly Ghanaian from the north, hundreds of people began dancing to Armstrong's music. Then Armstrong suddenly stopped playing. He was moved by the fact that one of the dancers resembled his mother, who had died twenty years before. Armstrong said: "I know it now. I came from here, way back. At least my people did. Now I know this is my country too."[9] For him, the significance of the crowds who had come to hear him in Accra was clear: "After all, my ancestors came from here and I still have African blood in me."[10] Armstrong the American embraced his African roots and caused Africans to embrace him.

The U.S. consulate in Accra was elated by what it called an "outpouring of press and public enthusiasm" for Armstrong and his All Stars. The consulate proudly cited the Ghanaian *Daily Mail,* which credited the U.S. government for the visit, applauding the "unbiased support for the African's course. . . . And they don't just talk thousands of miles away. They come to our land to see for themselves."[11] *Drum* magazine, read by people all over Africa, likewise remarked on the trip's global significance with its August 1956 feature: it both declared the trumpeter's virtuosity and made light of Cold War tensions, with the phrase "Satchmo Blows Up the World."[12]

But if Armstrong was moved and inspired by his experience of

6. *Armstrong wearing an African hat, Accra, Ghana, 1956.* Courtesy of the Louis Armstrong House and Archives, Queens College, New York City.

an African country on the eve of independence, this did not blind him to the struggles the Ghanaian people still faced as they grappled with the legacies of centuries of slave trading and colonial subjugation. While officials' fears of a riot did not materialize during his concert, Armstrong had been deeply distressed by the methods of crowd control. Police had periodically moved in with clubs to break up a crowd whose responses to Armstrong's trumpet, Barrett Deems's drum solos, and Velma Middleton's singing they had judged too disorderly. For Armstrong, it seemed to echo the American South's vigilante violence against black people. Worse still, his concert had been an occasion on which force was used against black people by other black people. It recalled a recent concert in Germany where police had used clubs against the crowds, a scene reminiscent of Nazi repression.[13] It was perhaps Armstrong's sympathy with the struggles of black people in a state slowly making its way out of colonialism that inspired him to play Fats Waller's

"Black and Blue." If he related to the sense of struggle among a people who were emerging out of decades of colonialism with optimism but were not yet free, that sense of shared struggle was reciprocated. Among the scenes captured by the film crew was a shot of Nkrumah as Armstrong sang "Black and Blue." The prime minister had tears in his eyes.

Since the visit to Ghana had been a spectacular success from the U.S. government's point of view, plans were quickly under way to send Armstrong on an official State Department trip through the Soviet Union and South America the following year.[14] But even as high-profile negotiations for a Soviet tour were in progress, Armstrong abandoned his plans for the trip after an event that had profound significance for the cause of civil rights: on September 2, 1957, Governor Orval Faubus of Arkansas ordered units of the National Guard to surround Central High School in Little Rock and block the entry of African American students.[15] Armstrong's experiences in Ghana in 1956 and his identification with the Southern civil rights movement provided the context for his strident criticism of Eisenhower during the Little Rock crisis. Having visited an African nation on the eve of its independence, and in the wake of the actions of civil rights activists, Armstrong was able to speak out in ways that would have been unthinkable a decade earlier. In Armstrong's opinion, the government, by failing to support desegregation, had violated its end of the tacit agreement that underlay his role as Ambassador Satch. "The way they are treating my people in the South," Armstrong declared, "the Government can go to hell." Calling Faubus "an uneducated plow-boy," Armstrong also denounced Eisenhower for his foot dragging, accusing the president of being "two-faced" on civil rights and allowing "Faubus to run the government." "It's getting so bad a colored man hasn't got any country."[16]

The impact of Armstrong's not only denouncing Eisenhower and refusing to tour for the State Department but announcing that black people in America had no country sent a very alarmed State Department scrambling to get "perhaps the most effective unof-

ficial goodwill ambassador this country has ever had," to recon-
sider.[17] The State Department immediately issued a statement expressing hope that Armstrong "would not let the segregation issue
keep him from making a musical mission to Moscow." Despite
pressure from his manager to recant and patronizing attempts to
downplay his anger, (manager Pierre Tallerie nervously told the
New York Times that "Louie isn't mad at anybody. He couldn't stay
mad for more than few seconds anyway"), Armstrong stood his
ground.[18] A week later, when Eisenhower finally sent in federal
troops to uphold integration. Armstrong praised his actions as "just
wonderful." Indicating that he might change his mind about refusing to tour for the government, Armstrong sent the president
a telegram saying: "If you decide to walk into the schools with
the colored kids, take me along, daddy. God bless you."[19] But if
Armstrong could endorse Eisenhower's change in policy, amid a
flurry of attacks and canceled concerts and television appearances,
he continued to express outrage over Little Rock. He remarked
in October 1957 that he'd rather play in the Soviet Union than
Arkansas, because in Arkansas "Faubus might hear a couple of
notes—and he don't deserve that."[20] The University of Arkansas
student senate was especially alarmed that Armstrong didn't want
Faubus to hear any of the "beautiful notes coming out of my horn."
Accusing Armstrong of creating "an issue where none existed," the
students canceled his scheduled concert.[21]

"Sick at heart" over Little Rock, Secretary of State Dulles told
Attorney General Herbert Brownell that the situation was "ruining
our foreign policy. The effect of this in Asia and Africa will be
worse for us than Hungary was for the Russians."[22] If Armstrong's
coming out publicly against Eisenhower and overtly linking his
own willingness to represent the U.S. government to its position on
civil rights hardly made him the ideal ambassador in the government's eyes, he was already Ambassador Satch in many parts of the
world and was much too valuable to lose. Thus, the State Department was delighted to claim him as an ambassador in November
1957, when he made a commercial tour of South America just six

weeks after the launch of the Russian satellite Sputnik—an event that had stunned Americans.

In "Hot Jazz Trails Hot Jets to Rio," the *New York Times* reported that the United States was "pitting hot jet pilots and the hot jazz trumpet of Louis (Satchmo) Armstrong against the Russians in a continuing propaganda contest in South America."[23] According to the *Times,* the "almost simultaneous" appearance of United States Air Force stunt fliers and Louis Armstrong was "an unplanned coincidence." But with U.S. prestige suffering in the wake of Sputnik, "jets and jazz are having a favorable impact and the United States is again the talk of the day here."[24] As President Juscelino Kubitschek, two cabinet ministers, and high-ranking Brazilian military leaders watched "the acrobatics of the Thunderbird Squadron of F-100 Supersabres and formation flying by jet bombers and KC-97 tanker planes," U.S. officials emphasized their intent to provide "all possible help" during Armstrong's visit.[25] Officials had to contend not only with Sputnik but also with the Bolshoi Ballet, which had recently visited Rio and had topped opinion polls as the cultural highlight of the year.[26] Armstrong did not disappointment the U.S. officials who hoped for a propaganda coup. In Caracas, Venezuela, as he had in Rio, Armstrong emphasized and embraced the change that was occurring in his country, telling audiences that "the situation in general for Negroes is far better than it used to be, despite what happened at Little Rock."[27]

If issues of civil rights had been relatively contained in the early jazz tours, Armstrong's Ghana trip and his subsequent denunciation of Eisenhower during the 1957 Little Rock crisis dramatically illuminated the connections between the domestic and foreign policies underlying the tours. As State Department officials responded to international charges of U.S. racism by pointing to change within the country, and attempted to counter and contain negative publicity about white resistance to the civil rights movement, they were increasingly forced to respond to criticisms of escalating U.S. involvement on the African continent. From World War II onward, U.S. officials had designs on mineral-rich Katanga Province in the

Belgian Congo.[28] When Louis Armstrong and his band embarked on their 1960–1961 tour of Africa, he, like almost all Americans, was unaware of the fact that CIA director Allen Dulles had transmitted an order in late August from Eisenhower to the CIA station in Leopoldville (Kinshasa) in the Belgian Congo: the recently elected prime minister, Patrice Lumumba, was to be eliminated.[29] Yet the centrality of the Congo crisis set the tone for the Armstrong tour and is fundamental to understanding the rationale for the trip and its unusual expenditure of resources.

The Congo had declared its independence from Belgium in 1960 under Lumumba's leadership. Belgium was not willing to lose Katanga Province without a fight. Through Belgian scheming, Katanga seceded from the Congo almost immediately after independence in June 1960, under the anti-Communist leadership of Moise Tshombe. U.S. officials were thus compelled to navigate their way through the Congo crisis with the utmost determination to retain control over the region's mineral wealth. While U.S. dependence on Katanga's Shinkolobwe uranium mine had diminished after the discovery of accessible uranium in the American West in 1952, American officials still had high stakes in limiting Soviet access to new sources of uranium and retaining Western access to the region's many others minerals, including cobalt, chrome, copper, and platinum.[30] For the fledgling nation, Katanga's resources were critical to any future economic and political viability. In his efforts to reunite the country, Lumumba sought help from the United Nations, and then from the Soviets when UN help did not materialize. While American officials ideally wanted a pro-Western and united Congo, they did not want to jeopardize access to Katanga's minerals.[31] Most fundamental to the administration's decision to assassinate Lumumba however, was that Eisenhower, Allen Dulles, and others distrusted Lumumba's nationalist and socialist politics and did not believe that a black African was capable of independent political thought.[32] The Eisenhower administration had hoped to maintain a separation between issues of foreign policy and those of domestic racial politics. But the international spotlight was now trained on its relationship with a new black nation.

As international criticism of U.S. economic ambitions mounted, officials with an all-too-spotty record on civil rights at home were forced to fight it out in Africa with Armstrong and his All Stars.

Armstrong began his twenty-seven-city tour of Africa in October 1960, accompanied by trombonist Trummy Young, clarinetist Barney Bigard, pianist Billy Kyle, bassist Arvell Shaw, drummer Danny Barcelona, and singer Middleton. Exemplifying the public and private sponsorship of the tours, the first two weeks of the tour—in Ghana and Nigeria—were sponsored by Pepsi-Cola, and the State Department sponsored the remaining nine weeks. Blurring the lines between commerce and war, *Down Beat* termed the first leg of the tour "a Madison Avenue Mission for Pepsi." The magazine reported that "Armstrong and his Pepsi Six are shock troops battling Coca-Cola for the African soft drink market."[33] The first stop on the trip was a return trip to Accra, where Armstrong was again met by Ghanaian musicians and dancers. Pepsi-Cola saturated Accra and Lagos with Armstrong's picture and the syllogism: "You like Satchmo. Pepsi brings you Satchmo. Therefore, you like Pepsi."[34] Armstrong's visit to Lagos coincided with Nigerian independence celebrations. With posters announcing "Pepsi Brings You Satchmo," the concerts "could be attended by anyone with the admission fee of two shillings sixpence and five bottle tops."[35] For some, Armstrong's presence underscored the significance of independence as a unique moment in history.[36] But for the Martiniquean intellectual Frantz Fanon, such transparent linkages between market and political freedoms were unsettling. He observed of Africa that "the United States had plunged in everywhere, dollars in the vanguard, with Armstrong as herald and American Negro diplomats, scholarships, the Voice of America."[37] If Fanon saw Armstrong as representing the American Century, others would not concede jazz to the United States or its current politics. In "We Claim Jazz, Listen to Africa," a South African writing in a Ghanaian newspaper celebrated jazz and the fact that "the voice of Africa comes to us from thousands of miles away," even if "under the splutter and meretricious ornament of the Voice of America."[38]

The State Department–sponsored leg of the trip took place in two parts. In the first segment, October 24–December 4, 1960, the band played in Cameroon, the Republic of the Congo, Uganda, Kenya, Tanganyika, Rhodesia, and Nyasaland. In an article titled "Satchmo Plays for Congo's Cats," the *New York Times* described Armstrong's arrival in Leopoldville by ferry; he crossed the Congo River from Brazzaville, in the French-controlled Congo, where he had performed the day before. Armstrong was met by "tom tom drummers and dancers of the Baboto, Ekonda, and Nkokongo tribes" as he "was carried on a red throne" by men "painted in ochre and violet."[39] Armstrong and his All Stars were greeted by 10,000 Congolese, "among the true devotees of 'chahss,' as jazz is pronounced here," continued the *Times*.[40] USIS-Leopoldville had set up special national broadcasts featuring agency-supplied tapes and records, and had distributed 2,000 posters.[41] That Armstrong was also welcomed by Clare H. Timberlake, the U.S. ambassador to the Congo, and escorted throughout by "an entire police company," was certainly no accident, given the controversial role of the United States in the unfolding tragedy of the Katanga secession crisis.[42] Indeed, several weeks later the band arrived in Elisabethville in Katanga Province, where they performed and stayed at the palace with Prime Minister Moise Tshombe.[43] Typifying what Arvell Shaw described as their regular program in the States, the Elisabethville concert featured "My Bucket's Got a Hole in It," "Tiger Rag," "Now You Have Jazz," "High Society Calypso," "Ole Miss," "Perdido," "St. Louis Blues," "I Love You So," and "When the Saints Go Marching In." Looking back on the concerts, Armstrong liked to comment that he had stopped a civil war, when a day-long truce was called so both sides could hear him perform. He did not know, however, that at the time of his visit to Leopoldville at the end of October and to Katanga in November, Lumumba had been arrested and was being held and tortured by Tshombe's army, with American assistance. Lumumba would be assassinated in January 1961 with the CIA's help, while Armstrong and his band were still playing on the continent.[44]

Whether State Department officials were engaged in a strategy

7. Armstrong being carried on a throne, Leopoldville, Republic of the Congo, October 1960. Courtesy of the Louis Armstrong House and Archives, Queens College, New York City.

of plausible deniability about this shameful episode in U.S. history, or whether they were unaware of what the CIA was involved in, their accounts of Armstrong's visit were unabashedly self-congratulatory. Reporting that an audience of 10,000 had come to see Armstrong perform in a stadium, U.S. officials in Leopoldville stated that "Louis 'Satchmo' Armstrong brought the first happy event to this trouble-torn city since independence on June 30. There is wide evidence that the Congolese appreciated this friendly gesture by the United States and that the impact of this visit will leave a sweet taste in Leopoldville for a long time to come."[45] Before leaving the Congo, Armstrong and his group also played before an audience of 6,000—consisting of United Nations troops, Congolese workers, and their families—in a "double airplane hanger" at the Kamina U.N. military base.[46] Amid Soviet accusations (reported in the New York *Times*) that "Louis Armstrong was sent to the Congo to 'distract' the Congolese from the crisis there," the USIS post at Brazzaville was pleased that Armstrong had deflected "politically oriented questions" about the trip with "a simple statement: 'Music's the same anywhere.'"[47]

The *Kenya Weekly News,* published in Nairobi, echoed this sentiment explaining that "Satchmo Armstrong has gone over tremendously well everywhere for the reason, as he puts it, that 'a note's a note in any language.'"[48] Arriving in Nairobi, Armstrong and his band were greeted by nationalist leader Tom Mboya, with a Kenyan band playing "Blueberry Hill." *Drum* magazine emphasized the differences in musical traditions between East Africa and black Americans, but American officials were thrilled with the responses from local press.[49] The *Sunday Nation* in Nairobi, for example, used the occasion of Armstrong's visit to reflect on the events in Little Rock. Little Rock, the editorial argued, showed America in a good light because it demonstrated that the United States was ready to "legislate against ignorance" and "enforce that legislation with armed force if necessary. . . . Ambassador Satchmo comes to us as the living testimony that the United States constitutes a large slice of this world wherein opportunity of advancement is not governed by inherited position or colour."[50]

Though Armstrong was certainly unaware of the U.S. government's political machinations in the Congo, and though he did embrace music as transcending politics, careful attention to his statements reveals a much more complex critique of that relationship than many of his contemporaries and subsequent critics have acknowledged. The *New York Times* reported from Nairobi in November 1960 that "Mr. Armstrong showed his diplomacy when he ruled out political questions from newsmen. 'I don't know anything about it; I'm just a trumpet player,' he said with a laugh in his gravelly voice. 'The reason I don't bother with politics is the words is so big. By the time they break them down to my size, the joke is over.'"[51] Through self-deprecating (if not self-demeaning) humor, Armstrong expressed cynicism and frustration in suggesting politics was a "joke." For Armstrong, like the African audiences for whom he played, freedom remained an aspiration, not an achievement. The civil rights struggles had considerably widened the boundaries of political expression; but if we are to fully appreciate the militancy of Armstrong's 1957 actions, as well as his statements while on tour, we must also emphasize the constraints that limited his choices. The long arm of McCarthyism, with its worst excesses seemingly past, left many singers and actors black-listed well into the late 1960s. Indeed, after Armstrong's angry denunciation of Eisenhower, an overt disavowal of politics while on his later State Department tour may well have been the price he had to pay the government for continuing to work.

A similar critique of American race relations was evident in Armstrong's 1961 essay in *Ebony* magazine, "Daddy, How the Country Has Changed," written shortly after his return from Africa. At one level an optimistic endorsement of integration, the essay also provides a scorching indictment of Jim Crow America through candid thick description.[52] Emphasizing the warmth and respect that existed between himself and such white performers as Bing Crosby, Armstrong makes clear the limits of this friendship: "But we weren't social. Even in the early days we didn't go cabareting together. I didn't go out with the Hollywood colony then— and still don't. I don't go out with the modern stars, even though

I've played with a lot of them—Danny Kaye, Sinatra. I don't even know where they live. In fact, I've never been invited to the home of a movie star—not even Bing's."[53] Discussing the South, Armstrong noted that he still could not play in his hometown of New Orleans, and explained: "I don't socialize with the top dogs of society after a dance or concert. Even though I'm invited, I don't go. These same society people may go around the corner and lynch a Negro. But while they're listening to our music, they're not thinking about trouble. What's more, they're watching Negro and white musicians play side by side."[54] Armstrong always embraced change in American race relations, and the power of music to effect that change, but he pointed to the current limits of that change.

Armstrong had arrived in Kenya "visibly worn," according to the *New York Times. Drum* magazine reported that Armstrong was annoyed with the press for making much of his weary aspect, reportedly asking, "Well, don't *you* get tired too?"[55] On the orders of a physician, who judged Armstrong to be suffering from "intense fatigue" after giving three concerts in Abidjan (Ivory Coast), Armstrong and his band took a break in Paris beginning December 5, before returning to Africa in January to finish the tour.[56] Tragically, it was too late for singer Velma Middleton, who had been warned by her physician not to travel, because of the risk of life-threatening illness due to high blood pressure and excessive weight. Middleton suffered a stroke and did not survive the trip. Arvell Shaw recalled the paralyzing loss felt by the band. "It was one of the few times that I saw Louis cry."[57]

Even the stop in Paris was hardly a respite from the demanding schedule. While in Paris, Armstrong worked on "Paris Blues," and interrupted the filming to fly to Gstaad, Switzerland, to play before a ski-resort audience that included the jazz-loving King Bhumibol Adulyadej of Thailand.[58] On January 9, 1961, the band flew to Dakar, where they began the tour's final leg, which lasted until January 30 and took them through Senegal, Mali, Sierra Leone, Liberia, Sudan, and the United Arab Republic. Armstrong won the praise of American officials in Dakar, who argued that "the presentation of the great American Negro artist added measurably to the prestige of the United States and at the same time gave jazz lovers the thrill of a lifetime." State Department officials in Bamako (Mali) celebrated what they saw as an effective challenge to criticisms of American racism: the "spectacle" of Armstrong's integrated band. The trip, the officials argued, marked "many firsts for . . . the young republic of Mali . . . : the first major concerts of any kind ever held in Bamako, . . . the first cultural presentation undertaken here by a foreign mission, . . . their first exposure to original American jazz, and . . . their first glimpse of an American Negro." In Cairo, in what was then the United Arab Republic, officials were especially delighted with Armstrong's "extracurricular" performance for five hundred children at a tuberculosis sanatorium.[59]

The All Stars returned home in February 1961, triumphant and weary. They were met with news of African American protests at the United Nations over the murder of Patrice Lumumba that month and an accelerating Southern civil rights movement, with its sit-ins and freedom rides. Jazz musicians Max Roach and Abbey Lincoln were among those who scuffled with guards in the UN gallery as hundreds of protesters gathered outside the UN and marched through Times Square later that night.[60] As U.S. officials sought grounds for a plausible denial of CIA involvement in the assassination of Lumumba, the white resistance to the Southern sit-ins and freedom rides drew increasing international censure. In May 1961, an interracial group of freedom riders left Washington, D.C., on Trailways buses for New Orleans. When riders were savagely attacked en route from Birmingham to Montgomery, the USIA reported the incident to be "highly detrimental" and a "severe blow to U.S. prestige."[61] By August of that year, "more than seventy thousand people had participated in sit-ins and more than three thousand had been arrested."[62]

Armstrong himself continued to express his sympathy for the movement and for a younger generation of black radicals. Two years later, he posed for a photo in *Ebony* magazine sitting in a chair in his home reading *Blues People,* by Amiri Baraka (LeRoi Jones).[63]

8. Armstrong performing outdoors at Tahseen Al Saha, Cairo's largest health center, January 1961. Courtesy of the Louis Armstrong House and Archives, Queens College, New York City.

9. *Armstrong assisting a student at a school in West Africa, January 1961.* Courtesy of the Louis Armstrong House and Archives, Queens College, New York City.

His self-conscious pose with *Blues People,* a critique of the commodification of black music by the white-dominated music industry, is striking. Armstrong had revolutionized the role of the jazz soloist in the 1920s, and his stature as an innovator in jazz was unquestioned. But in more recent years, his path-breaking image had suffered as a result of his criticisms of modern jazz. In addition, a younger generation of musicians was accusing him of reducing jazz to entertainment in Uncle Tom roles. By publicly associating himself with *Blues People,* Armstrong refused the role of generational adversary, and, perhaps more subtly, marked himself as an author and a critic. While some scholars have questioned Armstrong's part in his 1936 autobiography (written with a ghost writer), researchers have unearthed Armstrong's prolific if unorthodox writings, which range from articles, book reviews, and two book-length autobiographies to jokes, prose narratives, recipes, pornography, and song lyrics.[64] His 1936 autobiography is fundamentally concerned with the corruption of jazz by the market and with "the artistic possibilities of jazz and the contributions of African American musicians."[65] With these concerns—shared by the later bebop artists, as well as with Baraka in *Blues People*—Armstrong places himself in the tradition of intellectuals grappling with power and race in cultural production. Armstrong has been consistently claimed by those writing in the tradition of Ralph Ellison, who, as Farah Griffin has argued, critiqued Baraka's *Blues People* "for paying attention to politics and ideology at the expense of art and poetics."[66] While one should not elide the complexity of Armstrong's "absurdist humor," through which he could inhabit the trappings of the "grotesque jester" as well as the "self-assured modernist" (to use Brent Edwards' words), in this instance the photograph marks an endorsement of a specific moment in black cultural production linked explicitly to politics and the black freedom movement.[67]

Securing Ambassador Satch for an African tour had seemed the ultimate prize to U.S. officials. But it was only the beginning of increasingly visible U.S. political and military interventions in Africa that led the State Department to make further cultural efforts on the continent. These would include such black artists as the Golden Gate Quartet (a gospel group) and the Cozy Cole Jazz Revue. Even more extensive than the Armstrong tour (though not nearly so high-profile) was the Golden Gate Quartet's 1962 State Department–sponsored tour, which lasted a full four months, from January 17 (Morocco) to May 18 (Cairo), and included fifty-four cities across every region of Africa. The group had been well known in the 1940s not only for their gospel and spirituals, but for their popular-front ballads such as "Stalin Wasn't Stallin," which paid tribute to the heroic Russian sacrifices in defeating Hitler. The State Department had already drawn on the populist appeal of the group's spirituals and folk songs in a 1958–1959 tour of South Asia, Southeast Asia (including Laos and Vietnam) and the Middle East.[68] During that tour, it is likely that the "left-leaning" popular-front-style material was played. Officials had noted the group's success in Trivandrum and Cochin (India), stating: "This is the *red state* of India—very excellent."[69]

Performances in Brazzaville and Leopoldville (March 11–15) drew especially enthusiastic praise from U.S. officials. The quartet, along with pianist Herman Flintall comprised Clyde Riddick, first tenor; Caleb Gynard, second tenor; Frank Todd, baritone; Orlandus Wilson, bass. Playing a full repertoire of black American spirituals including "Joshua Fit the Battle of Jericho," "Nobody Knows the Trouble I've Seen," "Swing Low, Sweet Chariot," and "Deep River," the Golden Gate Quartet was applauded for its ability to convey the struggles of black Americans. Commenting on "Joshua Fit the Battle of Jericho," an insightful embassy report noted: "The name 'Joshua' can be considered as a real symbol in America where the trumpet of Armstrong, Gillespie, and others has brought forth from the depths of the suffering Negro people the heartrending tones, which, under the name of jazz, have caused several walls of racial discrimination to break down."[70] Officials praised the black spirituals as an ideal vision of America: "so dynamic, so full of zest, that their interpreters would deserve being named God's minstrels or jesters by celestial decree."[71] In the continuing Congo crisis, U.S. officials were determined to distinguish the United States from the former colonial power, Belgium. In this context, African American culture could be highly valued for its ability to convey to the Congolese people a sense of shared suffering, as well as the conviction that equality could be gained under the American political system.

In the context of U.S. attempts to woo African trade unionists, U.S. officials were equally delighted with the quartet's rendition of "Sixteen Tons." Described by one official as being "about a miner who has to load sixteen tons of coal each day and who complains about his inhuman lot," the song was useful for Americans, since it suggested the brutal Belgian labor practices in the mines. The official's embrace of the pro-labor song stands as a striking cultural corollary to the widespread American efforts to support anti-Communist African trade unions.[72] Yet had the song been performed in an American context, it would quickly have betrayed the quartet's popular-front past. And given the primary objective of protecting access to the region's uranium, cobalt, and tin mines, this otherwise insightful official seems to have missed the irony in his choice of a mining metaphor when he argued: "The appeal of the Golden Gate Quartet is a regular blow-torch which would melt spectators made of the grouchiest metal."[73]

Not surprisingly, the quartet's program was not well received in Salisbury and Bulawayo, Southern Rhodesia (Zimbabwe), during concerts for white audiences. But the group had great success with a concert in the "African sector" of Bulawayo and in Lusaka, Northern Rhodesia (Zambia), which officials noted had "not as much segregation as Southern Rhodesia."[74] In such an extensive tour, the group faced wildly inconsistent venues and promotions. In Conakry (Guinea), where the United States was openly hostile to the nonaligned politics and avowed socialism of President Sékou Touré, they had "a very uncomfortable engagement" due to what officials cryptically referred to as "the political atmosphere." Concerts were especially successful in West and Central African countries, such as Ghana and Dahomey, and in Kenya.[75] Yet even in Ghana, where the State Department cultural programs had made their debut with Armstrong's unofficial trip in 1956 and where the Golden Gate Quartet had been warmly welcomed, the honeymoon was about to end. U.S.-Ghanaian relations showed significant strain by 1963. That year, Cozy Cole toured Ghana with his jazz revue. Greeted by 3,000 people and five Ghanaian bands, Cole was embraced and renamed "Kwesi" Cole. He generated much enthusiasm for his plan to do a "West African High Life" album upon his return to the United States. Yet such highlights were offset by what the USIS in Accra described as "renewed attacks" on the United States. These included charges that the United States was attempting to undermine Nkrumah's government and criticism of the American role in the Congo crisis. The attacks also included "flat charges of CIA instigation" of the 1963 Iraqi coup that ousted (and killed) 'Abd al-Karim Qassim, the Iraqi leader whose seizure of power in the 1958 coup had so disturbed U.S. officials.[76] Increasingly in Africa, as well as across the globe, cultural programs were forced to contend with criticisms of America's foreign policy and its race relations at home.

A half-decade after the beginning of the jazz tours, the jury was still out as to their achievements and effects. In the words of the writer and lyricist Iola Brubeck, "The entire jazz community was elated with the official recognition of jazz and its international implications." Yet jazz artists who had participated in the tours had experienced first hand the uneasy juxtaposition of the arts and less than transparent foreign-policy agendas. And as members of integrated bands, they were uniquely steeped in the ironies of the export of jazz ambassadors at a time when America was still a Jim Crow nation and civil rights activists were faced with violent resistance and the inaction of the federal government. Following their own tour through Eastern Europe and the Middle East in 1958, Dave and Iola Brubeck addressed these ironies in the satirical musical *The Real Ambassadors,* a 1961–1962 collaboration between the Brubecks and Louis Armstrong.[77] The bands of both leaders came together for the production, and many of the musicians—including drummer Joe Morello, trombonist and vocalist Trummy Young, and pianist Billy Kyle—had been on the State Department tours. A jazz musical revue performed to critical acclaim at the Monterey Jazz Festival in September 1962—with Brubeck and Armstrong, joined by vocalists Carmen McRae and Dave Lambert, Jon Hendricks, and Yolande Bavan—*The Real Ambassadors* satirized State Department objectives, personnel, and protocol, and voiced a powerful and unequivocal indictment of Jim Crow America.[78]

The Real Ambassadors received much praise in the music world for its swinging juxtaposition of disparate musical styles. As Leonard Feather described it: "Often witty, sometimes poignant words [are] eloquently matched with melodies that are simple, totally suited to the artists, and generally of unusual melodic charm."[79] But it was also an important work of cultural and social criticism and a provocative political intervention, lauded by critics for its powerful "social message" that avoided propaganda and pretension.[80] *The Real Ambassadors* brilliantly captured the often complex (and contradictory) politics of the State Department tours at the intersections of the Cold War, African and Asian nation building, and the U.S. civil rights struggle. On the one hand, the Brubecks saw many

10 *Full cast of The Real Ambassadors, Monterey, California, 1962.* Copyright © by Dave Brubeck. Courtesy of the Dave Brubeck Collection, Holt-Atherton Special Collections, University of the Pacific Libraries, Stockton, California.

of the State Department personnel with whom they had worked as their allies in the promotion of the arts. For these government cultural workers, like the musicians, the State Department tours offered a unique opportunity to follow in the best traditions of countries (such as France) that made culture, and not simply defense, a fundamental part of their foreign relations. In satirizing the tours, Iola Brubeck guessed that "we were saying things a lot of the cultural personnel would probably have liked to say themselves."[81] On the other hand, as in Gillespie's tour of the Middle East, not all U.S. foreign-service personnel were as enlightened as those encountered by the Brubecks. Despite the overarching State Department strategy of supporting civil rights, individual officials abroad often mirrored the racial views of President Eisenhower and his segregationist allies, who were profoundly uncomfortable with the pres-

ence of African Americans. Thus, honoring the perspectives of the
musicians, the Brubecks allude to the ways in which the tours, like
world events, could sometimes spin out of the control of the State
Department.

Set in a mythical African country named Talgalla, *The Real Ambassadors* opens with the narrator explaining how the hero, mod-
eled on and played by Armstrong, had "spoken to millions of the
world's people" with his horn. He and other musicians had "inadvertently served a national purpose, which officials recognized and
eventually sanctioned with a program called cultural exchange."[82]
We are reminded that the tours were fundamentally a product of
Cold War foreign policy. The foreign policy of the tours, as well as
the ironic background of racial unrest in the United States, is captured in the song "Cultural Exchange" (lyrics by Iola Brubeck):

> *Yeah! I remember when Diz was in Greece back in '56.*
> *He did such a good job, we started sending jazz all over the world.*
>
> *The State Department has discovered jazz.*
> *It reaches folks like nothing ever has.*
> *Like when they feel that jazzy rhythm,*
> *They know we're really with 'em;*
> *That's what they call cultural exchange.*
>
> *No commodity is quite so strange*
> *As this thing called cultural exchange.*
> *Say that our prestige needs a tonic,*
> *Export the Philharmonic,*
> *That's what we call cultural exchange!*
> *. . . And when our neighbors call us vermin,*
> *We sent out Woody Herman.*

Note the telling observation that "no commodity is quite so
strange / as this thing called cultural exchange." Indeed, in the
tours by Armstrong and the Brubecks, cultural exchange was a

commodity that closely paralleled the quintessential Cold War commodities, oil and uranium. An appreciation of the musicians' critique of State Department notions of cultural exchange must begin with the fact that both artists had participated in the tours. They had deliberately been sent into the front lines of major foreign-policy crises.

Iola Brubeck's lyrics indicate that the scope of these programs involved many realms of the performing arts, yet emphasize that jazz was the pet project of the State Department. That U.S. officials could claim jazz as a uniquely American art form gave it more diplomatic cachet than classical music, theater, or ballet.[83] And the inferiority complex of government officials and supporters of the arts toward the classical music and ballet of Europeans and the Soviet Union could be used as an argument to fund the arts, and thus could be turned to the advantage of the American arts.

In *The Real Ambassadors* the Brubecks addressed the glaring contradiction in a U.S. strategy that promoted black musicians as symbols of the triumph of American democracy when America was still a Jim Crow nation. Brubeck was concerned that Armstrong's contribution to the civil rights cause was being largely overlooked even though official attempts to showcase Armstrong as a symbol of racial progress had imploded when Armstrong denounced President Eisenhower during the desegregation crisis in Little Rock in 1957. Despite Armstrong's outspokenness, as the struggle for equality accelerated he was widely criticized by civil rights activists as an Uncle Tom, and compared unfavorably with a younger, more militant group of jazz musicians.[84] Written as a tribute to Armstrong, *The Real Ambassadors* recovered his submerged militancy and paid homage to him as a political actor. It also expressed Brubeck's own commitment to desegregation. Throughout the 1950s, Brubeck had refused to play before segregated audiences in the South or to accede to segregationist demands that he replace his African American bassist, Eugene Wright.[85]

The musical opens with a suggestion of the militancy concealed behind Armstrong's mask, countering the perception that Arm-

strong hewed to whites' stereotypes of black cheerfulness and do-
cility. The narrator's claim that the hero possesses the "ability to
keep his opinions to himself," is challenged when a voice (Armstrong) declares, "Lady, if you could read my mind, your head
would bust wide open." Moreover, the audience learns precisely
what was on the hero's mind: "Look here, what *we* need is a goodwill tour of Mississippi." And in a sharp reminder of Armstrong's
denunciation of Eisenhower: "Forget Moscow—when do we play
in New Orleans!"[86]
    Nevertheless, the hero is persuaded to begin yet another tour.
"The morning of their departure, members of the President's
Committee . . . for Cultural Exchange appeared to give the musicians a last minute 'briefing.' . . . When you travel in a far-off land /
Remember, you're more than just a band. / You represent the USA
/ So watch what you think and do and say."[87] Here, as well as in the
song "Remember Who You Are," the Brubecks evoked and evaluated the briefing they received before embarking on their tours:

> [Armstrong]: Remember who you are and what you represent.
>   Always be a credit to your government.
>   No matter what you say or what you do,
>   The eyes of the world are watching you.
>   Remember who you are and what you represent. . . .
> [Trummy Young]: Remember who you are and what you represent.
>   Never face a problem, always circumvent.
>   Stay away from issues.
>   Be discreet—when controversy enters, you retreat.

As we have seen with Quincy Jones's scathing indictment of the
Gillespie Band's briefing, musicians were often quite taken aback
by the directives they received. But if Gillespie was able to dodge
his, briefings were an inescapable part of the tour, providing, in the
words of Brubeck, "a long list of how we should act."[88] With
briefings so focused on the prevention of potentially embarrassing
behavior, the Brubeck Quartet had had no warning about the tur-

bulent politics they encountered. Moreover, like the Gillespie band, the musicians sometimes encountered unsympathetic cultural personnel, and in those circumstances they could be overwhelmed by the politics of the tours. Expressing a frustration with the emphasis on elite audiences, trumpeter Clark Terry, who toured India and Pakistan in 1978, explained that they "coined a phrase to describe the official receptions musicians were expected to attend: 'time for us to go to the grinner.'" Terry added that "our escort officer was very uptight, very strict about time, appearance, and behavior. . . . 'If these guys blow it, it's my neck.'"[89]

Indeed, the last stanza of "Remember Who You Are" alludes to the musicians' allegiance to something other than the American government—namely, jazz and the history that gave birth to the music. Armstrong sings:

> Remember who you are and what you represent.
> Jelly Roll and Basie helped us to invent
> A weapon like no other nation has;
> Especially the Russians can't claim jazz. . . .

Here, the artists' burden of representation is to remember Jelly Roll and Basie and to represent jazz, even as the lyrics celebrate the gift of that music to America and proclaim pride in the music's status as a unique Cold War weapon.

As the tour, free of political drama (no wars, no political assassinations), comes to a close in *The Real Ambassadors,* the hero's story has just begun. In his travels throughout Africa, the hero had heard stories of Talgalla, "the newest of new African nations." Talgalla's portrayal in the musical satirizes the political motives for the African tours. "It had been unknown and unrecognized as a nation until the two great superpowers simultaneously discovered its existence. Suddenly Talgalla was a nation to be reckoned with." The Russians had built roads; "U.S. equipment had cleared the airfield."[90]

On the one hand, Talgalla is imagined as a product of superpower rivalries. Its mythic status as a repository of "tradition" and utopian dreams displaces actual African politics, just as the revue's subplot, a love story, displaces the story of U.S. interests in Africa and other formerly colonized areas (Armstrong's actual trip through Africa as well as Brubeck's actual trip through the Middle East). Yet Talgalla is also a place where a new social order can be ushered in—a symbol of democratic and utopian aspirations. The hero has been drawn to Talgalla by tales of an annual ceremony in which the social order in this "tiny tribal monarchy" is "turned upside down" for a week. Thus, as they approach Talgalla, the hero dreams of being "King for a Day."[91]

Despite the hero's superficial aspiration to be king, the song "King for a Day" unfolds as a satire on authority and a critique of political (civil rights) gradualism; the hero affirms a revolution in social relations against a voice that tells him, "You're expecting too much too soon." The opening passage illuminates the inspiration for the collaboration between the Brubecks and Armstrong and the fact that the Brubecks wrote the revue specifically for Armstrong. Constantly rewriting the libretto over a period of nearly five years to keep it topical, and writing with Armstrong in mind, the Brubecks incorporated Armstrong's playful statements before embarking on his six-month African tour in 1960. Armstrong was quoted in *Down Beat* commenting on the chance that the trip might extend behind the Iron Curtain: "Yeah, I'd like to slip under the Curtain. Let all them foreign ministers have their summit conferences—Satch just might get somewhere with them cats in a basement session."[92]

> *[Armstrong]: Man! If they would just let me run things my way, this world would be a swingin' place!*
> *[Trummy Young]: Yeah, Pops! What would you do?*
> *[Armstrong]: The first thing I'd do is call a basement session.*
> *[Trummy Young]: Uh, Pops, you mean summit conference.*
> *[Armstrong]: Man, I don't mean a UN kind of session. I mean a jam session.*

11. *Brubeck and Armstrong consulting on* The Real Ambassadors, *1962.*
Copyright © by Dave Brubeck. Courtesy of the Dave Brubeck Collection,
Holt-Atherton Special Collections, University of the Pacific Libraries,
Stockton, California.

Presenting jazz as a model for democracy, the lyrics move deftly between civil rights themes and international relations:

> *[Armstrong]: I'd go and form a swinging band*
>   *With all the leaders from every land.*
> *[Young]: Can't you hear that messed up beat?*
>   *I'll tell you now you'll meet defeat.*
> *[Armstrong]: Why they will fall right in a swinging groove*
>   *And all the isms gonna move.*
>   *Relationships is bound to improve.*

As the debate between the hero and the skeptic continues, it alludes to symbols of monarchy and authority. In the playful discus-

sion of the oppositional black politics of self-naming, Iola Brubeck is referencing bassist Eugene Wright's sobriquet "Senator," a nickname that stuck from the time of their 1958 tour, as well as riffing on an Armstrong interview where he explained his attitude toward the title of "Ambassador."[93] During his 1960 Africa tour, Armstrong told *New York Times Magazine* reporter Gilbert Millstein: "We used to call one another that when we was broke and hungry. That's where the Duke got his name, Duke Ellington. And the Count—Count Basie."[94]

> [Trummy Young]: Pops, you got eyes to wear a crown?
> [Armstrong]: I might enjoy being king.
>   After all, Buddy Bolden was king.
> [Trummy Young]: And there's King Oliver.
> [Armstrong]: There's Count Basie.
> [Young]: And Duke Ellington.
> [Armstrong]: And Earl "Fatha" Hines.
> [Young]: Man, quit jiving me! You know that cat ain't no Earl.
>   That's his first name!
> [Armstrong]: No? Man, he had me fooled all these years!

The United States has recognized the importance of Talgalla by appointing an ambassador, due to arrive momentarily. When the hero arrives—trumpet in hand—he blows his horn as a sign of greeting. Mistaking Armstrong for the officially appointed American ambassador, the Talgallans ask, "You are the American Ambassador aren't you?" The hero replies: That's what they call me, Ambassador Satch." The Talgallans are thrilled that "out of all the Americans such a wondrous man should be chosen as their Ambassador." Everyone is happy for several days, but the arrival of the U.S. ambassador sparks a flurry of confusion: Who's the real ambassador?[95]

In the studio performance of the number "Who's the Real Ambassador?" the singers Dave Lambert, Jon Hendricks, and Annie Ross make appropriately stiff and sanctimonious State Department personnel, with the lyrics repeated a second time at breakneck tempo, parodying the uptight frenzy perceived by many musicians.[96]

> *It is evident we represent American society,*
> *noted for its etiquette, its manners and sobriety.*
> *We have followed protocol with absolute propriety.*
> *We're Yankees to the core.*
> *We're the real Ambassadors,*
> *Though we may appear as bores.*
> *We are diplomats in our proper hats.*

Fortunately, Armstrong steps in and clears up the confusion. But in doing so, he challenges the legitimacy of government policy and asserts his authority, grounded in something deeper than mere state sanction.

> *I'm the real Ambassador!*
> *It is evident I wasn't sent by government to take your place.*
> *All I do is play the blues and meet the people face to face.*
> *I'll explain and make it plain I represent the human race and don't*
> *   pretend no more.*
> *Who's the real Ambassador?*
> *Certain facts we can't ignore.*
> *In my humble way—I'm the USA.*
> *Though I represent the government,*
> *The government don't represent some policies I'm for.*
> *Oh, we've learned to be concerned about the Constitutionality.*
> *In our nation segregation isn't a legality.*
> *Soon our only differences will be in personality.*
> *That's what I stand for.*
> *Who's the real Ambassador? Yeah, The real Ambassador.*

With the central political tension of the drama resolved, the narrative turns to a romantic subplot, yet continually revisits the animating theme of civil rights. The poignant number "They Say I Look Like God," singled out by the *Saturday Review* as "moving and daring" and by critic Ralph Gleason as "one of the most moving moments in Monterey's history," opens with the lines:

> *They say I Look like God.*
> *Could God be black? My God!*
> *If all are made in the image of Thee,*
> *Could thou perchance a zebra be?*

Brubeck praised Armstrong for his ability to transform some of the more trivial lyrics—those written for a laugh—into pathos or political commentary. The Brubecks had written the lines for a laugh, "to show how ridiculous" a religious conception of racial hierarchy was. But, Brubeck continued: "Louis had tears in his eyes. He didn't go for a laugh, and the audience followed him away from our original intentions. And all through the night, he took those lines that were supposed to get a laugh and went the other way with it. And at the record session he cried. You can hear it at the end, when he says 'Really free' for the last time. He broke down a little."[97] After years of demeaning roles, the collaboration in *The Real Ambassadors* offered Armstrong material that was closer to his own sensibility and outlook. And while Armstrong had often managed to rise above racist material by the sheer force of his artistry, the production allowed him a chance to make a statement about a life-long struggle for control over his own representation—a struggle that had hardly ended with the Little Rock incident. For Armstrong, freedom remained an aspiration, not an achievement. And the power of *The Real Ambassadors,* which was performed during the most turbulent years of the civil rights movement, lay in its articulation of that yearning, as well as in its satirical wit and musical accomplishments.

After the Monterey Jazz Festival, *The Real Ambassadors* was never again performed.[98] (The studio production, released on LP and reissued on CD, was recorded before the festival.) At Monterey, Joe

Glaser, Armstrong's longtime manager, prevented the TV crews from filming it. Attempts to get it produced, including plans for a Broadway production, failed; it was consistently viewed, at the height of violent resistance to the civil rights movement, as too political and controversial.[99] In the utopian finale, "Swing Bells, Blow Satchmo"—rich with Old Testament biblical imagery of black Christianity—the hero's horn ("Joshua had just a horn") has announced a new world:

> *Ring out the news! The world can laugh again.*
> *This day—we're free! We're equal in every way. . . .*
> *Lift up thy voice like a trumpet*
> *And show thy people their transgressions and their sins. . . .*
> *Let the oppressed go free. . . .*
> *Blow Satchmo! Blow Satchmo!*
> *Can it really be, that you set all people free?*

That day had certainly not yet arrived in 1962—a year marked in the United States by the deaths and casualties inflicted by those protesting James Meredith's registration at the University of Mississippi, Oxford, and in the Belgian Congo by the start of many decades of U.S.-backed dictatorships. And it would appear no closer in the following year, when dogs and hoses were turned on demonstrators in the campaigns of the Southern Christian Leadership Conference (SCLC) in Birmingham, Alabama, and when four children were murdered in the bombing of that city's Sixteenth Street Baptist Church.

Even as the U.S. government recognized the power of jazz and African American culture and tried to harness it to Cold War foreign policy by projecting abroad an image of racial progress, the State Department jazz tours also provided a global platform from which to celebrate the subversive wit of jazz, and to announce to the world: "Been waitin so long for . . . the day we'll be free."[100] The international power and appeal of jazz did not lie in the fact that it represented the music of a free country, as the State Department would have it. Rather, as brilliantly and forcefully articulated in *The Real Ambassadors,* it was conveyed through the instruments and voices of the jazz ambassadors. The epitome of these, Louis Armstrong, expressed his aspirations for freedom in a world where he, like so many of the people for whom he played, was still awaiting the day when he would be "really free."

CHAPTER 4

Getting the Soviets to Swing

In the period between the Berlin crisis of August 1961 and the Cuban missile crisis of October 1962, Benny Goodman became the first jazz musician to tour the Soviet Union for the State Department, making thirty appearances in six Soviet cities from May 28 through July 8, 1962. Goodman's tour could not have come at a more inauspicious time. As President Kennedy ratcheted up Cold War rhetoric to new heights, Soviet Premier Nikita Khrushchev jammed Voice of America broadcasts and declared support for national liberation movements worldwide. Any possibility of a genuine cultural exchange was threatened by mutual suspicion and by the aggressive propaganda campaigns carried out by both sides.[1] But if the tour came at a particularly awkward time in U.S.-Soviet relations, the battle over tradition versus innovation in jazz that broke out during the tour rivaled Cold War hostilities in intensity. Among jazz devotees, Goodman might have seemed an unlikely figure to land in the midst of such a battle. With questions of free and avant-garde jazz versus bebop and West Coast cool jazz versus East Coast jazz dominating the style controversies of the day, any style-related question about Goodman had long appeared settled.[2] For most critics and contemporary musicians, Goodman's 1930s vintage swing was considered so out of fashion as not to warrant debate. But issues that may have been resolved in the United States were reopened overseas—exacerbated by the unexpected twists and energy of a global youth rebellion—as Soviet jazz fans passionately entered the fray.[3] Soviet officialdom was deeply suspicious of "decadent Western jazz"; the State Department was eager to woo

Soviet fans; and, most important, Goodman's musicians and the Soviet fans saw jazz as representing personal expression and the possibility of freedom. For all three of these interested parties, what got
played, and how it was played, mattered deeply.

Issues of race complicated the views of musicians, fans, and State
Department officials in multiple ways. On the one hand, the fierce
battles over style were not overtly about race and did not break
down along racial lines. Only four of the nineteen members of the
band were African Americans, and many of Goodman's main an-
tagonists, such as saxophonists Phil Woods and Zoot Sims, were
white (the antagonisms mainly concerned stylistic and generational
differences). On the other hand, matters were complicated by the
fact that the bebop revolution against swing was viewed by many
musicians as asserting a black style against the commercialization
and predictability that had come to characterize swing. As Nathaniel Mackey has argued, "The white appropriation and commercialization of swing resulted in a music that was less improvisatory, less
dependent on the inventiveness of the soloists, than was the case
with music played by African Americans."[4] It is no accident that
Woods had played with bebop innovator Dizzy Gillespie and was a
veteran of his 1956 Middle East tour.[5] For Woods, the freedom to
improvise and express himself—"to blow"—lay at the heart of his
disputes with Goodman, and it was Gillespie, not Goodman, who
epitomized the modern sensibility of jazz.

Issues of race likewise shaped the interpretations of the tour by
both governments. President Kennedy felt that the white attacks
on Freedom Riders in Alabama had embarrassed him during his
meeting with Soviet premier Khrushchev in Vienna. Reports from
Moscow claimed that the white resistance to racial integration was
"indicative of the American way of life."[6] For U.S. officials, it became just as important to show democracy in action through an
integrated jazz band as it was to woo Soviet citizens with the dynamism of jazz. While the jazz tour represented a breakthrough
in U.S.—Soviet cultural exchange, it ultimately revealed far more
about the international dynamics of dissent against ingrained hier-

archies than it did about the happy democratic American family supposedly embodied in Goodman's band.

Goodman had already established himself as an effective jazz ambassador during his 1956–1957 tour of Asia. Yet the decision to send him to the Soviet Union reflected the Soviets' official ambivalence toward jazz and the centrality of race in their criticism of the United States. State Department officials had picked up on the fact that there was avid interest in jazz in the Soviet Union and Eastern Europe; they saw the tour as a unique opportunity to fight the cultural Cold War.[7] Through informal polls taken at exhibitions, State Department and USIS officials learned that Soviet citizens tended to resent what they regarded as the heavy handed propaganda of Radio Free Europe. In contrast, they welcomed the cultural programming of Voice of America, and Willis Conover's jazz programs ranked as the most popular—to the consternation of Soviet officials, who tried to jam the broadcasts.

The fortunes of jazz in the Soviet Union had waxed and waned along with the periodic openness or repressiveness of the Soviet government. Enjoying wide acceptance in the 1920s, jazz was driven underground during the purges of the 1930s, revived again in the more tolerant years of World War II, only to be officially proscribed with the renewed clampdowns of the Cold War; many jazz musicians were arrested and sent to labor camps during the repression of the late Stalin years.[8] Despite their expressions of sympathy for the plight of black Americans, Soviets resisted jazz, considering it "in the vanguard of a Yankee cultural assault."[9] As U.S.—Soviet relations thawed under Khrushchev, the Cold War rivals began an official program of cultural exchange in 1956. The Soviets now accepted "symphonic" jazz, while still rejecting modern or "decadent" jazz.

Although the two countries entered a landmark cultural exchange agreement in 1958, the years immediately preceding the Goodman tour were especially volatile. The already limited agreement was "regulated" by both sides.[10] The *New York Times* reported that the State Department "refused to sanction the appearance of the Soviet Army's chorus and ensemble. The Soviet Union has not accepted any leading jazz band."[11] A proposed visit by Louis Armstrong to the Soviet Union was rejected outright, without explanation, by the head of the State Committee for Cultural Exchanges with Foreign Countries.[12] The Soviets blocked the participation of jazz musicians at the 1959 Moscow Fair, which ran from July 25 to September 5 in the Soviet capital's Sokolniki Park, despite concerted efforts on the part of Marshall Stearns, the jazz critic on the State Department music committee who had accompanied Dizzy Gillespie on the first jazz tour.[13] Previously, Stearns had taken a Soviet cultural delegation, led by N. N. Danilov, deputy minister of culture for the USSR, to a Duke Ellington concert at Wilton High School in Wilton, Connecticut. On the drive to Wilton, Stearns had attempted through an interpreter to convince the delegation that jazz should be part of the program, but he had quickly concluded that "it was like trying to explain a transistor to a cave man."[14] When the Russians heard Ellington, Stearns felt as though his "favorite child had been spit upon." And when, at intermission, "the entire delegation rose, in established Soviet style, and walked out of the concert," Stearns had refused to follow, explaining, "Hell, no—you can't leave Duke's playing when there is more to come." The conversation was over.[15]

The Soviet rejection of jazz was multifaceted. Given the widely acknowledged excellence of Soviet classical music and ballet, Soviet officialdom promoted a rigid hierarchy in art. Classical forms were deemed the only true art, and any modern form was considered not simply inferior but degenerate and decadent. As Uta G. Poiger has argued, from the time of the Soviets' First Five-Year Plan in 1928, tolerance toward jazz "soon evaporated." Throughout the 1930s and 1940s, "periods of greater leniency were followed by vicious xenophobic persecution of jazz fans and musicians. Attackers associated the music with unbridled sexuality, homosexuality, degeneracy, and bourgeois decadence."[16] Even the new official tolerance toward "symphonic jazz" rested on an assessment of its proximity to classical forms. Despite the shift toward openness, the pejorative associations of jazz as profligate and immoral still carried deep resonance. The profound unease with jazz also points to contradictions in Soviet racial ideology. The Soviets' aversion to jazz rested, in part, on a racist recoiling at black American cultural expression even as they were relying on claims to racial equality within the Soviet Union and exposure of American racism as perhaps their most effective Cold war weapons.[17] Yet it is important to recognize that even at the worst of its Cold War excesses, the Soviet Union was not a monolith. In what might be seen as a parallel to the differences between the antimodernists and modernists in the U.S. Congress and the State Department, some Soviet officials evidenced repugnance toward black culture while others genuinely sympathized with black Americans as another class of oppressed workers—and may even have enjoyed jazz. In the Cold War, both sides had their modernists and antimodernists, even when the balance was tipped in radically different directions.

But the banning of jazz from the Moscow Fair led many in the jazz world to question the State Department's commitment to the music. While *Down Beat*'s questioning of the State Department's interest in jazz may have been misplaced, confusing State Department views with those of conservative members of Congress, at stake was the question of what constituted art and culture in America. *Down Beat* objected to the American entertainment package at the festival, organized by Ed Sullivan. When asked about the absence of jazz, Sullivan's spokesman Gene Schott explained "they want a high type of 'typical American' entertainment, not an intellectual program."[18] This "high-type" entertainment, *Down Beat* sarcastically pointed out, turned out to be "a troupe of novelty snake dancers, saucer-spinners, and tightrope walkers, some accordion and harmonica music, one opera star, . . . three girl singers, a man who spits out lighted electric bulbs—and Ed Sullivan." Ironically, Louis Armstrong's manager, Joe Glaser, defended Sullivan and insisted that he had done everything possible to interest the Russians in jazz. A State Department spokesperson confirmed that "we tried very hard to interest the Russian delegation in jazz. The impact of jazz on the peoples of other lands is well known to us." But for *Down Beat,* "the question of how hip the State Department really is remains an open one." The State Department, charged *Down Beat,* had also neglected to book jazz into the World Youth Festival, scheduled for July 26–August 4 in Vienna. With the Soviets' budgeting $4 million for the festival, anti-Communists in Vienna feared that the festival would be "a perfect platform for Communist propaganda." Yet others tempered their criticism of the State Department, blaming Congress instead for its meager allocation of funds for cultural exports. Describing the congressional attitude as "simply chintzy," *Down Beat* reported that Representative John J. Rooney of Brooklyn "blew his top because Jack Teagarden's recent (and very successful) tour of the Orient had cost $102,000, instead of the estimated $66,350."[19] For these writers, the failure of many in Congress to appreciate what the State Department and the jazz world saw as the spectacular successes of the jazz tours over the previous three years made staunch supporters such as Representative Joseph Holt of California seem "a very small voice in the wilderness."[20]

New snags in exchange negotiations threatened to make the issue of sending jazz to the Soviet Union a moot point. As the acrimonious year of 1959 neared its end, with the cultural-exchange agreement set to expire, suspicious Soviet officials regarded the exchange "as a 'Trojan horse' whose stomach could be filled with "anti-Soviet material."[21] Georgi A. Zhukov, chairman of the State Committee for Cultural Relations with Foreign Countries, explained that "anti-Soviet material" included Western newspapers containing anti-Soviet propaganda; it also comprised "corrupted" films and art. Citing West German officials who had forced a Ukrainian choral group to delete from its program a song entitled "Peace and Friendship," Zhukov claimed that Western nations regulated everything that came from the East and "pretend they do not understand that cultural ties are bilateral." Carefully keeping score in the cultural volley, Max Frankel, writing from Moscow for the *New York Times,* surmised that "Moscow has probably made a greater impact with such companies as the Moiseyev folk dances and the Bolshoi Ballet than has the United States with major symphony orchestras."[22] Yet in the summer exhibitions, "the United States probably compiled a greater propaganda score, since many of the goods and much of the art had never been seen here before."[23] As Cold War hostilities raged, cultural exchange had become cultural competition and both sides jockeyed for control over what would be deemed appealing and ideologically correct.

Despite these considerable tensions, the United States and Soviet Union extended the cultural agreement at the end of November 1959, paving the way for the opening toward jazz that occurred in early 1961.[24] The receptivity of the Soviets to jazz in 1961 and 1962—just before the two superpowers brought the world to the brink of nuclear war during the Cuban missile crisis—is one of the many small ironies of the Cold War. As bootleg discs taped from *Voice of America* and *Radio Tangier* circulated throughout the Soviet Union, this clandestine swinging seemed to suggest that Willis Conover's prediction—"jazz is a door opener everywhere, a Pandora's box of friendliness totalitarians won't easily be able to close" —was coming true.[25] In 1959 *Down Beat* agreed, citing anecdotal evidence from across the music world: *New York Post* columnist Leonard Lyons, who had been in Moscow covering the *Porgy and Bess* production, described a debate between *Porgy* orchestra trumpeter Junior Mignott and a Russian trumpeter over the relative merits of Louis Armstrong and Dizzy Gillespie. The Russian preferred the modern trumpet style of Gillespie. A group of Polish musicians who had visited Moscow described a jazz group led by Nikolai Kapustin that was heavily influenced by Gerry Mulligan and Shorty Rogers. Finally, "when the Bolshoi Ballet visited America recently, its members were reported taking home staggering armfuls of jazz records." *Down Beat* concluded: "The State Department believes that the Russian turn-down of an American jazz tour was made *because* of, not despite, the popularity of jazz in Russia."[26]

This wellspring of enthusiasm for jazz in the Soviet Union began to exert pressure on Soviet official policy. In early 1961 Leonid Osipovich Utyosov—one of the Soviet Union's most popular orchestra leaders, designated "People's Artist of the Russian Federation"—sided with the people by declaring, "We need jazz." Utyosov's insistence that "good jazz is art" was featured prominently in *Sovietskaya Kultura*, the official organ of the Soviet Ministry of Culture. Representative of the Soviet modernists, Utyosov claimed in the article that to prohibit jazz as "a forbidden fruit" was "dangerous and interfered with the education of youth in musical taste." Utyosov's endorsement of jazz was praised by Osgood Caruthers, who shared his approval with readers of the *New York Times*, arguing for the "considerable significance" of the article in light of the recent "official taboo on most forms of Western jazz."[27] In response to what Caruthers characterized as "severe attacks, including charges that jazz was a Western imperialist weapon to sabotage the morals of young people," Utyosov declared: "I must say that jazz is not a synonym for imperialism and that the saxophone was not born of colonialism." Invoking official Marxist-Leninist sympathies with the poor to defend a broader modernism, Utyosov defended jazz as having roots "not in the bankers' safes but in the poor Negro quarters." Yet he was also adamant in his defense of contemporary "commercial jazz."[28] Rejecting the hierarchies that had long dominated the official Soviet stance toward art, Utyosov insisted that good jazz was good art, transcending the contamination of the market.

Much of the pressure for change came from the growing dissent among Soviet youth. As the historian Jerimi Suri has argued, "young men and women in the expanding Soviet universities stood at the center" of 1960s dissident culture in the Soviet Union, a rebellious stance that was no doubt encouraged by the large number of foreign students in Soviet Universities.[29] Two months after Utyosov's defense of jazz, the official newspaper of Soviet youth, *Komsomolskaya*, which had been denouncing jazz for years as a capitalist evil, proposed a nationwide network of jazz nightclubs.[30] An Associated Press journalist writing from Moscow speculated that the shift in attitude may have been influenced by the high number of foreign students frustrated in their attempts to find places for leisure activities.[31] In this concession to internal as well as international pressure, *Komsomolskaya Pravda* argued the merits of tables, "sunken dance floors, and platforms for student jazz bands." Many considered it "astonishing," noted the Associated Press reporter, that the newspaper should admit "there are students familiar enough with jazz to play in such bands."[32] "American jazz," wrote John Tynan in *Down Beat* later that year, "long condemned by USSR cultural commissars as a manifestation of decadent bourgeois culture, is fast attaining official toleration."[33] Pandora's box had been opened.

Just as these reports of a new Soviet openness toward jazz reached the United States, Benny Goodman, who had long been lobbying for an engagement in the Soviet Union, got in on the act by "scolding" Soviet scholars over the fact that he had not been allowed to play there. Goodman, who had demonstrated considerable diplomatic charm and grace on his 1958 State Department tour, now displayed a rather more contentious side. In the words of *New York Times* writer Arthur Gelb, he "wasted no time on diplomacy."[34] Upbraiding the two prominent Soviet musicologists— Konstantin K. Sakva, editor-in-chief of the State Music Publishing House, and Izrail V. Nestyev, biographer and deputy editor in chief of the magazine *Soviet-skaya Muzyka*—Goodman demanded to know the fate of the "several hundred dollars worth of his records" that he had sent to Moscow through official and unofficial channels "as part of his campaign to be invited to play in the Soviet Union." Goodman charged that "he understood his records could be purchased in the Soviet Union only through the black market and were usually played in secrecy." Brushing aside the scholars' attempts to compliment his music, Goodman asked: "If I'm so popular, why can't I get in to play there?"[35] Citing Leonid Utyosov's call for jazz in the Soviet Union, Goodman said his ambition to play in Moscow had become a "near-obsession." Attempting to downplay the tensions between modernists and antimodernists in the Soviet

Union, Nestyev and Sakva insisted that the "statement had been given too much prominence in the United States and that Mr. Utyosov had really said nothing new." A petulant Goodman opined that "by the time the Russians got around to issuing an invitation he would have a long beard."[36]

In March 1962, one year after Goodman had chastised the Soviet musicologists, his tour to the Soviet Union was announced with much fanfare. It was to be a highlight of an expansion of the U.S.—Soviet cultural exchange agreement. With a front-page *New York Times* headline proclaiming, "U.S. and Soviet to Expand Their Cultural Exchange: Benny Goodman to Tour," the paper discussed the details of the agreement. Trips to the Soviet Union by Goodman, the New York City Ballet, and the Robert Shaw Chorale were planned. From the Soviet side, the Bolshoi Theatre Ballet, the Leningrad Philharmonia Symphony Orchestra, and the Ukrainian Dance Ensemble would tour several cities in the United States.[37] As *Newsweek* reported, "Nyet, nyet, nyet"—that "inevitable Soviet response" to jazz as "too decadent"—had finally become "da," as the Soviets accepted "Benny Goodman, that epitome of capitalist decadence."[38] Underlining the excitement in the broader world of the intelligentsia, as well as in that of diplomacy and jazz, a page-two *Times* story documented Goodman's romantic American rags-to-riches tale: the son of an impoverished Chicago tailor who had learned to play clarinet at Jane Addams' Hull House, honing his skill in a synagogue band. Distinguishing himself by integrating black musicians into a white band and bringing jazz into concert halls, Goodman had earned the title King of Swing "when he assembled a large band and began to play special arrangements in a style that made cheering listeners out of dancers."[39] On the same day, Alan Rich wrote in the New York *Times* that "after more than seven years of frustrated hopes, Benny Goodman is being allowed to take his music to the Soviet Union."[40] Goodman's aggressive lobbying on his own behalf may have been instrumental in the decision to send him to the Soviet Union.

What was termed Goodman's "eight-year campaign to go to the

Soviet Union" quickly erupted into controversy in the jazz world, as critics wondered why Duke Ellington, Louis Armstrong, or Dizzy Gillespie hadn't been chosen instead. In retrospect, the attacks on Goodman's selection might have appeared as mere gossip or sour grapes, had they not so clearly prefigured the pronounced tensions between Goodman and his band during their time in the Soviet Union. Calling Goodman's brand of music "highly commendable" but "awfully narrow" in scope, pianist George Shearing "wondered why the State Department continued to think in a 'swing bag.'"[41] Gillespie, who had been viciously attacked by segregationists and conservatives in the United States after his triumphant tour of the Middle East in 1956, was even stronger in his questioning of Goodman. Admitting that he wanted to take a band to Russia "so bad I can almost taste it," Gillespie said: "Nobody here is playing Benny Goodman's music today. What does he represent about today's jazz?" Yet Gillespie added, with his famous humor: "Goodman would at least give the lie to any Russian propaganda about exploited jazz musicians. 'You can't knock a millionaire, can you?'"[42] While Gillespie did not invoke his own history or the issue of race directly, he had been attacked as an unworthy representative of America *because* he was black. Still, he called attention to the politics of race subtly, by noting that the clarinetist had prospered in a way few black musicians could. In the selection of Goodman—with the State Department all too aware of congressional conservatives' scrutiny of their cultural programs, and with the high-profile Soviet tour at stake—some critics believed that race mattered.

Despite State Department concern with congressional critics, it was the Soviet officials, not the State Department personnel, who were crucial in the decision to send Goodman. Enacting their elaborately imbricated views on style, race, and modernism, the Soviets did not want a black bandleader. Soviet officials had declined the suggestion of an Armstrong tour in 1961. According to the *New York Times,* a U.S. government source said that Goodman and Armstrong were both proposed to the Soviets in the Washington negotiations and that "the Soviet officials expressed a preference for the former." A State Department source reported that "Mr. Goodman appeared to be more palatable to the Soviet officials because his jazz style was . . . more conservative, . . . and they were interested in the possibility of Mr. Goodman's appearing with the Soviet Symphony Orchestra for the performance of classical music during his tour."[43] Implicit in this preference was the Soviets' desire to play to their strength—classical music—and the feeling that African American jazz was more distinctive and thus more dangerous to present to Russians.

The approach of the Goodman tour summoned a defensiveness on the part of the Soviets that manifested itself in expressions of cultural one-upmanship against the West. Soviet artists, it was argued, needed to fight against the West's cultural onslaught. As the last-minute arrangements fell into place for the Goodman tour, Igor Moiseyev, the leading Soviet master of folk dancing denounced "the disgusting dynamism of rock 'n' roll and the twist." Moiseyev's admonishment of Soviet choreographers and composers for failing to create culturally grounded "modern dances to oppose the influences from the West" paralleled the call in the Soviet Union for composition of Soviet-style jazz to challenge American dominance."[44] Goodman's traditional jazz and his facility with classical music were more palatable to the Soviets and less threatening than the torrid, hyperkinetic blues of jazz. The latter was more improvisational and, perhaps, more explosive. Goodman's swing— "sweet" music, in 1930s jazz parlance—was seen as smoother and safer. The very style of jazz that had been officially proscribed during the 1930s now became acceptable a generation later. Moreover, the Soviets' most effective criticism of the United States in the Cold War battle for the hearts and minds of African and Asian peoples had been race. At the height of Soviet propaganda skillfully targeting America's Achilles heel of racism, hosting African American entertainers might undermine their case.[45] This, indeed, had been the hope of some in the U.S. State Department. Yet the State Department acceded to Soviet demands and settled on a white-led but integrated band. Much to their dismay, however, the skirmishing over style was not over.

As the tour approached, the "mild dissent" in the United States over Goodman's selection became a "Teapot Tempest."[46] Goodman's fondness for classical music may have made him acceptable to Soviet officials, but it did not sit well with jazz musicians and critics, who felt he was engaging in a cultural snobbery that demeaned jazz. Many jazz musicians did not appreciate the fact that in his publicized lobbying to tour the Soviet Union, Goodman had emphasized his classical training and recordings and "expressed the hope that he would have the opportunity to 'sit in' on serious music performances in the Soviet Union."[47] Moreover, according to *Down Beat* associate editor Bill Cross, "there are some who insist that no one really wants to play in a Goodman band anyway. The reason given is the Goodman 'Ray,' a reputed way of expressing disapproval toward musicians in his band by the way he looks at them."[48] Goodman's supporters rebutted those who questioned the appeal of Goodman's style or his suitability for the task by defending Goodman's record as an accomplished band leader: Goodman, the *Down Beat* editorial continued, was chosen because "he has shown himself capable of handling a large group of musicians . . . [and] getting the best out of them. . . . Goodman is a man who can do this quite important job—and do it with honor to the country and to jazz."[49] Asking the jazz world to put aside its differences and "rise to its responsibilities," the editorial concluded with the plea: "Let it rejoice that *jazz* is being sent to Russia. For it is jazz that has made a major break-through, not Benny Goodman."[50] If *Down Beat* can be applauded for taking the high road and defending Goodman's record, the editorial's comment that it was "malicious" to suggest that Goodman was sent because of his race overlooked the centrality of race in the broader Cold War–civil rights context. The meaning of race was a major bone of contention in U.S. and Soviet propaganda—indeed, the raison d'être of the jazz tours from the American perspective—and, for Soviet officials, was clearly a major factor in their acceptance of Goodman.

Concerns over style continued as Goodman announced the first twelve musicians to be signed for the trip. Critic Nat Hentoff noted that the "prevailing composition is young and modern" and presciently wondered "how he'll adapt his style to that group." Hoping for the best, critic John Wilson, a member of the State Department's Music Selection Committee, described the incomplete ensemble as "a good, capable, big band."[51] The integrated band, as described by the journalist Milton Bracker, "includes ten white musicians, one Negro musician, and a Negro vocalist, Joya Sherrill, who used to sing with Duke Ellington."[52] Seven musicians were signed at a later date, completing the nineteen-piece orchestra, which eventually included four black musicians.[53] The members were: Johnny Frosk, Jimmy Maxwell, Joe Newman, Joe Wilder, trumpet; Jimmy Knepper, Willie Dennis, Wayne Andre, trombone; Jerry Dodgion, Phil Woods, alto sax; Tommy Newman, Zoot Sims, tenor sax; Gene Allen, baritone sax; John Bunch, piano; Turk Van Lake, guitar; Mel Lewis, drums; Bill Crow, bass; Joya Sherrill, vocals; Teddy Wilson, pianist with sextet only (he had been a member of Goodman's 1930s quartet); Victor Feldman, vibes with sextet only.[54]

On May 27, after a sendoff reception hosted by the American Federation of Musicians at New York International Airport, Benny Goodman and his band boarded a Scandinavian Air Lines flight for Copenhagen en route to Moscow.[55] Landing in the "blindingly sunny" Sheremetyevo Airport after the twenty-four-hour flight, the band was greeted by Aleksei Batashev, a twenty-seven-year-old physicist and the president of Moscow's largest jazz club. Immediately, the governments' carefully hammered out notion of cultural exchange as a controlled presentation of concerts was disrupted by the common language of jazz artists. Batashev quickly struck up a conversation with the musicians and invited the sidemen to "make a jam session with us" at the club's headquarters at the House of Culture of Power Workers. Phil Woods immediately agreed; the "unofficial contacts" had begun. And it didn't take long to get a sense of the seriousness of Soviet fans. When tenor saxophonist

Zoot Sims asked where the musicians could get a drink, Batashev replied: "Our jazz fans don't drink. They are fanatics."[56] Tickets for the orchestra's premiere the following day (Goodman's fifty-third birthday) at the 4,600-seat arena of the Central Army Sports Club had been sold out for days. As Batashev jumped on the bus with the musicians, beaming—"Who would have thought that I would be riding on the same bus with Teddy Wilson?"—the cultural exchange seemed to be off to a glorious start.

But the band escaped neither Cold War intrigue nor the demanding perfectionism that had earned Goodman a reputation in jazz circles as being difficult to work with. In an immediate assertion of Cold War diplomatic bravado, Goodman's publicity package contained a *New York Daily News* editorial calling for American spies to be included in the band. Though the provocation was initiated by a privately owned newspaper, and it is highly unlikely that the State Department or Goodman would have approved the inclusion of such an appeal, it is understandable that Soviet officials took offense. Fortunately, reported the *New York Times*, Moscow newspapers "exonerated the Goodman musicians from responsibility for what it called 'provocative appeals.'"[57] Plans were disrupted by what cultural attaché Terrence F. Catherman described as Goodman's propensity "to improvise off-stage as well as on-stage," throwing into "disarray some Soviet and other plans." "Obviously dismayed at the prospect of playing in a gymnasium," Goodman immediately demanded to look over the premises of the Central Army Sports Club, despite protests that the facilities were not yet ready. "The Soviets," Catherman reported, "quickly learned that Goodman does not readily accept 'no' for an answer," and when Goodman "mistook a dingy side entrance for the main hall," he walked out, declaring that he would "rest" in Moscow, since he could not play in such a place. Fortunately, a group of "desperate Soviet officials" persuaded him to look at the hall, and he agreed that it would do.[58]

For Catherman, "it was obvious from the outset that Goodman was tense, exhausted, and out-of-sorts. After supper on the night of his arrival he took four sleeping pills and disappeared into a hotel room, refusing to discuss anything."[59] Things began to turn around the next day, when during rehearsal Goodman found the Soviet sound and lighting technicians to be of "such high professional calibre that he could do nothing but praise them." In Catherman's estimation, however, the technical excellence "did nothing to protect his musicians" from Goodman's demands and constraints. The battle over style emerged at the very first rehearsal. The problem, as one perceptive State Department official saw it, was that "all his soloists are well-known modern jazzmen. They want to 'blow,' whereas he wants to present the band more-or-less in the context of his arrangements from the thirties. The musicians feel that they are being cheated out of chance to show the Soviets real American jazz; Goodman feels that some of the soloists are trying to sabotage his music by injecting a modernist treatment into it."[60] Moreover, in what the sidemen saw as a question of style but Goodman insisted was a question of quality, Goodman "called several musicians to task for their musicianship." This intensified the anxiety surrounding opening night in the Soviet capital, where exceptional behind-the-scenes confusion was caused by the presence of NBC film crews which had been forbidden. With the sudden arrival of Soviet bodyguards and last-minute permission to film, Mr. and Mrs. Khrushchev arrived with three First Deputy Premiers, all members of the ruling Presidium. As the film crew stumbled around, setting up, "harassed Soviet officials" hustled some correspondents out of the building but allowed others to "wander at will backstage."[61]

The orchestra opened with "Let's Dance" and "Greetings Moscow," a number based on a Russian folksong. Initial audience response was cautious. Young fans seated near the jazz critic Leonard Feather called out the names of musicians they recognized. European and African diplomats seated in the first rows applauded for Joe Newman's "Moscow" solo. After what most observers agreed was a slow start, the audience being intimidated and awed by Khrushchev's presence, enthusiasm picked up with the introduction of the sextet and with Teddy Wilson at the piano. "The group shook the hall," reported the *Times,* with "Avalon," "Body and Soul," "Rose Room," "Stompin' at the Savoy," and "China Boy." After intermission, the program moved to an "anthology of jazz." Vocalist Joya Sherrill "charmed audiences" and even impressed Khrushchev with "The Thrill Is Gone"—the first number that drew substantial applause, in Feather's opinion.[62] Sherrill was recalled for the encore, "I'm Beginning to See the Light." "Benny Goodman's Moscow Concert Pleases but Puzzles Khrushchev," announced a front-page headline in the *New York Times* the following day. Reportedly smiling, applauding, and chuckling as U.S. ambassador Llewellyn E. Thompson Jr. and Mrs. Thompson explained what was happening onstage, Khrushchev commented: "I enjoyed it. I don't dance, myself, so I don't understand these things too well."[63] Exiting at intermission, Khrushchev later sent a note to Goodman saying that he had been "very pleased and delighted to be at the concert" and that he had been compelled to leave on a matter of "state business."[64] Most Americans, cultural attaché Catherman surmised, believed that Khrushchev's presence had dampened the enthusiasm of the crowd, whose reaction was described as "mild enthusiasm" by the State Department, and "lukewarm" though with plenty of "respectful cheers" by the *Times.* Moreover, explained the *Times,* "among those attending were more of the elite and well-connected of Moscow than the thousands of Soviet jazz fans who have been eagerly awaiting the arrival of the Goodman orchestra."[65] The second concert, with a primarily young audience, was received with more vigorous applause and enthusiasm.[66] Yet from the very first concert, Goodman had his critics among Soviet jazz fans. "As much as they relished Mr. Goodman's performance," reported the *Times,* "many Soviet fans were frank in saying that the King of Swing was now regarded in the Soviet Union as passé." One "well-known orchestra leader" wondered privately why Goodman could not have "come here fifteen years ago. He would really have taught our musicians something."[67]

Despite these reservations, Soviet and American commentators alike judged the concert a great success, and Khrushchev's presence demonstrated the "new respectability of jazz in the Soviet Union." *Tass,* the Soviet press agency, described the concert as "a great hit."[68] In grand diplomatic mode, Goodman declared the Soviet audience "wonderful" as he graciously accepted the praise. The band, Goodman declared, was "on the ball."[69] Ambassador Thompson had planned a reception in honor of Goodman and his orchestra— complete with a large birthday cake for Goodman—at his residence at Spasso House after the concert. In what the State Department was quickly learning was Goodman's penchant for erratic behavior, Goodman first refused to play at the reception, asking if he were being required to "sing for my supper." Conceding that he would play for a few minutes on the condition that there was "absolutely no dancing, and that people be silent and listen, as if at a concert," Goodman proceeded to arrive at the reception, insist that the rugs be pulled back, and got a jam session underway. When he saw that no one was dancing, he "swept" the ambassador onto the floor, "completely breaking the ice. The musicians jammed until three o'clock and the last of the delighted guests straggled out at four o'clock."[70]

The next day, Goodman first embarrassed U.S. officials and "ruffled feelings" by canceling scheduled classical concerts because the Russian orchestras were not, in his estimation, good enough, and simply ignoring an invitation by the Moscow Conservatory to visit the institution and play music with the students. But then he surprised the Russians with an impromptu solo performance in Red Square. In a "Kremlin Serenade," Goodman "became for a few tuneful moments today the Pied Piper of Red Square" as "children swarmed about" the clarinet player. When Goodman saw the squad of soldiers marching stiffly by to relieve the guard at the red-marble Lenin Mausoleum, the "temptation was too much" for him and he broke into a rendition of "Pop Goes the Weasel." He then "caught the rhythm of the passing boots and the King of Swing began beating time with the Red Army."[71] He was winning the hearts of the Russians in his own way, not according to the State Department plan. Moreover, he somehow managed to get

12. *Benny Goodman outside the Kremlin, June 1, 1962.* Courtesy of the Institute for Jazz Studies, Rutgers University.

Soviet authorities to retract their rigid positions on a series of disputes, on matters ranging from the itinerary to recording rights. This was unfortunate in the eyes of the State Department, however, because it gave Goodman the "misapprehension" that he knew "precisely how to handle the Soviets"—a perception that took "weeks of bureaucracy, bungling, delay, and sometimes downright meanness to allay."[72]

As Goodman continued to keep Soviet and U.S. officials on their toes by making, breaking, and ignoring agreements and appointments, the band members were busy sightseeing, meeting Moscow jazz fans, visiting youth clubs, and, according to the State Department, "having a quite successful jam session at the local jazz club."[73] But at the same time, for many musicians the official ban on fraternization with ordinary Russian citizens lent a bizarre and eerie quality to the Moscow experience. Remembering Moscow as "dour and depressing," Phil Woods described going for "walks to relieve the boredom. . . . As we strolled through the park by the hotel we would hear the bushes and trees talking. 'Dizzy Gillespie' a begonia would cry; 'Thelonious Monk' an elm would answer. We responded to these hip vegetable matter with our own primal cries. 'Dodo Marmorosa,' 'Vido Musso' (Zoot's favorite), 'Harvey Leonard,' 'Phil Arabia.'"[74] For the musicians, this was part of the process of getting to know some of the USSR's very knowledgeable jazz fans.[75] For the State Department, these highly unofficial interactions were valuable, marking a pattern of success with individual contacts that would continue when the band flew to Sochi on June 2, where they were scheduled for three concerts. As the group relaxed on the beach for the first two days, "an articulate group of jazz fans and musicians amazed the Americans with their expert knowledge of jazz in general and, specifically, of the careers of the Americans themselves." One musician remarked: "These cats know more about us than we do!" Trombonist Willy Dennis sat "open-mouthed" as a Soviet fan questioned him about his *Down Beat* "new jazz artist" rating. In two after-concert sessions, band members jammed with a Soviet band at Gorka, a local restaurant. Nowhere, judged Catherman, was the influence of the Voice of America more in evidence. Several band members visited the apartment of a local aficionado to listen to tapes of VOA broadcasts.[76]

Such detailed knowledge on the part of local fans had its downside, however. Reaction to the public concerts—in the 1,600-seat Summer Theater, "an open-air theater with excellent acoustics and a good sound system"—was, in the view of the State Department, "puzzlingly mild."[77] The State Department noted "practically no whistling and shouting," empty seats and almost "no crowds outside the theater." Catherman speculated about the reasons for this lack of enthusiasm: "The band members were bombarded by the local modern jazz musicians with criticism of the Goodman style, as being too old-fashioned, so that most of them blamed Goodman's 'intransigence' in not allowing more modern music on his program as reason number one."[78] Catherman, like many State Department people who worked closely with jazz bands, developed a deep sympathy for the musicians and became something of a jazz critic in his own right. He agreed with the band that Goodman's "timing is . . . atrocious; he often stands for minutes on end after announcing a tune, trying to find the 'beat' with a blank expression on his face which defies description." Some thought this had contributed to the poor reception. Others, including Goodman, believed that the audiences were "loaded with anti-jazzites or indifferent people to prevent access for the real fans." The State Department in fact argued that there was evidence of this in each city.[79] The "overzealous uniformed militia" very much in evidence in Sochi could have intimidated audiences.[80] Goodman was forbidden by Soviet authorities to use Catherman as an interpreter to replace the Soviet interpreter, who was "missing his [Goodman's] patter and giving only the titles of numbers."[81] More dramatically, on the night of the final concert in Sochi, trumpeter Joe Newman and Catherman were talking with the chair of the local jazz club and several members when "three motorcycle policemen roared up." The police "arrested the chairman, confiscated all the phonograph records and Benny Goodman books" which had just been distributed, and then "roared off with their arrestee." After aggressive intervention with the Soviet authorities by Catherman, the young man appeared the next day to say goodbye to the orchestra. He explained that the arrest had been a mistake, but left the musicians and Catherman to wonder whether he was still at liberty.[82]

With these numerous complicating factors audience criticism of the Goodman style appeared as part and parcel of the internal tensions that racked the band and blew up in Sochi. As reported by Catherman for the State Department, on the morning of June 3 "Goodman told trombonist Jimmy Knepper to pack his bags and go home." The dispute had begun in Moscow when "Knepper played a solo chorus which was too modern for Goodman's taste." According to Goodman, Knepper then "made a face at him."[83] During the afternoon rehearsal, first saxophonist Phil Woods "'quit' the band when Goodman made some slurring remark" about Woods's playing ability. Then, said Catherman, came the "fateful" night of June 3–4. After the concert, several band members gathered in the room directly above Goodman's "and proceeded to have a party until daylight. All of Goodman's demerits were discussed in loud detail, every word of which was clearly audible to the band leader through his open window. A typical statement was, 'The King Is Dead; Long Live the King.'"[84] For Woods, the worst moment came the next morning when Goodman insisted on punishing the band with a noon rehearsal where, Gene Lees has recounted, Goodman humiliated Woods by "poking his clarinet right in Phil's ear."[85] U.S. officials feared that Goodman would send the whole band home. Although this "disaster was averted, . . . it was clear that the whole band was united against Goodman."[86]

Following the debacle in Sochi, the professionalism and good humor displayed by the band during long delays en route to Tbilisi, Georgia, "forever endeared" the musicians to Catherman. Capricious weather kept the band at the airport for fourteen hours, then delayed their departure till the next day. Arriving in Tbilisi, they found the "official attitude . . . much warmer" than in Sochi. Appollon Kipiani, an old friend of Catherman's, met the band at the airport and presented a local television program on Goodman that evening. But the tensions over style appeared inescapable. Kipiani lobbied to make the Goodman program "more lively" after hearing reports from Moscow and Sochi, requesting more "modern jazz in addition to some twist and rock and roll." The State Department was now in the position of "briefing" the Soviets. Catherman confided in his report to Washington that "the facts of life about Goodman were explained in a diplomatic manner and Goodman drove them home less diplomatically during the next few days." Attendance was disappointing, and the audience reception was "polite." Only on the last night (when there were as many as 2,000 empty seats) did "the band catch fire with the audience; and everything came to a roaring finish to the blare of Dixieland horns, shouts, whistles and stomping."[87]

As if the band's own internal conflicts and the official Soviet am-

13. *Poster advertising Goodman performances in Tbilisi,
Republic of Georgia, June
1962.* Translation: "Georgian
State Philharmonic Presents
at the Palace of Sports—June
8, 9, 10, 11, 12—Benny
Goodman and his Jazz Or-
chestra." Courtesy of the Institute for Jazz Studies,
Rutgers University.

bivalence toward jazz had not been enough, the group stumbled
into Soviet regional tensions when Joya Sherrill sang the Russian
song "Katyusha" in Tbilisi. Sherrill had learned the song phoneti-
cally, and her rendition had delighted audiences in Moscow and
Sochi. But in Georgia the hooting and clamor of the audience led
Goodman to cut the song off after one chorus. Soviet officials tried
to explain that the "acoustics were bad," but audiences made it
clear that they were "very nationalistic and do not speak Russian
willingly."[88] The Georgian audience resented the Russian language,
not Sherrill—they "cheered heartily" after her next number, "Riding High."[89]

The low point of the tour came in the city of Tashkent, where
musicians encountered "the most apathetic audiences" of the
whole trip, along with police harassment of jazz fans and a full-scale

air raid alert.[90] But Leningrad was the undisputed high point. The band had no sooner arrived when Phil Woods hit it off with a local Soviet saxophonist and then with a local jazz pianist, started an "international" jam session. The next night, they jammed until three in the morning at the university, with even more Soviet artists participating. By this time, reported Catherman, the feeling was "that we were no longer in the same country that we had been performing in previously." A greater atmosphere of freedom seemed to prevail. Soviet musicians visited band members in their hotel rooms, "Phil Woods had become fast friends with the Soviet alto man, the city officials seemed eager to set up meetings with musicians, and the tickets to the performances were sold out."[91]

Despite the "acoustical horror chamber" of the 6,000-seat Winter Stadium—converted for the concert from an indoor track stadium by adding wooden seats and rough bleachers—the audience reaction was "what the band had been waiting for. . . . Long ovation followed long ovation." On opening night, the *New York Times* reported, the "band was forced to do forty minutes of encores."[92] Joya Sherrill repeatedly "scored an overwhelming triumph," doing three encores after the first performance. Winning audiences with such numbers as her medley of "The Thrill Is Gone," "Summertime," and "Fascinatin' Rhythm," Sherrill "nearly brought the house down" when she acknowledged the applause with "Spasibo bolshoye!" ("Thank you very much!"). And the Russian audience "went wild with approval" over her rendition of the Russian classic "Katyusha."[93] After the last concert, the "audience simply stayed, clapped, yelled, stamped, whistled, and demanded encores." Clearly relaxed and enjoying himself, a good hour after the conclusion of the performance Goodman "came out in a sweater and slacks and played a solo."[94]

Unfortunately, what the State Department termed "the typical Soviet atmosphere" gradually asserted itself against the warm informal contacts between American and Soviet musicians. Catherman reported: "Soviet jazz fans stopped coming to see Americans at their hotel, requesting, instead, surreptitious meetings in parks. The

Soviet alto sax player was warned not to see too much of Phil Woods. There were some reports of arrests. *Druzhiniki,* strong-arm men, were obvious and active during and after the concerts, to keep the fans away from the players. People were led off by plainclothesmen."[95] Moreover, the spectacular success of the Leningrad reception was not enough to alleviate tensions between the band and Goodman. As Catherman's sympathy with the band members grew, so, too, did his annoyance with Goodman. Catherman said that the reception was marvelous, "despite the fact that Goodman often seemed to forget where he was on the stage and constantly picked on some of his best musicians."[96] By the end of four performances in the 10,000-seat Palace of Sports in Kiev, despite an enthusiastic reception, "the band was becoming jaded."[97] Having remained in relatively good humor about the uneven quality of the food, the band now endured "bad and often spoiled food" at the Moskva Hotel, with "despicable" service, unsatisfactory rooms, miserable weather, and more noticeable police action than ever before. As the musicians' morale plunged, they found themselves surrounded by a ubiquitous Soviet camera crew. "Goodman," who (Catherman explained) "never eats with the band and prefers not to even see the members when not performing," considered the Soviet crews a photo opportunity. He "had all the tables for the band arranged around his, sort of family style, so that the camera crew could film the happy group. As usual, the Goodman table was loaded down with delicacies which the other members of the group did not receive, and this added to the general feeling of disgruntlement."[98]

That this "happy family," an idealized image of America, was in fact dysfunctional was becoming apparent to far more people than Catherman. From Kiev, the *New York Times* reported that members of Benny Goodman's touring band "expressed their discontent today over the music that the King of Swing is settling for" and reported that some would quit the band when they got back to New York. Labeling the music "older than what the Russians are entitled to hear," drummer Mel Lewis declared that "if I had known we were going to play music like this, I would not have come."[99] *Life* magazine reported, in an otherwise celebratory treatment of the tour, some "sour notes" as the band spread "friendship and harmony" throughout the Soviet Union. The band, according to *Life*, "complained that Benny cut short their solos [and] made them play old-time arrangements when they would rather have gone modern." Noting that "things got really bad" in Leningrad, *Life*'s article entitled "Stompin It Up at the Savoy-Marx" reported that "trumpeter Jimmie Maxwell went on a hunger strike, singer Joya Sherrill couldn't sleep, and alto sax Jerry Dodgion took sick for days."[100] One of the few black Americans and the only woman in the band, Sherrill experienced the tensions with Goodman in a particularly acute way. "Goodman was a beast," she recalled, describing the experience as a "cultural shock." Like Phil Woods, Sherrill felt that Goodman was resentful of her rapport with Soviet audiences. Coming from her experience with Duke Ellington, who Sherrill said "always showcased the talent of his musicians," she found the temperamental Goodman abusive.[101]

Arriving for the final six concerts in Moscow "feeling generally worn-out, dejected, chased by cameramen, and hungry," the band managed successful performances in Moscow.[102] Audiences there were as enthusiastic as those in Kiev, though not quite as lively as those in Leningrad. As spirits gradually improved at the prospect of returning home, a last-minute mutiny was averted after nine band members refused to play at the penultimate concert until they received their paychecks. Goodman and the band somehow agreed to disagree on the timing of the pay, and the concert went on. Although there were few informal contacts, several musicians did participate in a "lively jam session one evening at the Molodyezhnoe youth club." And Goodman, whose spirits seemed to improve as the tour neared its end, chaired a meeting with members of the Moscow State Symphony, where he played classical solos, and then met with a group of twenty jazz composers, arrangers, and orchestra leaders.[103] Premier Khrushchev visited the U.S. Embassy's Fourth of July reception. Given his well-known penchant for "graphic diatribes" against young Soviet artists, Khrushchev was polite but candid in his conversation with Goodman.[104] "Ah, a new jazz fan," said Goodman. "No," Khrushchev replied, "I don't like Goodman music. I like good music." Both men agreed that they liked Mozart, which led Khrushchev to wag his finger reproachfully at Goodman, saying: "And yet you play this bad music."[105]

By the tour's end, the band had played thirty concerts before 176,800 people (an average of 6,000 per concert). In the eyes of the State Department, "despite all of the arguments, misunderstandings, and hard feelings involved," the tour had boosted the respectability of jazz in the Soviet Union and had been an important success. For all of his sympathy with the band and his thinly veiled criticism of Goodman, Catherman ultimately concluded that Goodman had been "the best choice to bring live American jazz to the Soviet Union for the first time." For Catherman, the fact that Goodman played a style of jazz acceptable to Soviet officialdom (even if they didn't admire it as music) and was a competent classical musician—along with his "impeccable" personal habits, which put him above reproach—was decisive. Perhaps Goodman's personal style was a fair match for that of cantankerous Soviet officials. (In the Soviets' unwillingness to reschedule the canceled classical concerts, even the State Department could not "help but consider the possibility that the Soviets were giving Goodman some of his own medicine.")[106] Though Catherman had observed no definitive resolution of "the argument about 'modern' vs. 'classical' jazz" that was "fought out in the midnight hours throughout the trip," he concluded: "If the Soviet jazz fan is to be pleased in the future" (as opposed to Soviet officialdom and the general Soviet public), "we should concentrate on sending over modern jazz stars."[107] By shunning innovation and improvisation, Goodman had managed to alienate his own band, Soviet jazz fans, and even Catherman.

Goodman, basking in the limelight upon his return to New York, said the success of the tour could be measured in the response of Soviet audiences "and in the impressive sum of $500,000 that the tour had grossed for the Soviet Union."[108] Chatting with President Kennedy, Goodman learned that Kennedy had sent another message to Premier Khrushchev thanking him for attending a Goodman concert and saying that "he was looking forward to seeing the Bolshoi Ballet when it comes to Washington in the fall."[109] Music critic John Wilson reported that Goodman dismissed complaints by some members of the band that he concentrated on old arrangements at the expense of new material. "Mr. Goodman indicated that he had little sympathy for musicians who felt they did not receive adequate solo opportunities in his band. 'I'm not a devotee of playing eighteen choruses on a solo,' he said. 'I call that practicing on the job.'"[110]

In a *Down Beat* postmortem, members of the band gave their side of the story. Vic Feldman said that he'd gotten sick from "all the tension and the bad food" and ended up in the hospital. "I was literally sick and tired of the whole thing. . . . [Goodman] doesn't care how the men feel about him anyway. He doesn't care about his band or even care for any other bands; like, he put down Duke Ellington as being 'too much a band of stars.'" Still, for Feldman, a gig was a gig. "He paid us good money, and I accepted the deal, and I'm glad I made the trip." "All those newspaper stories about discord in the band," drummer Mel Lewis said. "That was nonsense. We all got along fine; the only trouble was between all of us and Benny." Moreover, claimed Lewis, after all of Goodman's talk about helping Soviet jazz musicians by letting them perform with the band, "he never even went to hear them." Lewis outlined what, for most, had been the crux of the problem: "He doesn't like sidemen to shine too much. After I got a big hand with my 'Sing, Sing, Sing' solo, he took the solo away from me. After Phil Woods took a solo one night on 'Greetings to Moscow' and got a great hand, the same thing happened." Asked if he would do it over again, Lewis replied: "Sure, but next time I'd take Dizzy along as leader."[111]

As Goodman's rejection of innovation and improvisation was perceived as violating the spirit of jazz, the bandleader's authoritarian style inflamed already pronounced differences. Confrontations between band leaders and sidemen were scarcely unusual in the jazz world. But the musicians inhabited a scene permeated by the new challenges and militancy of the civil rights movement, which transformed individuals, if not the inequitable structure of the music industry.[112] As musicians already influenced by the changing youth culture and civil rights challenges were spurred on by Soviet rebels against the status quo, Goodman's hierarchical sensibilities appeared singularly antiquated. Through the tour, the band entered an international forum where Soviet polemics exposing U.S. racism had become a very potent weapon. The band was sent to ameliorate this by standing for interracial unity, but its interracial harmony was drowned out by Goodman's discordant persona. Instead of Americans' successfully countering Soviet criticism, in what might be described as a transnational dynamic of rebellion, modernists and critics of the political state and existing social orders on both sides of the Cold War divide encouraged and inspired each other in their desire for change. The members of Goodman's band, noted Catherman, had been "constantly surrounded by jazz fans with a phenomenal knowledge of modern jazz."[113] As Soviet artists risked reprisal from the repressive Soviet state by jamming with or even meeting with American musicians, the depth of knowledge and devotion to jazz on the part of Soviet fans no doubt fueled the musicians' dissatisfaction with Goodman.

In the shadow of the Cuban missile crisis just three months after the Goodman tour, any new "official" legitimacy for jazz in the Soviet Union was precarious. Exacerbated by this dramatic breakdown in U.S.-Soviet relations, the tumult created by Goodman's tour led, in the winter of 1963, to a renewed party edict against jazz within the Soviet Union.[114] But succumbing to pressure for freer expression, Khrushchev backed off the following spring.[115] The Soviet line toward the arts remained contradictory, as the Soviet public was increasingly exposed to styles attacked as "Westward-looking."[116] The Soviets stopped jamming Voice of America, and by the summer of 1963, according to *New York Times* reporter Max Frankel, "jazz—good, bad, and atrocious—is everywhere now in the Soviet capital." As one Soviet "youngster" put it: "You Americans couldn't hold down the Negro, and we Soviets couldn't suppress their music."[117] Indeed, the dynamism of black culture and the contests over civil rights and race that had always animated the tours were now at center stage.

CHAPTER 5

Duke's Diplomacy

Less than two weeks after the march on Washington on August 28, 1963, the Duke Ellington Orchestra left New York City for Damascus embarking on the first of its numerous State Department tours. The three-month tour of the Middle East would include Syria, Jordan, Afghanistan, India, Ceylon, Pakistan, Iran, Iraq, Lebanon, and Turkey.[1] The tour followed on the heels of Ellington's production of *My People,* "a music and dance revue written to commemorate the hundredth anniversary of the Emancipation Proclamation."[2] A collaboration with choreographers Alvin Ailey and Tally Beatty, *My People* opened a week and a half prior to the march on Washington and ran daily at the Arie Crown Theater in Chicago until September 2. Joining the dance groups, a choir, and the band, Joya Sherrill, who had toured the Soviet Union with Benny Goodman the previous year, was among the singers. As Ingrid Monson has demonstrated in her path-breaking work on jazz and the civil rights movement, the production included a segment which "refashioned the spiritual 'Joshua Fit the Battle of Jericho' into 'King Fit the Battle of Alabam,'" and "described some of the most dramatic moments of the spring 1963 SCLC campaign."[3]

Indeed, the Birmingham Campaign in May of that year and the march on Washington in August provided a dramatic political backdrop for the tour. Television footage of Police Commissioner Bull Connor's vicious dogs and hoses turned on black children was broadcast around the globe. The turmoil in Birmingham, more than any other single event, embarrassed the administration in

Washington and pressured Kennedy to take unprecedented action in favor of civil rights. One Nigerian journalist observed that the United States appeared to be becoming "the most barbarian state in the world." As African leaders discussed a rupture between the United States and African nations at the founding meeting of the Organization of African Unity, Prime Minister Milton Obote of Uganda wrote an open letter to President Kennedy protesting the treatment of black protesters in Birmingham. Such pressure led Secretary of State Dean Rusk to conclude that "there is no effective substitute for decisive action on [the] part of the United States government."[4] The State Department warned that pictures of dogs attacking black Americans and of "a police officer pinning a Negro woman to the ground . . . have a dramatic impact on those abroad who listen to our words about democracy and weigh our actions against those words." Kennedy, in a nationally televised address, fervently declared civil rights a "moral crisis."[5]

Edward Kennedy "Duke" Ellington was perhaps the ideal ambassador for one of the first tests of cultural exchange under the heightened international scrutiny of American race relations and the new official endorsement of civil rights. Born on April 29, 1899, in Washington, D.C., and now sixty-four, Ellington had achieved international recognition as a composer, pianist, and bandleader. His stature matched that of Armstrong, and after the tension-filled Benny Goodman tour it was hardly accidental that the State Department turned to Ellington. His brilliance as an orchestra leader was legendary, and he was renowned for getting the most out of musicians by featuring their talents in extended solos. His instrument of choice, it was said, was his orchestra. In an era dominated by rock and roll, when most big bands had broken up long ago, Ellington had managed to keep his orchestra together. Not only did he need a band to test his newest compositions, but his orchestra exemplified the success of big bands in providing gainful employment for African American men facing otherwise meager opportunities. Unlike Goodman, who had hastily assembled his band for his tour, Ellington's band on the State Department tour included such veteran members as Billy Strayhorn, Johnny Hodges, Paul Gonsalves, Cootie Williams, Sam Woodyard, Harry Carney, Ray Nance, Cat Anderson, and Russell Procope.[6] From the time the tour began, the State Department escort immediately discerned that "Ellington writes for his soloists" and "the members of the band are strongly individualistic not only as musicians but as personalities."[7] For the State Department, an orchestra filled with "stars" who were "all in a position to consider themselves exceptional artists" made for spectacular performances. It also led to conflict, difficulties in scheduling, and distinctly different views of the politics of the tours on the part of musicians and the State Department.

Ellington's cosmopolitanism—his worldliness as an international celebrity and his experience in leading a black band in Jim Crow America—meant that he was uniquely situated to contend with the enormous tensions in the Cold War project represented by these government-sponsored tours. Between his first government-sponsored tour through the Middle East in 1963 and his death in 1974, Ellington toured the Soviet Union, made two trips to the continent of Africa, appeared in Eastern Europe, and toured South America and South Asia—all under the auspices of the State Department.[8]

This senior statesman of jazz brought a singularly complex perspective to the tours. He appears to have been not only a patriot but a sincere believer in the American Cold War mission of promoting the superiority of American democracy (a perspective not necessarily shared by the members of his orchestra). Along with Lionel Hampton, he was one of the very few Republican jazz musicians involved in the tours. Ellington's Republicanism might best be understood as a generational phenomenon, a residual effect of early twentieth-century Washington, D.C., where he had been born and raised in a relatively privileged middle-class black world. In Ellington's youth, the Republican Party was still the party of Abraham Lincoln. The Democratic Party was not only the party of the solid South but the party of Woodrow Wilson, the president who had brought legal segregation to the nation's capital and to the black Republic of Haiti after the U.S. invasion in 1915, when Ellington was an adolescent.[9] Thus, however anomalous in the jazz world, Ellington's "Republicanism" was consistent with his life-long commitment to civil rights and the struggle over the control and representation of black cultural production.

Though Ellington relished his role as ambassador, as late as 1957 he had expressed profound reservations about the possibilities for America. In his essay "The Race for Space," Ellington dispassionately observed that "America's inability to go far ahead or at least keep abreast of Russia in the race for space can be traced directly to this racial problem."[10] Noting that science and the arts were both fundamentally creative endeavors, Ellington compared Sputnik to "a work of art in the sense that I view a great painting, read a great poem, or listen to a great work of music." Although he condemned the "regimentation of thought and the brutal subjugation of the individual to the state" in the USSR, he believed the achievement of Sputnik had been possible because the USSR "doesn't permit race prejudice . . . to interfere with scientific progress." The United States, in contrast, was held back by racism, lacking the "harmony of thought [that] must have prevailed in order for the scientists to make a moon [satellite] that would work."[11] In other words, the United States couldn't be modern because of racism.[12] For Elling-ton, Americans needed a "new sound. A new sound of harmony, brotherly love, common respect, and consideration for the dignity and freedom of men."[13] When Kennedy endorsed the civil rights movement six years later, it meant that Ellington had witnessed, in his own lifetime, the imposition of Jim Crow in Washington and the unprecedented challenge of the movement in the late 1950s leading to Kennedy's condemnation of segregation. It was this dra-matic shift that made him optimistic about the prospects for Amer-ican liberalism. Thus, as Ellington embarked on his first ambassado-rial trip in 1963, it was the civil rights movement that created the conditions under which he could endorse the potential of the United States to enter the modern world.

Given Ellington's characterization of repression within the Soviet Union, it is understandable that he could endorse Cold War liberalism once the United States had made an overt commitment to racial equality. But far more important to him than any direct consideration of U.S. Cold War foreign policy was the fact that he was being asked to serve as a cultural ambassador—belated, long-overdue recognition of his artistry. While many considered Ellington the quintessential American composer, critical acclaim from the nation's cultural establishment continued to elude him. But if Ellington did not share the critical perspectives on U.S. foreign policy of many in the jazz world, this did not make him "apolitical," as many of his peers suggested he was.

A master at the politics of representation, Ellington had long resisted the restrictive categorization of black music by white critics, maintaining that "the music of my race is something more than the American idiom."[14] His resistance to being defined contributed to the irony of this highly successful jazz ambassador's repeated rejection of the term "jazz." During one State Department sponsored tour, Ellington explained that "we stopped using the word in 1943. . . . The whole scene outgrew the jazz category many years ago."[15] Ellington consistently told audiences listening to his State Department lecture demonstrations that "jazz" was a misnomer, and American officials cringed as he denied the very existence of their prized cultural export. Yet if Ellington's explanations for his refusal to use the term "jazz" could be frustrating to the State Department, they are critical for understanding Ellington's rejection of the exclusionary modernist canon—a canon admitting no place for his hybrid musical sensibility, which encompassed African American and Western classical musics and ran the gamut from popular dance numbers to ruminative extended-form compositions.[16] Over time, as the tours enabled him to make further connections to African and African diasporic forms, his own struggles against appropriation would influence the way he approached new experiences and new musical influences.

Moreover, amid an ongoing battle over the politics of represen-

tation of black people, Ellington, like other black musicians and
their allies, perceived the State Department jazz tours as a platform
from which to promote the dignity of black people and their culture throughout the world in the era of Jim Crow. On the 1963
tour, the moral authority that accompanied the high-tide of the
civil rights movement allowed musicians to assert egalitarian principles that challenged the State Department's priorities in cultural
exchange. And for some musicians, these even ramified into questions about foreign policy. In exploring some of the tensions that
arose between the State Department and the musicians during the
tour, we might see the Ellington organization as a political entity
unto itself, engaged in diplomatic relations and often advancing an
interpretation of events that ran counter to those of the State Department.

After what Ellington remembered as "thirteen shots and vacci-
nations," the orchestra left New York City on September 6 and
flew via Rome to Damascus.[17] The Ellington Orchestra was the
first cultural attraction to appear in the Middle East under a reorganized cultural-presentations program. Reflecting the increasing
diplomatic priority given to cultural exchange, as well as an acknowledgment of the logistical difficulties that had arisen in earlier tours, the State Department dropped its partnership with the
American National Theatre Academy and now was the sole administrator of the tours (in cooperation with local USIS personnel).

As part of the reorganization, the band traveled with a State
Department escort officer, Thomas W. Simons Jr. The son of a
foreign-service officer, Simons held a Ph.D. from Harvard in Western and Central European history. He joined the foreign service
shortly after earning his degree, in 1963, and the Ellington assignment was one of his first.[18] Ellington took an immediate liking to
Simons. He became the young man's mentor and turned the tables
on the escort officer's usual function as supervisor, interpreter, and
guide. Ellington recalled in his autobiography, *Music Is My Mistress*:
"I am soon talking to him as if he were a relative, warning him

against making the kind of mistakes that are all too easy, especially since the whole trip is east of Greece. If one is not socially aware, it is very easy to be caught in a position where one's chauvinistic shirttail is showing."[19] Punctilious in his attention to logistical and political details, Simons protected the musicians from some of the excessive demands and disorganization that had burdened musicians on earlier tours. While Simons experienced his share of frustration with the band members, he also developed a sympathetic bond with them, sometimes positioning himself as an advocate and interpreter. At times he adopted the musicians' language, discussing scheduling problems, for example, by explaining that the orchestra never "hit"—that is, began their performances on time.[20]

Beginning with two performances in Damascus, the tour had an outwardly successful but nonetheless shaky start. It brought the Duke Ellington Orchestra into the most tumultuous U.S.–Middle East and intra-Arab relations since the overthrow of the Iraqi monarchy and the formation of the United Arab Republic in 1958, at the height of U.S-Egyptian tensions over the Saudi-Egyptian proxy war in Yemen.[21] The Eisenhower Doctrine of 1957 had declared the need to defend the Middle East against the aggression of states "controlled by international Communism."[22] CIA operatives had covertly intervened in Syria in 1957—just a year after Dizzy Gillespie's visit—to support a military coup against a pro-Communist government. This time, the band arrived just after yet another Syrian coup, which had disrupted newspaper publishing and therefore publicity.[23] In Syria, as in Iraq, the U.S. supported the Ba'athist Party, which they judged to be their best hope as an ally that would oppose the Communists and Egyptian president Gamel Abdel Nasser.[24] The band appeared as the American representative at the Damascus Fair, playing to audiences of more than 1,500 people each night. State Department officials had been able to publicize the event using direct mail, compensating for the lack of newspaper advertisements.[25] Reflecting the State Department's new emphasis on youth audiences, as well as a continued focus on elites, the band attended a reception with 150 students and jazz fans at the American Library.[26] The next stop, however—in politically tense Jordan, where the embattled pro-American monarchy had reached yet another nadir in its relations with Egypt and its other Arab neighbors—brought more "official" and somewhat less enthusiastic audiences than the youthful fans of Damascus. On the first night, Simons reported, "Mr. Ellington noticed the front row stopping their ears." The audience at the Officer's Club in Zerqa, judged by the State Department to be "one of the tour's most crucial audiences, given the political situation on Jordan, . . . ate throughout and applauded little."[27] Under such circumstances however, Simons considered the "mere fact" of the concert a success.[28]

But for the American participants, the political intrigue and logistical problems of the initial part of the tour paled in comparison to the tragic personal problems that ended trumpeter Ray Nance's participation in the tour. Throughout, State Department officials' not so subtly coded discussions of "behavior" revealed prevailing anxieties about race, sexuality and drug use. These anxieties erupted early on the tour, in Amman, Jordan, where Nance suffered an emotional breakdown, apparently brought on by drinking, stress, and fatigue. Nance's erratic behavior culminated in his refusal to stand for the national anthem while playing a concert at the Roman Theater in Amman.[29] Since officials were angered by conduct they attributed to drug abuse, Ellington and band members spent hours with State Department officials, insisting that Nance was not using drugs. The stakes were very high, as Nance had served time on a narcotics charge in 1955. To the contrary, they argued, he was drinking and depressed because he was *not* using drugs. Simons, clearly moved by the musicians "sorrow" over Nance's problems, explained in his letter to Washington that "they had been with him for years and valued his true worth as a person and as a performer." Positioning himself as an advocate for the musicians and a buffer against official reprimand, Simons argued to Washington that "the embarrassment and harm which America has suffered as a result of Nance's conduct pales beside the tragedy of a fine American and a fine man."[30] All parties agreed that Nance should be sent back to the States.[31]

Simons was relieved that Nance's illness did "not spoil the excellent impression" made by the orchestra. *Al Manar,* a local Amman paper, reported that "Duke Ellington—that charming American face—is preaching love and visiting people in the name of humanity." Accentuating his humanist appeal, the paper argued that "Ellington is extending his hands to greet other people on behalf of the United States, and indeed on behalf of humanity as well."[32] Judging this coverage to be favorable, the State Department was *not* pleased and filed as "unfavorable" the same paper's praising of Ellington's ability as a "Negro" to "surmount the whites' prejudice and obliterate it." *Al Manar's* argument that, "with a smile of love, the Negro can transcend the inequity of his white brother and erect a bridge of security and peace through which humanity can pass" was precisely the kind of sentiment the State Department hoped Ellington's integrated band would counter.[33] Hoping that the image of an integrated band would rapidly transform overseas audiences' perceptions of American race relations, the State Department was uncomfortable with the paper's frank acknowledgment of continued racism on the part of white Americans.

After performances in Beirut, the band flew to Kabul, Afghanistan—a ten-hour flight on a converted cargo plane.[34] In an extremely rare demonstration of anger on the part of Ellington, the composer furiously dubbed the plane "a cattle-car for Negroes" and argued that better arrangements would surely have been found for a classical orchestra.[35] Despite the trauma, musicians demonstrated the professionalism that consistently impressed State Department officials. Members of the band impressed the Kabulis with "their warmth and friendliness" and their "readiness to talk to students and other young people on equal terms." In this "northern perimeter" country, U.S. officials sought to impress Afghans as well as Russians. While acknowledging the high number of "entertainment-starved and wildly aficionado" foreigners in the audience, a State Department official remarked that "never before has there been such a 'favorable' proportion of Afghans to Americans." Moreover, among the foreigners, Russians turned out in high numbers.[36] Ellington however, in an incident that foreshadowed later differences on the tour, was perturbed to be playing before a small elite, along with some Germans and Americans—an audience amounting to only 4,000 in a hall with 15,000 seats.[37]

The next leg of the trip, lasting more than a month and a half and taking the band through India, Pakistan, and Ceylon, constituted, in Simons' words, "almost a different world for the orchestra." The "strong indigenous musical tradition" enabled audiences to appreciate Ellington's music.[38] Although Ellington suffered from health problems throughout the tour, missing half of the performances in New Delhi and the entire Hyderabad-Bangalore-Madras portion because of illness, for the State Department there was no question that he was an "enormous success in India."[39] The Delhi performances were "widely acclaimed as one of the most successful cultural undertakings in recent years," said State Department officials in New Delhi. They summed up student reaction to the lecture demonstration by quoting a young jazz fan: "This has been the greatest moment of my life."[40] The Hindustan Times declared that "each of the soloists" had "surpassed himself in inspired performances." Similarly calling attention to the magic of the orchestra, the Indian Express of Madras judged the concerts "a triumph for every player, each no less important than the other. . . . Duke Ellington's Orchestra played the poetry of jazz. We lost our hearts." Clearly sensitive to strong Indian criticism of U.S. political policy, one State Department official took care to note that "the leftist-leaning Patriot was unreserved in its praise."[41]

In marked contrast to the delight that U.S. officials in the Soviet Union took in the spontaneous rapport between American and Soviet musicians, the consular post in New Delhi lamented that the orchestra "preferred all-night jam sessions with local jazz groups" over the informal activities arranged by the posts.[42] The post in Ceylon, in contrast, declared a reception and jam session with musicians and the staff of Radio Ceylon to be the highlight of the visit. U.S. officials noted especially the Ceylonese Music Group's rendition of the Ellington orchestra's theme piece, "Take the A Train," played on traditional instruments.[43] In Pakistan, the band arrived

14. *Ellington studying a sitar performance, October 1963.* Courtesy of the
Duke Ellington Collection, Archives Center, National Museum of American
History, Smithsonian Institution, Washington, D.C.

during a period of strained relations between the United States and
that important ally. The American Consul General in Lahore declared that the "aura of good feeling generated by the visit" had a
"welcome mitigating" effect on the tensions. In Karachi, U.S. officials felt that informal contacts in particular had "fortified post
contacts among target groups." In other countries, such as Iran,
where officials believed that there was a low level of interest and
knowledge about jazz, the posts were happy with exposure reaching some of the targeted audiences, such as students and local elites.
A telecast performance on November 5 helped to overcome a lack
of exposure and made Ellington "the talk of the town."[44]

Following the Iranian performances, the band traveled to Iraq,
where in February of that year, according to journalistic and diplomatic lore, the CIA had masterminded a coup led by General
Ahmad Hassan al-Bakr, a mentor of Saddam Hussein. The grue-
some coup had overthrown 'Abd al-Kaim Qassim and brought the

Ba'athist party to power.[45] Roy Melbourne, U.S. chargé d'affaires, gloated that "the Russians give every sign of knowing what we do—namely, that they have received a serious defeat in the Middle East."[46] Six months earlier, President Kennedy, anxious to see Iraq's dependence on the Soviet Union reduced, had asked his National Security Council staff "what we're doing for the new Iraqi regime." While advisers were surely more occupied with the possibilities of the Pentagon selling the "Bakr regime twelve helicopters for use against pro-Qassim insurgents" than with jazz bands, the Ellington visit in November was part and parcel of the U.S. strategy. In July, "White House Middle East expert Robert Komer told Kennedy" about "making [the] most of [this] Iraqi opportunity."[47]

The band's eventful visit to Baghdad began auspiciously with a performance at a party celebrating the founding of the U.S. Marine Corps. The gathering was held at the home of the U.S. ambassador, Robert C. Strong. Noting that the 188th birthday was being fêted in a 1,200 year old city, one U.S. official reported that "the ambassadorial residence rocked" as four hundred Iraqis and Americans "danced to such old favorites as 'Take the A Train,' 'Mood Indigo,' 'Sophisticated Lady' . . . or crowded around the orchestra for a closer look at the ageless Duke."[48] Local sponsors had been skeptical about selling tickets, but the first concert on November 12 not only sold out but was broadcast in its entirety by the Baghdad television station, Iraq's sole station. "An enthusiastic first-night audience," reported U.S. officials, "watched the concert at Khuld Hall, near the presidential palace, while all over the city thousands sat around television sets in open-air cafés and restaurants or in the comfort of their own homes and enjoyed the artistry of one of the great contemporary figures in American music."[49]

Early the next morning, while most of the musicians were asleep in their hotel across the Tigris, the presidential palace was attacked by Iraqi air force jets. This attempt by rightists in the Ba'athist Party to overthrow the moderate Ba'athist government sent the city into crisis, and a curfew was imposed.[50] While the musicians and the escort officer somewhat guiltily welcomed the imposed rest at a point when the physical demands of the tour were taking their toll, two members of the band "insisted on visiting a local nightclub." "They could only have been prevented by force," lamented Simons, "and all Marines were at the embassy. Asked afterward, they said it was wonderful: two men and twenty girls, shaking like leaves, and 'all those cats with submachine guns sitting around outside.'"[51] The Iraqi capital quickly returned to normal, and when phone service was restored at the U.S. Embassy "they were swamped with calls from Iraqis who had to wait twenty-four hours to congratulate them on the Duke's dazzling first-night performance."[52] The scheduled concert went on, and, like the first, was a sellout.[53]

On November 18, just three days after the orchestra departed the country, the Iraqi army revolted and overthrew the Ba'athist government.[54] While the late 1963 coup might best be characterized as factional Ba'athist infighting in which the military wing of the party had colluded with the government to form a military dictatorship, the Ba'athist Party and the ousted Ahmed Hassan al-Bakar did not regain power until the coup of 1968, and then only with the help of Saddam Hussein.[55] American policymakers did not have the power or influence to halt the evaporation of the opportunities represented in the first coup. Yet in an eerie echo of Louis Armstrong's visit to the Congo during the 1960–1961 crisis, here, clandestine CIA involvement in Iraqi politics had been complicit in further undermining stability in the country and sabotaging the moment of goodwill and possibility exemplified by the Ellington orchestra's visit.[56]

As poignantly illustrated by the band's ease of movement in Baghdad, 1963 was a promising moment with potential for favorable relations with many of the world's nations. Ironically, the worldwide scrutiny of American race relations provided an international as well as domestic opportunity for the Kennedy administration to claim the moral high ground. Thus, the 1963 Ellington tour represented the peak of shared interests between black artists and civil rights activists on the one hand, and State Department personnel on the other. Ellington did not hesitate to promote his

15. *Ellington and Paul Gonsalves relaxing in Ctesiphon, Iraq, November
1963.* Courtesy of the Duke Ellington Collection, Archives Center, National
Museum of American History, Smithsonian Institution, Washington, D.C.

civil rights agenda abroad. Convalescing from dysentery in a New
Delhi Hospital, he played a tape of *My People* for the nurses.[57] The
New York Times reported from Tehran on November 6, 1963, that
"Ellington . . . tonight condemned racial segregation in the United
States. He said he hoped the race problem in the United States
would soon be resolved in favor of the Negro." Reflecting on the
significance of the tour, the *New York Herald Tribune* reported later
in November that Ellington emphasized that "aside from jazz, the
people he met were most interested in talking about the United
States' civil rights struggle."[58] Throughout the tour, Ellington debated with Billy Strayhorn and Simons over the character of racial discrimination. For Ellington, the problem was fundamentally
economic and would disappear with greater economic equality.
Simons agreed with Strayhorn that the issue went beyond eco-
nomics.[59] It was perhaps not surprising that, as a composer, Elling-

ton might analyze racism structurally; but in terms of form, his optimism in 1963 stands in sharp contrast to the views he had expressed only a few years earlier as the tours began. For Ellington, as for other jazz ambassadors, U.S. government support of the civil rights movement was critical to his enthusiastic endorsement of the tours.

Ellington placed his frank discussion of the civil rights struggle in the context of his explicit defense of American freedom. Remembering the 1963 tour, Ellington was impressed that as the "various dos and don'ts which we are expected to observe are enumerated" during the briefings, "we are not required to restrain ourselves in the expression of our personal, political, social, or religious views. As citizens of a free country, there are no restrictions on our tongues. We are to speak as free men. They are very explicit in advising us that we should always say what we think in or out of favor of the U.S."[60] While in Delhi, India, Ellington took the offensive when confronted by a critic of U.S. racial and economic policy:

> "The United States has an extremely accurate news service and the press enjoys almost complete freedom," I claim. "Did you, incidentally, hear about the five little girls who were burned up in that church down in Alabama the other day?"
>
> "Yes," he says with great triumph.
>
> "Well, that was only a couple of days ago, and I'm not sure anybody else would have let such news out that quickly if it had happened in their backyard."[61]

Interestingly, as Ellington fielded responses to the murder of the four girls in the Birmingham church bombing, back in the States Dizzy Gillespie was using his diplomatic capital to respond to the bombing. Gillespie had turned what was initially a joke—the production of "Dizzy for President" buttons—into a campaign for world peace, disarmament, and civil rights. An early high point of the unconventional campaign came in Monterey in September 1963, just after the firebombing of the Birmingham church. Gillespie helped to raise funds for the NAACP, and jazz vocalist Jon

Hendricks "called for a moment to honor the dead children of Birmingham" before singing "the thinly veiled rewrite of 'Salt Peanuts' called 'Dizzy for President.'"[62] Ellington was named as Gillespie's intended Secretary of State (though Gillespie replaced "Secretary" with what he regarded as the more dignified term of "Minister").[63]

In the immediate aftermath of the assassination of Medgar Evers, the Birmingham campaign, and the Kennedy administration's belated embrace of civil rights, the State Department gave Ellington unprecedented latitude in the expression of his political views. Along with his forthright comments to the press, Ellington recounted in a 1963 interview having been deeply upset when asked, "Why hasn't the Negro artist done more for the cause?" Along with his defense of artists, Ellington affirmed his personal investment in the civil rights struggle, arguing that "we had been working on the Negro situation in the South since the '30s, that we had done shows, musical works, benefits, etc., and that the American Negro artist had been among the first to make contributions."[64] In a struggle far from won, Ellington declined to discuss strategy, arguing that publicizing strategy "would help our opponents to build up an even more formidable resistance than they have now."[65]

If the State Department agenda of emphasizing progress in civil rights and black freedom might allow artists to promote civil rights, the agendas of the State Department and Ellington and his band didn't always coincide. Band members felt that their own desires to perform and meet local musicians, as well as their eagerness to bring jazz to new audiences, conflicted with the State Department's focus on neocolonial elites as target audiences. Throughout India, Pakistan, and Ceylon, musicians encountered what Simons described as "a large, Western-oriented, and in many cases Western-educated middle-class"—people who often "provided the bulk of the enthusiastic and even nostalgic audiences."[66] In Calcutta, for example, the band played three concerts before "prestige audiences," the most "American" of the audiences on the tour.[67] If this familiarity with jazz facilitated an appreciation of Ellington, it was also a source of frustration for the musicians.

Members of the orchestra overtly challenged the State Department's views of cultural exchange. Both Simons and the musicians noted that in every case where sponsorship was binational, Americans were in striking evidence in the audience. This "USO character" of some concerts "came as a surprise to almost every member of the orchestra. They did not," explained Simons, "object to entertaining fellow-Americans far from home, but they felt that their primary task was to impress local audiences with the qualities of American culture."[68] Simons was deeply sympathetic to the musicians on this score. The musicians "quickly perceived that large parts of their audiences were splendidly dressed and were so familiar with Ellington music as to be nostalgic."[69] For the pragmatic Simons, the crux of the issue was: "Why should the U.S. taxpayer spend money preaching for the choir?"[70] The musicians, while agreeing with Simons, added an egalitarian twist.

When the musicians protested that they were playing only for elites already familiar with jazz, whereas they had expected to play for "the people," Simons struggled to reconcile his role in the State Department with the musicians' view of "the people." The band, Simons explained, had a "different conception of what they were to do," compared with the notions of the State Department. "The orchestra members," Simons reported tongue in cheek, "had misunderstood the word 'people,' and were disagreeably surprised."[71] Positioning himself as a mediator between the musicians and the State Department, Simons argued that the lower classes "do not in fact 'count' as much as they do with us" and were not necessarily the people the government was trying to reach. The State Department, he explained, was "trying to reach out to those who did count."[72] The pragmatic Simons also invoked the matter of finances and the need to earn back local expenses "in order to justify the expense of the attraction to Congress."[73] Nonetheless, musicians continued to assert their more democratic and egalitarian views of cultural exchange. Simons explained:

Band members continued to feel that they would rather play for the "people," for the men in the streets who clustered around tea-shop radios. More rationally, they believed that the lower classes, even if unimportant politically, were more worthy of exposure to good Western music than the prestige audiences for whom they played. . . . They saw that playing in the courtyard of a first-class hotel already demanded a coat and tie, and felt that it automatically excluded large numbers of people who would have benefited themselves and the United States by hearing Ellington music.[74]

Simons' ultimate assessment of the tour—that groups of this size and trips of this length were inefficient in reaching target audiences and achieving desired effects—seems to have been taken seriously, since there would be a hiatus in such tours. But the musicians had far more immediate civil rights concerns at stake.

Like many of their fellow civil rights activists, musicians even invoked Cold War arguments in favor of egalitarianism: they related stories they had heard "that the Soviets presented their folk dances before tens of thousands on the Calcutta Maidan."[75] At times, conflicts pointed to broader political differences over foreign policy. One African American army private based in Iran was delighted to be invited to dinner with drummer Sam Woodyard at the home of an African American couple who worked as technicians for the State Department. He was deeply hurt when Woodyard refused to sign the LP he had brought for him to autograph, making it clear that he disapproved of his military status.[76] In Woodyard's case, playing for the State Department did not imply an embrace of U.S. foreign policy or U.S. military service.

Duke Ellington's sense of his audience clashed with the State Department's when he learned while in Bombay of the black market for tickets and received numerous telephone calls and letters from musicians complaining of the impossibility of getting tickets. For Ellington, "all musicians are brothers in arms, and it distresses me terribly that they could not get into our concert, so we go about the business of readjusting the conditions. I insist that from now on, no matter how limited the space, all musicians are to be admitted."[77] The elitism inherent in State Department–organized functions remained distasteful to many African American musicians, who had themselves been all too often excluded from special events.

State Department officials were greatly impressed with the charm and diplomatic acumen of Ellington and many members of the band. Simons noted that despite illness and a taxing schedule, Ellington "in his offstage appearances was without fail gracious, articulate, charming, and absolutely winning, even when feeling poorly."[78] Paul Gonsalves demonstrated his diplomatic skills from the time of the first briefing in Damascus. After the U.S. ambassador finished briefing the band on its duties and local customs, Gonsalves (who Ellington recalled had been sipping a few drinks) went over and put his arm around the ambassador. "'Mr. Ambassador,' Paul says, 'you are absolutely right!' He then proceeds to make his own speech. His Excellency is astonished but feels it is wonderful and compliments Paul, telling him that he is a very good ambassador himself."[79] Gonsalves, Ellington concluded, "is a great diplomat, and sometimes, from the way he goes on, you think it is he who is really representing the government."[80] Indeed, the State Department judged the diplomatic achievements of the whole band to be considerable. As Simons reported, "the group as a whole worked very hard to make offstage functions a success. Its members were almost without exception excellent ambassadors and representatives of America. . . . They were vivacious, direct, informal, and intelligent. They were enormously friendly. They were excellent conversationalists."[81]

Lecture-demonstrations, in contrast, had mixed results in the opinion of the State Department. Simons judged the lecture element to be ineffective, because "Ellington is articulate about music, but no one in the band, including Ellington, is articulate in the way 'lecture-demonstration' suggests." Ellington would typically give a five- to ten-minute "homily" explaining that "jazz" was a misnomer and that music has no real categories but only the "sounds" of great musicians.[82] Those closest to the tours, such as Simons, did not view the concerts or demonstrations as propaganda; they saw them as giving the world "the best you've got and letting the chips fall where they may."[83] Nonetheless, it could be disconcerting to have one of America's most prominent jazz musicians questioning the very existence of jazz. What the State Department did appreciate about the lectures was that after Ellington introduced each member of the band and had him solo, they evolved into mini-concerts whose "spontaneity made the lecture-demonstration musically the most enjoyable events of the year."[84]

From the State Department's perspective, problems arose over time as the group became tired. With most members over forty or even fifty, the demands of travel in hot climates began to show after a month. Moreover, as Simons saw it, as jazz musicians they had two characteristics that clashed with the needs of the posts. First, "jazz musicians live at night and sleep through the day." Despite initial efforts to meet obligations and attend daytime functions, over time "they will return to their natural mode of living."[85] The combination of fatigue and their inclination to "indulge in activities which are congenial to them" meant that "it became progressively more difficult" to convince band members to attend parties held in their honor. They preferred spending time with other musicians, going to nightclubs, and sometimes, to the distress of the State Department, keeping company with "unmarried women."[86] Simons ultimately defended the musicians' desires to go to nightclubs and play with other musicians, recognizing its value for relaxation as well as for informal cultural exchange.[87]

But if there was diplomatic value in informal cultural exchanges, Simons repeatedly called attention to the State Department's and musicians' incompatible senses of time and duty, complaining that Ellington's "habitual tardiness was a constant burden."[88] Overall, "the most time-consuming, exhausting, and enervating job the escort had was to try to get the group anyplace on time."[89] Simons reported that inordinate amounts of time were spent in simply waking the musicians up. Telephoning was rarely enough; the "awakening process often involved the use of housekeys, and sometimes physical shaking as well."[90] Conflicts over time and scheduling were exacerbated by the logistical difficulties of the tour. Excess baggage was a constant hassle, as airlines were often unable to accommodate the 2,000 kilograms of cargo and baggage, meaning that the cargo had to precede or follow the group.[91] Flight accommodations depended on availability and varied from the first-class arrangements between New York and Damascus to the World War II–era DC3s that carried the group between Damascus and Amman, and Kabul and New Delhi, and the converted cargo plane that transported the band between Beirut and Kabul. Payment of salary, administered through the Ellington Company manager Al Celley rather than through the State Department directly, along with difficulties in converting money into and out of local currencies, provided a constant source of tension.[92] Simons judged that Ellington was so popular with his musicians in part because Celley was so unpopular and played the bad-cop disciplinarian when needed.[93]

The sheer length of the tour—nearly three months—provided ample opportunity for clashes over what constituted appropriate behavior. The State Department complained that members of the group "sought and found the companionship of persons with whom the State Department and local officials would have preferred them not consort." For the State Department, in addition to "moral objections," there was the practical matter of the image of the United States. "The image we seek to project," argued Simons, "is in general one of a people who are honest, good-willed, informal, hard-working, and chaste. Every member of the group had the first four characteristics in abundance; rather fewer possessed the last."[94] Despite his clear sympathy and bonds with many of the musicians, Simons viewed this problem as endemic to jazz musicians: "A symphony orchestra does not present a publicity problem, but because it seeks recreation in public a jazz band can." Yet while "possibly detrimental activities on the part of jazz musicians can never be entirely prevented," given that "jazz is one of our cultural showpieces," the State Department needed to "make the best of a possible dangerous characteristic."[95] Moreover, the real danger was only in places where the press "depends for its prosperity on the exploitation of scandal," and "only in Colombo and Ankara was the group involved with a press generally ready to exploit the nonscheduled activities of the group."[96]

Ellington himself appeared beyond reproach in the eyes of the State Department, engaging in "no reprobate public activities," following doctor's orders not to drink, and taking "all meals except 'official' ones in his room."[97] Always "charming" at functions, "if the conversants were ladies it was full of gallantries whose exaggeration was conscious and well-understood, it was impeccably polite." In Simons' opinion, Ellington was "a gentleman from head to toe, entirely concentrated on his music, his comfort, and his reputation."[98] From New Delhi on, however, Ellington was joined by his companion, Countess Fernanda de Castro Monte, "a lady whose presence was a constant source of acute embarrassment and apprehension to American officials." Simons went out of his way to explain the "abiding affection" between the two and maintained that the relationship could not "in any reasonable definition of the word be described as tawdry." Yet the possibility that Ellington might be seen or, worse yet, photographed with this "tall, impressive and always strikingly blonde and dressed" woman mortified State Department officials.[99] If the State Department benefited from promoting civil rights abroad, an interracial couple was far beyond the bounds of acceptable ways in which to promote an integrated society. If their relationship should become public, the damage to the State Department in the eyes of Congress would be considerable. Though Ellington's friend avoided photographs "like the plague," they were accidentally photographed together twice in "incidents" well documented by the State Department. The first— ultimately containable, since it involved a USIS photographer— was during a visit to Ctesiphon, outside Baghdad, and provoked embarrassed apologies. In a potentially far more damaging incident in Ankara, they were photographed together when they were both ill and had therefore "unwisely left the hotel for the hospital together." Ellington and the countess were greeted at the door by what the State Department described as "a barrage of hungry press photographers." Al Celley, who was nearly blind, was "tackled by a press representative in an effort to get him out of the way of the camera. The assistant cultural affairs officer struck the camera away but was photographed in doing so." The local paper was set to run "half a headline and half a photograph," but, as Simons described it, this "was destroyed when the news of President Kennedy's assassination was received." The "incident," Simons explained had "happily come to an end for unhappy reasons."[100]

The assassination of President Kennedy on November 22 brought an abrupt end to the tour. Herbie Jones, the trumpeter who had replaced Nance, recalled being at a special dinner for the band when "someone came in and yelled out, 'The President's been shot!'" Jones remembered thinking, "Yeah, well, okay. Everyone's always getting shot around here. The guy says, '*Our* president.' And you hear about a dozen plates fall on the table."[101] Ellington had retired for room service when a State Department officer called and insisted on coming to the room right away with the news of the assassination. Ellington remembered: "The food just sits there and gets cold. Nobody eats, nobody talks, nobody does anything for thirty minutes. When the news hits the city, it apparently has the same effect on the crowds in the street. The people all look as though they are numbed."[102] The State Department canceled the scheduled performances in Turkey, along with the remainder of the tour (Cyprus, United Arab Republic, Greece, and Yugoslavia) to "avert widespread censure and avoid offending local traditions," which forbade public performances in a time of mourning.[103]

Devastated by the news of the assassination, Ellington nevertheless wanted to continue the tour, arguing that his music expressed the spectrum of human emotions and the orchestra's performances "would signify tribute rather than disrespect."[104] His response to Kennedy's death was to stay up all night composing memorial music.[105] While Ellington was persuaded that the remaining countries on the tour "might have thought that a continuation of the tour was in poor taste," he continued to defend his desire to complete the tour with memorial concerts.[106] In an interview with Sally Hammond of the *Washington Post,* Ellington explained that "it would have meant a 'complete turnabout'" but that he had been "ready to sit up all night writing special memorial music." Outlining his vision of the music, he continued: "Of course I'd have cut out all the theatrical stuff and there wouldn't have been any swinging. But it would have had a beat. Religious music, you know, does have a beat."[107] The problem, Ellington argued, came down to the word "jazz": "This word has absolutely no meaning today. . . . If it hadn't been overplayed in the publicity, there would have been no reason to cancel the tour." For Ellington, jazz should simply mean "freedom of expression through music" but because of the "shady associations" people had given it, concerts were canceled as country after country went into mourning. "They thought jazz might be considered in bad taste."[108]

Cut short by the Kennedy assassination and disrupted by Ray Nance's departure, the tour turned out to be a strange, troubling, and ultimately tragic experience. The musicians had often been stunned and depressed by the widespread poverty they witnessed, and disturbed by political tensions manifested most dramatically in the Iraqi coup attempt. But like Gillespie, Brubeck, and others, Ellington responded to the sorrows and triumphs of the tour through composing music. As evidenced in his desire to compose memorials for Kennedy, Ellington remained an active composer who was constantly writing through the most grueling itineraries. The musicologist Travis Jackson argues that "Ellington was not engaged in an attempt to *imitate* the different musics he heard during the tours. Rather, his primary aim was to allow all the experiences he had—musical and nonmusical—to *influence* his way of composing."[109]

In the liner notes to his *Far East Suite,* Ellington explained: "I don't want to copy this rhythm or that scale. It's more valuable to have absorbed while there. You let it roll around, undergo a chemical change, and then let it seep out on paper in the form that suits the musicians who are going play it. But this takes quite a bit of doing; you don't want to underestimate or *understate the world out there*" (emphasis added).

Ellington's emphasis on the diplomat-artist's delicate relationship to "the world out there" offers a clue to his sensibilities as an ambassador. Recalling his warnings to Thomas Simons about the pitfalls of American chauvinism, Ellington's desire to let himself be influenced but not to imitate suggests his wariness of appropriation. This suspicion of appropriation, one might argue, was grounded in the resistance to being defined and categorized by critics—a resistance that had long animated Ellington's life and work. Writing about the tours, he made no pretense of authority or even comprehension. He embraced the stance of misrecognition, calling attention to his frequent lapses in understanding, as when in Bombay he had misunderstood the gesture for "yes" and proceeded to eat the worst item off the menu for seven days in a row.

Further clues to Ellington's concern not to "understate the world out there," are found in his insistence that "the music of my race is something more than the American idiom." The passage continues: "It is the result of our transplantation to American soil, and was our reaction in the plantation days to the tyranny we endured. What we could not say openly we expressed in music. . . . It expresses our personality."[110] Ellington's insistence on music as expression, and specifically historical expression that marks a reaction to slavery and oppression, is critical. For Ellington, *"stating* the world out there . . . takes quite a bit of doing,*" in part because music takes on the responsibility of representation. Indeed, Ellington's sense of music as historical expression mitigated against modernist forms of appropriation that posited art as pure expression abstracted from both history and its production through labor.[111] Not only is Ellington wary of misrepresenting "the world out there," but his music has to *state* the world, to capture a changing cultural scene that is new to him and goes beyond the questions of power and representation that he has grappled with in a primarily American context.[112]

Yet as Ellington's work expanded further beyond the nation-state, to be involved in the tours at all was to be steeped in a national project of power and appropriation. Travis Jackson helps to illuminate Ellington's complex position vis-à-vis influence and appropriation. In letting himself be "influenced" by other musics, Ellington was not engaging in a form of colonial appropriation. Ellington wasn't trying to invigorate a seemingly dead or lackluster form of expression with more "primitive" or "emotionally engaged" musics from places seen as "outside the West." Nor was he trying to give a flagging career a shot in the arm by coloring his work with exotica.[113] Rather than engaging in a colonialist form of appropriation, Ellington was mining what he heard and saw as a way of coming to think differently about composition. In doing so, however, he sometimes resorted to clichés that reduced the complexity of other people's music to a few musical signifiers. (For example, in his *Far East Suite* Ellington uses phrasings to suggest snake charmers and "drones.")[114] The metaphor of mining helps to remind us that while Ellington's State Department tours were not part of a colonial project, they were part of the U.S. pursuit of hegemony through policies of modernization and development. It was no accident that jazz tours moved through regions rich in those quintessential Cold War commodities oil and uranium, even as they hit the Cold War hotspots.[115] Ellington would later travel to mineral-rich southern Africa in a tour sponsored by copper-mining companies and the Zambian government; he would also perform in Laos and volunteer to perform in Vietnam. It would be wrong, however, to comprehend the tours and their significance solely within the context of the vast and multifaceted American efforts to secure global resources.

To export American culture was to export its hybridity, it complexities, its tensions and contradictions. To export jazz was to export, in the words of Ellington, "an American idiom with African roots."[116] And in 1963, that meant exporting the civil rights movement. If the curious convergence of interests between State Department personnel defending American "race relations" and black artists fighting for civil rights could at times benefit the State Department, it also allowed for the projection of the optimism and vitality of black American culture abroad. The conflicts within the tour—over the meaning of "the people," the audiences for the tours; over musicians' preference for interacting with other musicians and learning new musics over attending official functions; over the musicians' insistence on putting their stamp on diplomacy—all bespeak the impulse to refuse appropriation and the desire to project a cultural statement and musical expression that constituted "something more than the American idiom." In Ellington's long-standing fight against appropriation, in his attempt to be influenced but not to imitate, there was an uneven match between what he intended and what he achieved in "the world out there," just as there was for the State Department.

The Duke Ellington orchestra returned home to a rapidly evolving civil rights movement. The continuing white violence and resistance to civil rights—dramatized in the killing of four volunteers of the Student Nonviolent Coordinating Committee during the summer of 1964 and the refusal of the Democratic Party to seat the Mississippi Democratic Freedom Party—contributed to massive disillusionment. By the time President Lyndon Johnson succeeded in passing the 1964 and 1965 Voting Rights and Civil Rights acts, for many it was too little too late. As Gillespie carried on with his "Dizzy for President" campaign, he would joke before playing "Morning of the Carnival," introducing it as a song from the film "*Black Orpheus,* excuse the expression." Saxophonist James Moody would counter with, "Dizzy, you can say 'black.' Don't be ashamed to say '*black*.'" Gillespie would respond first with the rhetorical question, "It's all right, huh?" And when Moody replied, "Yah, Malcolm told me," Gillespie would come back with, "Everything must be cool if Malcolm say so, baby." When Gillespie concluded the introduction with the words, "From *Black Orpheus,* and I mean it!" Moody would add, "And if they don't like it, we can lay right down here and demonstrate!"[117] Gillespie's playful rendition of an assertive black culture was a harbinger of developments that would fundamentally reshape the State Department and the country as well.

CHAPTER 6

Jazz, Gospel, and R&B

Black Power Abroad

In 1963, at the time of Duke Ellington's tour of the Middle East and South Asia, few Americans had heard of Vietnam, the country their government had been pouring military aid into for a decade. That same year, Dizzy Gillespie could playfully invoke the authority of Malcolm X in his stage act and his mock presidential campaign. But one of the last acts of President Kennedy had been his approval of the coup to overthrow South Vietnam's president, Ngo Dinh Diem. The coup resulted in the murder of Diem and his brother Nhu, and deepened America's involvement in the Southeast Asian nation.[1] And on February 21, 1965, Malcolm X was killed by an assassin's bullet. By 1966, Americans were awakening not only to a growing antiwar movement at home but to extensive international censure of U.S. intervention in Vietnam, as critics from Africa and Europe to Latin America and Asia charged the U.S. government with racist imperialism. At the same time, urban rebellions throughout the country were making it painfully clear that despite the dismantling of Jim Crow legislation, the heroic sacrifices of the civil rights movement had done little to address the nation's poverty or to improve the lives of a great many black Americans.[2] Police brutality and discrimination in jobs and housing remained daily facts of life. So black activists began shifting their focus: they sought to gain control over the local institutions that shaped their lives—institutions ranging from businesses to schools to the penal system.

As the slogan "Black Power" became a rallying cry, as black activists demanded economic and cultural autonomy, a mood of "no compromise" with white liberals was expressed in strident critiques of social policy and a resurgence of artistic creativity.[3] Poets, writers, and artists created the Black Arts Movement. And there was a similar impetus in the jazz world: civil rights organizations provided a model for such new groups as the Chicago Association for the Advancement of Creative Musicians, the Detroit Creative Musicians' Association, and the Black Artists' Group in St. Louis. These groups advocated a free jazz aesthetic and cultural innovation, and were committed as community organizations to the cultural and political liberation of the masses.[4] Meanwhile, as the national audience for jazz continued to contract, the gospel-based sound of soul music, along with rhythm and blues, through such studios as the Memphis-based Stax and Detroit's Motown, was transforming American popular music and finding enthusiastic acclaim overseas.[5] In the two years following the assassination of President Kennedy, the international and domestic cultural and political landscape altered dramatically.

How did shifts in the civil rights revolution and the growing attention to America's international policies affect the State Department? Did its goals in sponsoring the tours change as the world altered so rapidly and radically? Liberals in the Johnson administration had hoped that the passage of the 1964 and 1965 Voting Rights and Civil Rights acts would usher in a new period of harmony. Instead, they found themselves on the defensive. Caught in a whirlwind of reaction to unprecedented attacks on U.S. policies, the State Department did not immediately rethink its cultural-exchange strategies in a systematic fashion. Yet as policymakers strove to answer harsh criticism of the nation's foreign policy, they attempted to reach larger audiences. Toward this end, officials began to take note of new musical developments, turning more and more to popular forms rather than insisting on the high-modernist art extolled in the early tours. The State Department employed such musical forms as gospel, soul, and rhythm and blues, but it did not push jazz aside. Rather, it embraced a multiplicity of black musical forms.

The First World Festival of Negro Arts, held in Dakar, Senegal, in April 1966, provided a forum for an international affirmation of African and African diasporic art, and was a catalyst for the State Department's shift toward a wider range of black music. For many black American artists, the festival was more than simply a counterpart to African American art. Animated by the ideas of Negritude advocated by Senegal's poet-president Léopold Senghor, the festival was a celebration of the formal and spiritual connections between African and Afro-diasporic art forms, reflecting both the African inspirations and international resonances of developments in black American culture.[6] But why the U.S. government embraced the festival is another story.

Throughout 1965 and early 1966, President Johnson, Secretary of State Dean Rusk, and Johnson's National Security advisers sought a strategy for confronting what they perceived as Johnson's image problem in Africa. The advisers worried that despite Johnson's success in passing civil rights legislation, the goodwill that many African leaders felt toward the late President Kennedy had not carried over to Johnson. For these advisers, it was critical that the president take steps to make sure he was identified with African aspirations.[7] They had ample reason for concern. In November 1965, the unilateral declaration of independence from Britain by Ian Smith's white minority government in Rhodesia (and the tepid American protest) had brought renewed attention to American coziness with apartheid in South Africa. Johnson faced charges of complicity with apartheid from the Student Nonviolent Coordinating Committee (SNCC), which staged a sit-in at the South African embassy in Washington, and from Senator Robert Kennedy, who delivered an anti-apartheid speech in Cape Town, South Africa.[8] And by the end of February 1966, it was clear that Johnson had far more than an image problem. In addition to continuing controversy over U.S.-supplied arms used by Portugal to maintain its colonial hold on Angola, the United States was widely suspected (accurately, as it turned out) of involvement in two coups d'état on the continent: a November 1965 coup in the Belgian Congo, in which General Joseph Mobutu assumed the presidency, and the Ghana coup that had ousted Kwame Nkrumah on February 24, 1966.[9] Given Johnson and Rusk's political problems, it is not surprising that the State Department rushed headlong into a cultural blitz of the African continent in 1966 and 1967, beginning with its sponsorship of numerous black American artists at festival in Dakar.

The festival, opening only two months after Nkrumah's ouster, must have seemed the perfect venue for showcasing the "nonmilitary programs" that Rusk deemed essential for "developing attitudes favorable to the West."[10] To emphasize Johnson's commitment to the continent, his wife, Lady Bird Johnson, served as honorary chair of the committee overseeing American participation. The festival, a celebration of African culture throughout the continent and its diaspora, was co-sponsored by the government of Senegal, UNESCO, and the American Society of African Culture (AMSAC), the U.S. wing of the French-based Society of African Culture. By the time of the festival, the U.S. Congress had formally dismantled Jim Crow with the passage of the Civil Rights and Voting Rights acts. For the State Department, this legislation, along with the presence of such black cultural dignitaries as Duke Ellington, Alvin Ailey, the gospel singer Marion Williams, and the writer Langston Hughes, represented the achievements and hope of American liberalism.[11] Yet far from exulting in the end of American racism and inequality, this post–civil rights moment witnessed unprecedented assertions of black cultural solidarity that far exceeded the cultural politics and vision of American officialdom. What the State Department had not anticipated was that black artists would bring their own agendas to the festival and the tours, and would interact with African audiences in ways that challenged the organizing principles of the performing-arts tours.

At the festival, gospel singer Mahalia Jackson was recognized as best female vocalist for her gospel recordings, and Marion Williams won international acclaim for her vocal virtuosity in performing gospel. Seeing this extraordinary enthusiasm, the Department of State got religion. Officials seized an opportunity to respond to

America's crisis of legitimacy in Africa by quickly signing up Williams for a tour of the continent later that year. The resounding success of the Williams tour led to a steady stream of U.S.-sponsored gospel, dance, jazz, and rhythm and blues (R&B) performances on the African continent over the next several years. These were followed by Mahalia Jackson's visit to India in 1971. The State Department embraced gospel for pragmatic reasons: African American religion and spirituality proved to have powerful resonance for African audiences. Williams and Jackson were not the first gospel artists to tour for the government, but as the cultural programs continued to shift their aim toward youthful audiences and away from elites, the State Department implicitly acknowledged the appeal of popular culture and Afro-diasporic forms. This pragmatic turn to gospel and other African diasporic forms would fundamentally challenge the ideological rationale behind the tours.

The prominence of gospel at the Dakar festival and Williams' subsequent trip to Africa reflected a major shift in the State Department's performing-arts tours. Previously, the tours had been animated by the twin ideologies of color-blind liberalism and a commitment to a modernist aesthetic. With the Dakar festival and the gospel, dance, R&B, and jazz tours that followed, these ideologies became less salient as the defining assumptions that promoted art over entertainment and insisted on the irrelevance of race unraveled. As American officials sought to enlist the international authority of black-movement culture in the wake of the Dakar festival, to proclaim America's color-blindness they had to confront the growing militancy of black artists abroad. Thus, the State Department's encounters with an assertive and increasingly globally defined black culture—through the performances of Marion Williams in Africa, the dances composed by Alvin Ailey, the work of jazz composer and pianist Randy Weston, and the performance styles of gospel and R&B—further exposed and exacerbated earlier tensions about traditional versus modern jazz, popular versus elitist audiences, official versus personal visits and encounters, and U.S. versus transnational goals.

At the Dakar festival, these tensions had already begun to manifest themselves. The State Department celebrated American progress in civil rights, but artists like Alvin Ailey didn't share the State Department's optimism about, or comfort with, Lyndon Johnson's civil rights legislation. In a live interview on the National Radio of Senegal during the festival, Ailey told Senegalese audiences of his own civil rights agenda:

> When I started to have a dance company, I decided I wanted to do something to show what the Negro had done. . . . In the United States, we have a little problem, as you know. They think we're not first-class citizens. . . . They don't recognize [our music and dance] . . . for what it is. So I made a dance company mainly to illustrate to them what the Negro had contributed to America, . . . what the Negro made out of adversity, what the Negro made out of his sorrow, what the Negro made out of being held down in America. That's what the blues are. . . . I've taken these beautiful things and put them in dance.[12]

Ailey felt that his art expressed the historical struggles and achievements of black America. He described himself as an "organic artist," alluding both to his life-long exploration of many forms of the expressive arts and to the fact that his major works, such as *Revelations,* came from the experiences of his family, who were "deep Texans, deep Negro Southerners." Calling attention to the profound moral and creative resources found in the experiences of his people, Ailey described his family: "They were sad; they were beautiful. They sang the blues and the spirituals because they felt them. When I became a choreographer and started putting things on the stage, these were the things I wanted to express."[13]

Though the State Department celebrated America's purportedly color-blind universalism, Ailey thought the festival represented global recognition and affirmation of black American culture. Indeed, Ellington, Ailey, and Williams were the undisputed hits of the festival, and African Americans were awarded first-place honors in numerous categories of the arts. Such recognition was usually based on the assumption that their art was rooted in their lives and experiences as African Americans. Best-film honors went to *Nothing but a Man,* Michael Roemer's gritty portrayal of gender relations among blacks in the Jim Crow South, with affecting performances by Ivan Dixon and Abbey Lincoln. Mahalia Jackson was named best female vocalist for her album of gospel hits. And in what might be considered recognition of an entire remarkable career, Louis Armstrong was named best male vocalist for the hit single "Hello, Dolly," a song whose artistic limitations were (in Armstrong's view) offset by the fact that it knocked the Beatles from their accustomed position at the top of the charts.[14]

While State Department personnel were intensely proud of the art of Williams, Ailey, and Ellington and of America's progress in civil rights, these artists gave credit to the African diasporic ties nurtured by the conference. Ellington began work on his *Senegalese Suite* on his way to Dakar (though the composition ultimately became "La Plus Belle Africaine"). If the State Department perceived the festival as a triumph of American culture, Ellington saw it as an affirmation of African diasporic ties. "After writing African music for thirty-five years," Ellington noted in his Dakar journal, "here I am at last in Africa. I can only hope and wish that our performance of 'La Plus Belle Africaine,' which I have written in anticipation of the occasion, will mean something to the people gathered here."[15] Ellington celebrated the Afro-diasporic spirit of the festival in his 1966 album *Soul Call,* whose title track was the Louis and Henry Bellson composition "Soul Call" and which included Ellington's "La Plus Belle Africaine," "West Indian Pancake," and the Othello-inspired Ellington-Strayhorn composition "Such Sweet Thunder."[16] Continuing to pursue Afro-diasporic connections on a 1969 trip to Jamaica—where, he recalled, "the band was uniformly dressed in dashikis"—Ellington would return to the African continent for the State Department in 1973 to perform in Ethiopia and Zambia.[17]

The political challenges facing Johnson and the State Department in Africa were evident at the Dakar festival. These contributed to the subsequent American cultural blitz of the African con-

16. *Paul Gonsalves watches as Sam Woodyard tries a Sabar drum, Dakar, April 1966.*
Courtesy of the Duke Ellington Collection, Archives Center, National Museum of
American History, Smithsonian Institution, Washington, D.C.

17. *Ellington with musicians in Jamaica, 1969.* Courtesy of the Duke
Ellington Collection, Archives Center, National Museum of American History, Smithsonian Institution, Washington, D.C.

tinent, with tours by Marion Williams, the Alvin Ailey troupe,
Woody Herman, Randy Weston, and others. The first controversy
to affect the American participants in the festival was the sharp divide in African politics between a more European-oriented and
American-accommodating Senegalese-led bloc, and the militant
pan-Africanism of Sékou Touré and Kwame Nkrumah. This divi-
sion was exacerbated by the overthrow of Nkrumah in a coup less
than two months before the festival. While Nkrumah's opponents
had legitimate grievances about the suppression of civil liberties in
Ghana, his ouster was primarily a result of his uncompromising
stance against neocolonial control of the continent's politics and
economy.[18] This divide in African politics found a parallel in the
controversies over the American attendance at the festival. Apart
from the artists themselves, American attendance ultimately con-

sisted of a delegation of 183 people from AMSAC, a co-sponsor of the festival. While AMSAC had been indisputably important in nurturing artistic and intellectual links between Africans and African Americans, critics of U.S. policy suspected the organization—correctly, as later reports showed—of accepting CIA funding. Thus, AMSAC's sponsorship of the festival associated it with U.S. foreign policy and made it suspect. Indeed, most American participants were firmly in a pro-Senegalese and anti-Nkrumah camp.

Although leftist critics of Senghor did not attend the festival, its organizers had inadvertently provided a forum for black diasporic and African critics of U.S. foreign policy in Africa. These critics indicted the United States and Senegal for their prompt recognition of the post-Nkrumah military regime in Ghana and their weak protest against Rhodesia's unilateral declaration of independence (UDI) as a white minority government.[19] Novelist James Baldwin and singer Harry Belafonte boycotted the festival, criticizing the "approach" of Senghor, by which they meant everything from the concept of Negritude to the U.S.-friendly politics of Senegal. (Ralph Ellison and the actors Ossie Davis and Sidney Poitier also boycotted.) Belafonte had visited Guinea several times as a cultural adviser to President Sékou Touré, and had criticized Senegal for failing to break off relations with Britain over Rhodesia's UDI, as Guinea had done.

A lively and contentious debate over the concept of Negritude dominated the festival. Lloyd Garrison, a *New York Times* correspondent, observed that "in hotel rooms and cocktail parties and in the gleaming white National Assembly Hall where the festival's colloquiums are held, the mere mention of negritude is bound to stir debate."[20] The Negritude movement had been founded by Senghor, Aimé Césaire, and Léon-Gontran Damas as a celebration of African cultural heritage in the Francophone world.[21] Though viewed by its supporters as a future-oriented and modern African alternative to Western modernity, Negritude was criticized for echoing Western ethnocentric beliefs about the essential nature of Africans and for celebrating a precolonial past.[22] Certainly, African

Americans entered this debate with views that were radically different from those of the Francophone intellectuals among whom the concept had emerged. For most black American artists, responses to Negritude had far more to do with a reading of contemporary American politics than with the long-developing West African and Caribbean positions.[23] Yet by 1966, many people found it impossible to separate Senghor's philosophical position on Negritude from the political and economic policies of Senegal, and saw Senghor's Negritude as politically accommodating rather than challenging Western hierarchies. What had begun as a debate about culture had become infused with politics. For Barry Farrell, a journalist writing from Dakar, Senghor "has carefully distinguished between the cultural theory of *negritude* and the economic reality of keeping his country going." Farrell pointed out that the economy of Senegal ran "almost exclusively through white bankers, businessmen, technicians, and planters." For Farrell, reconciling this arrangement with Negritude was a "delicate trick" that furthered economic prosperity. For critics of Senghor, it was no trick at all but a continuation of colonial relationships.[24] What Farrell saw as Senghor's political acumen, others saw as abject dependence and an evasion of politics.

Even among artists closely involved in the festival, many objected to Senghor's advocacy of Negritude. The African American choreographer Katherine Dunham, who served as an adviser to Senghor and the festival, insisted that the term was "meaningless."[25] And Ailey, while insisting on the African American origins of his art, also believed in its universal qualities, which he believed conflicted with Negritude. Ailey saw his art as potentially accessible to everyone, and he felt that the concept of Negritude rested on a restricted notion of blackness. "People are very eager," warned Ailey on Senegalese National Radio, "to say, 'Oh, those Negroes—they have such a sense of rhythm. They're the only ones who can do the blues, they're the only ones who can do jazz.' And that's not true. That's not true at all."[26] Ailey's belief in the universalizing qualities of his art fueled his missionary passion as a cultural ambassador.[27]

Langston Hughes, in contrast, defended Negritude as linked to the black American "soul": "Negritude has its roots deep in the beauty of the black people—in what younger American writers and musicians call 'soul.' Soul is contemporary Harlem's 'negritude.'"[28] As a critic of Negritude, Ailey agreed with much of Negritude's project—that of articulating a form of universalism and modernity distinct from Western modernity. But as the festival developed, the understanding of Ailey and many other African Americans of Negritude as restrictive, and the political fissures that emerged between Senghor and left-leaning Africans and African Americans, engendered deeply divided views.

Amid the controversies over the philosophical and political implications of Negritude, the State Department had not imagined that in supporting black performers at the Dakar festival, they would be exporting conflicts within America about the funding of the arts. But attempts to raise money for the festival had made it clear that black art in America lacked support. Government funding had gained visibility with the creation of the National Endowment for the Arts in 1965.[29] For the Dakar festival, an American committee under the titular authority of Lady Bird Johnson had raised only $100,000 out of a goal of $600,000. Several visual artists withdrew in protest against the American committee's unwillingness to pay each artist $1,000, half of which would go to a black college. Such funding, they charged, would have been readily forthcoming for white artists.[30] Though the shortfall was ultimately met by the government, which contributed $250,000 through the State Department and the Agency for International Development, critics saw these as paltry sums when compared to the support that had been extended to white artists over the years. The State Department funded the artists already involved in its tours. In addition to Ellington, half of Ailey's expenses were covered by the State Department when his troupe replaced Arthur Mitchell's Dance Theatre of Harlem at the last minute. The committee had been unable to cover expenses for Mitchell's much larger company.[31]

Not only did the Cold War intrude through the controversies

over U.S. and Senegalese foreign policy, but it also played out as a sideshow in Dakar. The Soviets sent their popular poet Yevgeny Yevtushenko, as well as a cruise ship to court the artists and supplement Dakar's limited hotel space. While the Soviets could not compete with America's contribution of black art and performance, they did serve vodka, and they mounted an exhibit highlighting the fact that (as the *New York Times* reported) "the Russians never engaged in the slave trade, while guess-who did."[32]

The controversies over U.S. participation in the Dakar festival marked the first significant moment during the jazz tours in which critics charged that jazz and black art were being coopted as Cold War weapons.[33] But for Ailey, numerous jazz musicians, and other participating artists, State Department funding of the black arts at the Dakar festival was long overdue and much deserved. In Ailey's opinion, the festival was first and foremost a global platform for demonstrating the beauty and dignity of black American culture. It is in this context that several of the participating artists at Dakar decided to return to the continent under the auspices of the State Department.

Criticisms of U.S. policies in Africa sparked a flurry of official "strategic" cultural presentations throughout the continent. In the wake of the Dakar festival, a State Department report described the power of African American artists to "perform [the] strategic role" of "relat[ing] to the young elite of Africa."[34] Franklin Williams, U.S. ambassador to Ghana, had tried hard to arrange a visit by Ellington to Ghana to help silence suspicions of U.S. involvement in the coup that had overthrown Nkrumah. Williams expressed relief that exchange and cultural programs "were no longer restricted by [Ghanaian] cabinet sanctions." Though Ellington did not return to Africa until 1973, many others would tour in the years immediately following the festival.

Marion Williams was the first American artist at Dakar to tour for the State Department. From the beginning of the tours, the State Department's view that jazz embodied a race-neutral expression of American freedom clashed with the musicians' belief that jazz was deeply embedded in African American history and culture. The tensions already evident in trying to dissociate jazz both from popular entertainment and from its origins in African American cultural settings—big bands, dance halls, nightclubs—were greatly exacerbated by the Dakar festival and the State Department's eventual turn to artists performing gospel, R&B, and soul. The gospel tours exemplify the anxieties inherent in the official definitions of a race-neutral American national culture and the attempt to demonstrate that the country had transcended racial divisions. Presenting gospel musicians—artists whose performance style is emblematic of black particularity—further undermined the assumptions of a color-blind universalism, which the State Department encouraged but which had always been contested. Praised by the State Department for its "connection" with foreign audiences, a connection made possible by its kinetic spirituality, gospel actually countered the government's claims of the unique character of American freedom. It was likely that African and Asian audiences identified with the African American struggles for freedom which the gospel songs reflected. The performance style of gospel, historically grounded in slave spirituals and distinguished by improvisation and Afro-diasporic rhythms, tended to convey an oppositional rather than racially integrated image of American culture.

Six months after the Dakar festival, the Marion Williams Trio (backed by pianist Marion Franklin and guitarist Clifton Best) toured East, West, and Central Africa (with a stop in the Middle East) for six weeks. They performed in Kenya, Ivory Coast, Niger, and the United Arab Republic. Williams, born in Miami, Florida, in 1927, had begun singing in a local West Indian Holiness Church at the age of six. She'd had to leave school after the ninth grade, when her father died. While working as a domestic and in factories and laundries, she had sung in storefront churches and streetcorner revivals on weekends. By the time she was in her mid-teens, she was known as the Queen of Miami Gospel. In 1947 she had joined the Clara Ward Singers as their featured soloist, and in 1958 had formed her own group, the Stars of Faith. Williams had received international acclaim for her performance in the gospel play *Black Nativity,* written by Langston Hughes in 1961 to showcase her talents. Premiering in New York City, the production had been enthusiastically received at Gian Carlo Menotti's Festival of Two Worlds in Spoleto, Italy, and in a subsequent forty-week European tour. After a performance at the new Philharmonic Hall at Lincoln Center in New York during the 1962 Christmas season, the production had returned to Europe for a 1963–1964 tour. During 1965–1966, Williams had starred in Hughes's *Prodigal Son* in Europe, and had given concerts in Paris and London.

From November 19, 1966, through January 3, 1967, the trio gave twenty-seven concerts and made twenty-five offstage appearances. Williams' gospel repertoire included "Peace in the Valley," "Who Gives Me Courage," and "He's Got the Whole World in His Hands." She ended every performance on the tour with "We Shall Overcome." For an embassy official in Cairo, Williams' performances and repertoire were "uniquely successful in that Miss Williams' repertoire was so basically All-American. She and her partners served the post's cultural objectives very well indeed."[35] Yet a local critic, writing in *Le Journal d'Egypte,* rather than seeing Williams' spirituals and gospel songs as All-American, asked: "Is her art a return to the sources or the expression of a suffering civilization? Who knows?"[36]

Throughout the tour, officials marveled at Williams' ability to connect with her audiences. Describing Williams' concerts in Lomé (Togo) as a "phenomenal success," the U.S. Embassy there emphasized the participatory nature of her performances. According to a State Department account of a Christmas concert in the Methodist Salem Church, "When she asked the people to sing with her, their voices rang out; when she asked them to clap their hands in time to the rhythm, the church rocked with enthusiastic hand-clapping and foot-stomping. This performance was climaxed with Miss Williams calling some small children up front to share the stage with her. The audience burst into wild applause as she sat down on the platform surrounded by the children and held a couple of them on her lap while singing."[37] In the tours by Williams and, later, Mahalia Jackson, officials frequently commented on their "natural" powers. The U.S. Embassy in Cairo claimed it could "hardly improve on an account in *Le Progrès Egyptien* that described Williams as 'a force of nature.'" She was "built like an athlete," and her voice sounded one moment "like a grounding volcano" and at another "like a peaceful river running to the sea."[38] Since there were relatively few women leading performing-arts tours, these observations on Williams and Jackson are striking. In sharp contrast to U.S. officials' perceptions of male artists such as Ellington, whom government officials were willing to grant a degree of diplomatic agency, officials overwhelmingly saw Marion Williams and Mahalia Jackson as natural vessels of spirituality and attributed their popular appeal to these supposed innate gifts.

Yet while the State Department delighted in, and depended on, Williams' rapport with audiences (one account boasted that "all the diplomats, *even* the French," were won over) it couldn't control the audiences' reception or the forms that performer-audience solidarity might take. In Lomé, in what an official described as the "pièce de résistance," Williams sang "We Shall Overcome" "while strolling with the Chinese ambassador, the second secretary of the Nigerian Embassy (both in native dress) and the [American] PAO [Public Affairs Officer], all with hands clasped and raised upwards."[39] Since Williams was wearing Togolese attire during the performance, it's likely that "We Shall Overcome" held third-worldist rather than pro-American resonance in that context. Similarly, did those French-speaking West and Central African audiences hear Williams' rendition of "He's Got the Whole World in His Hands"—in which she sang, "He's got France and Belgium in his hands"—as a simple naming of two countries or as a reminder that these colonial powers were subject to divine and human judgment?

The State Department's willingness to capitalize on artists' powerful rapport with African audiences was evident in their perception of the Alvin Ailey company. At the Dakar festival, Ailey clearly saw State Department sponsorship as a way of furthering a civil rights agenda. Moreover, since modern dance was the most finan-cially vulnerable of the art forms represented at the festival, Ailey regarded government tours as critical to the dance company's survival.[40] Following the success at the festival, Ailey brought the troupe back to Africa in 1967, and to Western and Eastern Europe in 1968, for State Department tours. He disbanded the company in 1970 for lack of funds, but reassembled it that same year for State Department tours of northern Africa and the Soviet Union. The Soviet tour had been scheduled first, and the State Department, be-sides wanting to meet its African objectives, was concerned at the prospect of losing a prestigious American company when the Sovi-ets were investing heavily in their own dance companies. The State Department felt that "keeping the company in performing status" with the African tour "would clearly enhance the nation's cultural exchange efforts."[41]

Events just before the 1967 tour violently demonstrated the con-tinued gulf between the image of black American life projected abroad and the reality of life at home. Ailey was walking home shortly past midnight, after dining with a friend near Lincoln Cen-ter. A police car pulled up, and a voice said: "This is the guy. I rec-ognize him." Ailey had been mistakenly identified as the murderer of four policemen in Cincinnati. He was taken to a police station, where he was handcuffed, thrown on the floor, and kicked. As Ailey was beginning to wonder if he would be killed, the police found his passport in his briefcase and decided they had the wrong man. But they charged him with pushing a policeman, and he spent the night in jail. Against the advice of his lawyer, Ailey did not press charges. Only two days later, he rejoined the company, catching up with it in Athens for the African tour.[42] State Department officials did not seem to note any signs of trauma arising from the incident. They were consistently impressed by Ailey's professionalism and skills as an ambassador. But Ailey's friend Edele Holtz "noticed that for a long time after, when Alvin was upset he would rub his wrists as if they were handcuffed."[43]

Preparing for the tour, the USIS produced a film, *Rock-a-My-*

Soul, with excerpts from the Ailey company's tour repertory in the summer of 1967. The film was heavily used in promotions and at press conferences to encourage large turnouts throughout the African tour. The tour began on September 14, 1967, in Addis Ababa (Ethiopia) and continued through the Malagasy Republic, Uganda, Kenya, Tanzania, the Belgian Congo, Ghana, and Ivory Coast. It ended in Dakar on November 4.[44] Venues varied from state-of-the-art theaters in Senegal and Ghana to rural community centers where the company tapped into municipal street lighting systems for power.[45] In Addis Ababa, 8,000 feet above sea level, the dancers had to have oxygen tanks in the wings so they could regain their breath.[46] Judith Jamison, a star dancer with the group, recalled that in Ghana they were "welcomed with a choreographic greeting where the celebrants danced right up to the plane. We were welcomed warmly by what we did for a living—dance."[47] The underfunded company did not own a portable stage and had many stages assembled at the last minute. In Nairobi, they "danced on a makeshift wooden stage, three inches off the ground and on the bias" in 110-degree heat.[48] Jamison remembered feeling "overwhelmed" at dancing in the presence of President Kenyatta, and Kenyatta was deeply impressed with the company. Jamison described herself as having "a deep yearning for African identity," and Kenyatta seemed to share her delight in the bonds across continents, telling Jamison that "there was a woman who worked for him who could have been [her] sister."[49]

Ailey, whom the State Department saw as having "special professional and personal talents," was extremely adept as an ambassador, dazzling audiences and State Department personnel in press conferences, television shows, and radio interviews, and—to the delight of officials in Francophone Africa—"speaking French when necessary."[50] He had always believed in making dance accessible. He felt that his company had an obligation to take dance "where it was needed most, unless it was an impossible situation that would have endangered the dancers."[51] Indeed, in Africa he was "able to fulfill his earlier dream and reach out to students with low-priced performances and lecture demonstrations in which the dancers presented examples of jazz, ballet, ethnic and modern dance styles." Ailey observed that African audiences readily understood such works as *Revelations* or dance pieces by Tally Beatty (whom Ailey had worked with during the production of Ellington's *My People*). Many Africans were surprised by the more experimental works, though Senghor made an astute cultural observation to the company: "You have discovered how to stylize your passions for a technological era."[52]

Throughout the tour, State Department officials reported the "outstanding success" of the formal presentations, with the company "filling houses and standing space time after time and inspiring prolonged ovations and repeated curtain calls." State Department officials thought that those numbers "in which African audiences felt a point of contact with their own traditions, such as *Roots of the Blues,*" made "an especially profound impact."[53] The Accra *Sunday Mirror* reported that "for a suspenseful two-and-a-half hour 'age,' a bridge . . . was thrown over the Atlantic, linking the people of Ghana to the people of the United States." In Kinshasa (Leopoldville), in the Belgian Congo, *Le Courier d'Afrique* enthused: "Four days of joy dominated the air. The Americans . . . were able to mix with our artists and discuss their common problems."[54]

While the Ailey dancers also remarked on the artistic connections they made in the Congo, Jamison was disturbed by the ongoing war. On November 25, 1965, backed by the CIA, General Joseph Mobutu had staged a coup d'état and usurped the presidency.[55] Two years later, Ailey and his dancers were blind-sided by the continued conflict as Mobutu fought to consolidate his power in the face of opposition. With mercenaries being brought in and "all sorts of little riots going on in the downtown area," remembered Jamison, "we found ourselves in the middle of a little war."[56] Like Louis Armstrong, who had visited the Congo when Lumumba was being held under house arrest with U.S. assistance, Ailey's dancers could not have known the extent of American complicity in this war. Not only had the CIA been involved in the ouster of two Congolese leaders, but the United States had supported the use of white South African mercenaries to bring peace to the Congo. This, noted journalist David Halberstam, was like "the Mayor of New York City bringing the Mississippi Highway Patrol to halt riots in Harlem."[57] In a frightening episode for the troupe, given the widely reported atrocities by both the rebels and Mobutu's mercenaries, Ailey dancers James Truitte and George Faison were detained for several hours because they were foreigners.[58] Diplomacy was getting close to the field of combat.

In the face of widespread criticism of its Congo policy, the State Department seized on the value of cultural exchange afforded by the company's connection to African audiences. Officials praised the Ailey dancers' "wholesome, vivid curiosity relative to African dance traditions"—a curiosity that "contributed greatly toward their own creations and sensitivity toward Africans."[59] It was the reciprocity of exchange that most impressed the State Department. Effective ambassadors in their demonstrations of modern dance, they also "took busmen's holidays to indulge, to the delight of local onlookers, in contemporary popular dancing."[60] In cities throughout Africa, the company encountered vibrant nightclub music and dance scenes. Even as African audiences connected to touring black American artists, the African Americans were energized by these local scenes.[61] As was the case with many jazz musicians, interactions with African dancers and nightclub patrons would influence the development of Ailey's art, as seen in such works as *Masekela Language* and numerous other pieces that incorporated West African traditional and social dance styles.[62] In a Congolese club where the walls were covered with black and white monkey fur, Ailey and Jamison witnessed dance steps that were later incorporated into the ballet *Cry.* "We were listening to music and enjoying ourselves," Jamison recalled, "when we noticed that there were young women in the club performing indigenous dances. They were from the bush. It was pure movement and it translated into the last crossover movement of *Cry.* When the young women in the club started doing that step, Alvin and I just looked at each other. It was fabulous. Next thing I know it's 1971 and it turned up in *Cry*."[63]

Officials at the State Department were uniformly pleased with the Ailey troupe's connection to African audiences. From their perspective, the company had excelled by stepping into a political hotbed and demonstrating the best of American creativity. The unambiguous recognition of the company's innovativeness by dance critics on the selection committee also ensured a smooth relationship with the State Department. Yet this enthusiasm about connection to African audiences, and the harmony between the needs and perceptions in the field and the modernist agendas of the selection committees, did not always prevail.

Despite the resolute endorsement of a range of African American artists from African posts, the music selection panelists in 1967 were still reluctant to send on tour popular forms of music they deemed too close to rock and roll. While the music panel admitted the potential appeal of R&B in West Africa precisely because it was "music close to [West African] highlife," they determined that it was "not in line with the kind of jazz that members of the subcommittee want to send abroad, since it is just entertainment."[64] Similarly insisting that performing groups meet their criteria for the highest-quality "art," the panel rejected the Golden Gate Quartet as "simply entertainment," despite its highly successful 1962 tour.[65] Though some officials sought to capitalize on the power of Afro-diasporic ties, many others in the African posts or on the music panel lacked an appreciation of African and African American forms beyond a limited understanding of jazz. Moreover, confusion in policy resulted when perceptions by State Department officials and escort officers that African audiences were "unsophisticated" clashed with the desire of the music panelists to present what they saw as the best of American modernism. Both views were predicated on a restrictive view of American modernism that excluded most Afro-diasporic forms, even as some State Department officials sought to exploit these forms.

That jazz did not escape this confusion was evident in the glaring failure of the 1966 Woody Herman tour. Officials consistently lamented that there was wider appreciation of Herman among European audiences than among Africans. This was the opinion of Arthur Tienken, the American consul in Elisabethville (Belgian Congo). Tienken's explanation stands out not only for its racial condescension, but also for omission of any mention that race may have been a factor in the white band leader's failure to connect with African audiences. "It must be concluded overall," argued Tienken, "that modern jazz is not readily understood by the mass of African listeners."[66] He continued in a self-congratulatory vein: "Mr. Herman's visit undeniably demonstrated the willingness of the U.S. government to share its cultural resources with others, and deeply impressed those listeners with a background in and appreciation for some of the finest jazz music available today." Yet "advanced groups" like Herman's could not "involve the hearts and minds of the mass of Africans," who found the band's arrangements incomprehensible but readily responded to "Mr. Herman's physical movements, to the flashing of a flash bulb, to the foot-stomping of a saxophonist." Tienken thought that neovaudevillean fare would be more appropriate for the Congolese, who were certain to appreciate "an American magician, a dance team, or some other artist with a strong visual impact."[67]

For Tienken to claim that jazz was too advanced for Africans entailed a repression of the recent memory of Louis Armstrong's triumphant tour of the Congo in 1960 and 1961. Indeed, his reading seems to constitute a willful denial of the appeal of African diasporic ties. During the 1966 tour, the State Department was forced into a damage-control operation when the AP wire service released a story from Elisabethville reporting that "the Herman Band played before an all-black audience for the first time on the tour" and that "in Morocco, Tanzania, and Uganda he played before European audiences only." The State Department denied the charges, giving long-winded descriptions of the demographics of northern and eastern African nations to account for the paucity of Africans in the audiences.[68] U.S. officials did not want the tours branded as white or elitist. Despite the experiences in the Herman tour, they recognized the power of diasporic ties and saw them in a positive light for America as a nation. Insistence on color-blindness was gradually yielding to an ambivalent embrace of black particularity and pride in roots.

That U.S. officials sought to use African diasporic connections to their advantage, even as they sought to control the terms of those connections, is illustrated in the experience of the black American pianist and composer Randy Weston, who toured North and West Africa in 1967. Weston saw his tour as part of a redistributive agenda, extending long-denied material support to black American art and artists. Coming from a family with a strong Pan-Africanist bent, he also regarded the tours as fostering ties between African and black American musicians. "My dad's people," he explained, "came from Jamaica, Panama, and Costa Rica. My mother's people came from Virginia." His father, "a great lover of Marcus Garvey," had told Weston as a child: "You are an African born in America."[69] The story of Weston's musical development underlines his sense of the complexity of the African diaspora and the interrelatedness of Africans and peoples of African descent. His father had made him take piano lessons to offset the fact that he was tall (nearly six feet, eight inches) and loved sports. In the 1940s, he had developed a fascination with the music of Thelonious Monk and had sharpened his playing by spending time with Monk at his house, visiting the home of drummer Max Roach, and hanging out at the Putnam Social Club in Brooklyn with Dizzy Gillespie, Roach, and Miles Davis. Weston had begun recording in 1954 under the Riverside label, and developed a profound interest in the music of Africa. In 1960, inspired by the African independence movements, Weston had made his famous recording *Uhuru Africa,* with the Nigerian percussionist Olatunji, trumpeters Clark Terry and Freddie Hubbard, and a large ensemble. "Uhuru" is the Swahili word for "freedom." Weston had been one of the first jazz artists to become interested in African music. This interest on the part of jazz musicians was evident in such works as Max Roach and Abbey Lincoln's *Freedom Now Suite* (1961), which included a song inspired by the Sharpeville Massacre in South Africa.[70]

Weston had first traveled to the African continent in 1961, when he'd visited Nigeria as part of a twenty-person AMSAC delegation. He would later return to Nigeria with the support of AMSAC. In Nigeria, Weston had studied traditional music styles and visited the Mbari Cultural Center in the city of Ibadan. There, he had recorded African musicians and had written the piece "A Night in Mbari," based on his experiences. By the time of the 1967 State Department tour, Weston had already composed African-inspired songs, including "African Cookbook." The Randy Weston Jazz Sextet included Ray Copeland, trumpet and fluegelhorn; Clifford Jordan, tenor sax; Bill Wood, bass; Edward Blackwell, drums; and Chief Bey (James Howthorne), African drums. Weston's fifteen-year-old son, Niles, accompanied the group at Weston's expense as an informal band-boy. From the tour's opening in Dakar on January 17 to its close in Rabat (Morocco) on April 10, the group gave forty-eight performances and traveled through Mali, Upper Volta, Niger, Ghana, Cameroon, Gabon, Liberia, Sierra Leone, Ivory Coast, Lebanon, the United Arab Republic, Algeria, and Morocco.

In Dakar, the sextet appeared at the Daniel Sorano Theatre, described by the group's escort officer as "the best in Africa, . . . complete with all modern and up-to-date mechanical devices."[71] The sextet's concert program included such Weston compositions as "African Cookbook," "Berkshire Blues," "Gospel Monk," "Hi-Fly," "In Memory Of" and "A Night in Mbari." The group's "History of Jazz" program linked jazz to African music and a variety of African diasporic forms. Beginning with a segment on African rhythms, the set continued with examples of calypso, spirituals, work songs, New Orleans marching-band music, and blues. It also included jazz from Count Basie, Duke Ellington, Tadd Dameron, Dizzy Gillespie, and Thelonious Monk, and concluded with a "Renewal of African Influences" section, which included Weston's "African Cookbook."[72]

Despite Weston's enthusiasm and the State Department's support, clashes over race and politics between the group and U.S. officials were evident after the Dakar concert, at the reception hosted by the American ambassador. Harry Hirsch, the sextet's escort officer and a veteran of several cultural-presentation tours on the continent, had traveled with the Golden Gate Quartet, Cozy Cole, and Marion Williams. Hirsch was puzzled by what he called the "rather strange observation of our own Ambassador, who asked Randy Weston in all seriousness why he doesn't think of integrating his sextet."[73] In an incident that sheds light on the nature of some officials' color-blind integrationism, the ambassador seemed to think an all-black group implied exclusionary practices aimed at whites. When Weston, who was upset by the question, raised the matter with Hirsch, the escort officer thought "it best to soft-peddle the situation." But he confided to Charles Ellison, the director of cultural presentations in Washington, that he thought it "strange for an American Ambassador, who incidentally had just arrived in Dakar, to speak that way."[74] Despite Hirsch's embarrassment at the ambassador's question, his own assumptions about Africans and his attempts to control and limit the definitions of black music would eventually become a cause of considerable conflict.[75]

The diasporic ties encouraged by the tour were evident in North Africa as well as West Africa. In April, as the tour neared its end with concerts in three Algerian cities, the paper *El Moudjahid* ran an article entitled "Randy Weston in Algiers" that clearly showed an identification with black Americans. "For the first time since independence we can hear jazz, true jazz, for . . . we cannot call Woody Herman's music jazz." Urging jazz fans to attend Weston's concert, the article stated: "This is the proof that jazz is most popular in Africa, its cradle. . . . Without 'transplanted' Africans, jazz would never have existed."[76] Under the heading "Return to Origins," the paper *An Nasr* carried an interview with Weston that asked: "Why African music?" "This music gave birth to jazz," Weston explained. "If there had not been any Africa there would not be any jazz."[77]

Weston's positive and constructive approach to performing-arts programs did not temper his criticisms of the ways the tours were handled. He was especially displeased with the escort officer, Hirsch, arguing that personnel with "colonial mentalities" had no business in African posts and were hurting the position of the United States.[78] Ironically, it was Weston's interest in connecting to Africans—something the State Department repeatedly noted as valuable—that led to much of the conflict. Even before the group had left New York, Hirsch had looked at a tape recorder Weston wanted for the trip and said: "I feel it is an awful lot of money to spend for *just* picking up native songs in Africa."[79] Years later, Weston would look back with amusement at his tension with Hirsch, describing them as being "at each other's throats." In one incident, Weston's strongmindedness, combined with officials' concerns about the appearance and behavior of artists, led to a battle with Hirsch. The musicians' contract stipulated that they had to wear American suits during performances and at official receptions. Conflict erupted over what they could wear during their "down time." When they wore dashikis, officials protested that they could not readily be identified as Americans, which for Weston was precisely the idea.[80] For U.S. officials, Weston's effectiveness as an ambassador was dependent on what they read as his difference as a black person, as well as his sameness as an American. Officials relied on Weston's blackness to reach out to African audiences, even as they tried to manage and contain its meanings.

Even as State Department personnel tried to reach broader audiences, they faced a problem not unlike that of many avant-garde jazz players within the United States. As Eric Porter has argued in his discussion of Archie Shepp and the avant-garde movement in jazz, "the fusion of avant-garde jazz and popular appeal was difficult to pull off." Even when music was an "avant-garde expression of popular sensibility," there could be a "a great distance between this music, inspired 'by the people,' and one that would actually reach a mass audience."[81] Yet State Department observations about the distance between avant-garde jazz and popular audiences didn't carry the same commitment to "the people," and appeared to some musicians as condescension toward Africans. Six weeks into the tour, Hirsch wrote to James Webb, a special assistant at the Office of Cultural Presentations identifying what he saw as "the sore point of the Randy Weston tour." Weston, Hirsch complained, "doesn't want to play anything but far-out jazz, and he says that he was hired to do just that, so the Africans who should be getting hamburgers and ice cream are getting pheasant under glass and cherries jubilee."[82]

At the close of the tour, Weston's manager, Georgia Griggs, was quoted in a *Down Beat* article describing the group's outrage at encountering such attitudes. On the one hand, Griggs took care to point out that her criticisms applied to "only a few, not by any means the majority" of State Department personnel. She nonetheless argued that "the main thing wrong was the attitude of our escort and some of the local U.S. personnel."[83] Outlining the "patronizing" and "colonialist" views the group encountered, Griggs charged that the group was "warned both before we left and enroute that African audiences would respond only to Dixieland numbers or to loud drum solos and had no comprehension of or affinity for any other manifestation of American jazz, especially modern jazz." The group was "told repeatedly" to "remember, they're not as sophisticated as U.S. audiences." Griggs held Hirsch especially responsible, calling him "a great jazz authority who wouldn't have been able to tell Coltrane from Beiderbecke, and undoubtedly had never seen a jazz audience in the U.S."[84] Griggs saw the "same patronizing attitude" in the "inability on the part of some Americans to understand why the band members were so eager to hear African tribal music and to meet local African musicians and people interested in African culture." After all, argued Griggs, "if you believed that Africans are culturally deprived—and anyone who hasn't been sufficiently exposed to U.S. culture, whether he's in Harlem or the Upper Volta, is automatically deprived as far as these people are concerned—what could they possibly do or achieve that could be of interest to Americans?"[85]

While particular animosity had clearly developed between Griggs and Hirsch (Hirsch at one point described Griggs as "useless"), her characterization of State Department attitudes offers insight into the shifting and contradictory State Department policies that the sextet encountered.[86] Here, as elsewhere, despite officials' budding recognition of the appeal of popular African diasporic forms, their insistence on the rigid opposition between art and entertainment and their dismissal of African art prevented some of them from resolving these contradictions. And it certainly prevented them from making sense of Weston, who was alternately seen as too modern and "far out" on the one hand, and too African on the other.

Just as it had made efforts to contain the meanings of Weston's blackness, the State Department attempted to appropriate his forthright criticisms of the U.S. government. The urgent need to address American policy in Africa was soon exacerbated by the growing international attention to the U.S. war in Vietnam. As the State Department attempted to celebrate the passage of civil rights legislation and the achievement of equality before the law as a moral victory, international scrutiny of the American war in Vietnam was rapidly eroding U.S. credibility, and global criticism of the United States was escalating. The issue of Vietnam affected black diasporic interactions in unexpected ways, giving a new twist to the conflicts between the State Department and the jazz musicians. With demonstrations against U.S. intervention mounting in Europe, Asia, and Africa, including several bombings of USIA libraries, the convergence of the civil rights movement and antiwar protests presented many faces. Declaring that "jazz speaks in a special idiom to many Algerians," an official at the U.S. Embassy in Algiers praised Weston's response to Algerian militants who were criticizing the United States. Following is an excerpt from the official's description of the incident:

Weston was approached by two twenty-year-olds, who rather belligerently asked him how he, a Negro, could be playing when his country was committing atrocities in Vietnam. Weston, who towers six feet seven, answered, "War, man, is a drag. There isn't just one Vietnam—there are lots of them. We have them in Mississippi, in Alabama, and in the North. We're not just mouthing about them— we're trying to do something about them. You can't just mouth— you've got to *do* something. Are *you*?"[87]

Although Weston's "we" referred to ordinary people who should have been doing something about the war and not simply complaining, the official heard the "we" as "the United States" and sought to appropriate his statement as a defense of the country. The delighted official explained that Weston, a "sometime scholar of Schoenberg, does not use 'jive talk' in ordinary conversation—but it was clear that the two interrogators got the message."[88] From Weston's perspective, he had succeeded in making a strong antiwar statement without the government being alarmed or even realizing it.

For the embassy, which was deeply invested in proving the tours' effectiveness at silencing critics, Weston's presence as an African American and jazz musician deflected critical scrutiny of U.S. policy. Officials viewed the tours as a legitimizing and humanizing force which was useful in the effort to make critics of U.S. policy identify with America or the idea of America, independently of American policies. But there is ample evidence that jazz and the cultural tours did *not* persuade those in Algeria, the Congo, or elsewhere to support U.S. foreign policy. Despite the triumphal accounts of Weston's Algerian visit, the State Department recapitulation of offstage activities from Algeria read: "Broke diplomatic relations before Embassy had a chance to provide statistical data."[89] Congolese and Ghanaian audiences may have identified with Williams, Ailey, Ellington, and Weston, and may also have identified these artists with America, but the America they identified with was that of African American culture and symbols of civil rights and black power.

After 1967, Weston, taking advantage of the tour to further his own long-standing Pan-Africanist project, relocated to Morocco, where he petitioned the State Department to set up more permanent programs to promote such collaborations. In Morocco, where he spent the next seven years, Weston sought to combine commercial work with the study of African music. While it was often difficult to get work and keep his projects going, Weston's attitude was that he had struggled for three decades in the United States, and he was willing to struggle in Africa.[90]

In other tours as well, officials' acknowledgment of the Afrodiasporic appeal of jazz clashed with the notion that it was a uniquely American form with a modernist aesthetic. For example, in a report on the Charlie Byrd Quintet, U.S. posts in Africa continued to emphasize "the high priority given to jazz as a uniquely American art form." Yet the State Department especially appreciated Byrd's strong ties to Brazilian music and the quintet's "execution of bossa nova compositions," because of the "particular meaning for listeners in Dahomey, which has strong historical and cultural ties with Brazil."[91]

As seen in the Williams and Ailey tours, as well as in the conflicts over jazz, attempts by the State Department to reach African audiences gradually made it receptive to a wider range of Afrodiasporic forms. It sponsored tours by Chicago-based blues artists Junior Wells and Buddy Guy and His Band in 1968 and 1969, respectively. The two would return to the continent as the Guy-Wells Blues Band in 1975 for a fourteen-country tour. The Jazz Dance Theater toured in 1969.[92] Manthia Diawara's account of a Junior Wells concert in Mali in his book *In Search of Africa* suggests how the tours worked through creative misreadings. Black transAtIantic communication was facilitated by the U.S. State Department via the tours. In a passage that playfully opens: "We were kitsch and we were living on the cutting edge," Diawara recalls his excitement when Radio Mali advertised a concert by Junior Wells. Diawara had records by saxophonist Junior Walker, and "in those days when my English was limited, Junior Wells and Junior Walker were one and the same to me."[93] Radio Mali's promotion of Junior

Wells and his Allstars as a group that played the hits of Otis Redding, Wilson Pickett, and James Brown added to his excitement. Diawara's memory of the electrifying content—including such songs as "Respect," "Midnight Hour," and "Say It Loud, I'm Black and I'm Proud," illustrates the ways in which state-sponsored tours became vehicles for the transmission of militant global black consciousness and Afro-diasporic culture.[94]

During the break, Diawara was able to talk to the musicians through the translations of "a white guy from the United States Information Agency." (These tours were State Department tours but USIA cultural officers were usually involved at specific locations.)But it was important to Diawara and his peers that he was able to bypass that translation, using his halting English—acquired during two years of education in English and summers in Liberia—to speak directly to one of the musicians. For Diawara, to speak directly to the musicians, to be seen a someone who spoke English as an American, put him "in the vanguard." In addition, "to be liberated was to be exposed to R&B and to be up on the latest news about Muhammad Ali, George Jackson, Angela Davis, Malcolm X, and Martin Luther King Jr., all of whom were becoming an alternative source of cultural capital for African youth and creating within us a new structure of feeling." For Diawara and his friends, this was a way to subvert the hegemony of *Francité* (French dominance) after the revolution. Diawara argues that James Brown, through his album *Live at the Apollo,* reconnected Malian youth to a pre–slave-trade energy after centuries of suppression by colonialism and Judeo-Christian and Islamic religions.[95] These black transatlantic cultural exchanges provided an alternative cultural capital for all parties involved. African American artists and musicians like Ailey and Randy Weston, as well as audiences, found new sources of cultural capital in their exchanges and new relationships with African musicians, in their exposure to the politics of independence and internationalism, and in their roles as cultural ambassadors.

The State Department considered the Junior Wells tour a spectacular success, celebrating the group's connection with African audiences, as they had during the Ailey tours. The following year they sent another Chicago blues band, led by Buddy Guy, on a tour that included Kenya, Tanzania, and Zanzibar. State Department officials in Tanzania explained that Buddy Guy's Chicago blues performances the following year "came at just the right psychological moment, when Aretha Franklin and her innovations of soul were starting to capture the masses."[96] The Dar es Salaam *Sunday News* reported that "teenagers all over the city are 'crazy' with soul. One is apt to meet 'soul brothers' and 'soul sisters' and the more intoxicated ones—the bishops of soul." And Buddy Guy "gave local soul-hungry fans their first real 'ear-witness' experience of the music they all wanted to dig."[97] In yet another *Sunday News* report, Guy was deemed all the more "incredible" as he stood up to comparison with the already revered Wilson Pickett, James Brown, Otis Redding, Aretha Franklin, and the Supremes.[98] The State Department complained that the "Party papers have yet to even mention Buddy Guy (apart from our fat ads) but did carry the news that the TANU Youth League on Saturday adopted a resolution that all schools should form cultural groups and not sing foreign jazz songs."[99]

Nation building in Tanzania did, in fact, have an ambivalent relationship with African American culture. Tanzania's president, Julius Nyerere, had welcomed black American expatriates who admired his socialist project and for whom Tanzania had become the destination of choice following the ouster of Nkrumah in Ghana. But soul music was banned in Tanzania in November 1969, just five months after Guy's visit. The Coast Regional Commissioner, Mr. Songambele, responded to teachers' complaints that "this type of dance . . . was a cause of bad manners in the country's youth" and banned all soul music in Dar es Salaam.[100] The ban led to a spate of protest, and enforcement was minimal. Andrew M. Ivaska has argued that the banning should be understood in the context of national anxieties over "decency" and the city, not "in reference to the way such culture enabled or disabled the black struggle worldwide."[101] But the banning did lead to a lively debate on what constituted the "foreign" and on the African roots of black American music—a debate similar to the ones that had occurred during Guy's visit. And for the State Department, the elaboration of bonds between Tanzanians and African Americans—especially those bonds which celebrated an ethic of pleasure and consumption—was very much the point. State Department officials had considered reservations about foreign music a minor glitch as they delighted in the debate on soul that was going on across Africa, from Tanzania to Kenya—"soul" sometimes being understood as American R&B, and often sketched more broadly as the sensibility found across Afro-diasporic forms. For the State Department, the comment of one Kenyan fan captured the value of the tour: "When he plays that soul, I know what he's doing. When he plays that slow stuff [blues], I don't know what he's doing, but I sure know what he's feeling."[102]

The State Department hoped that soul music would stand as an alternative to radical political affinities. U.S. officials saw Guy as an effective counter to criticisms of the United States by ordinary Africans, and even by African militants. In Dar es Salaam, U.S. officials were disturbed by encounters with militant black American expatriates. "The uninhibited appeal to soul brothers of Buddy Guy and His Band," wrote one U.S. official in Dar es Salaam, "naturally brought out all the resident, militant Afro-Americans who have come back to Africa and to whom soul means just those who spit in the eyes of whites." Admitting that the "number of militants who rallied around surprised our Embassy," the official nonetheless insisted on a pro-American reading of Guy's message. "The back-to-Africa Americans are in for a rude shock" when they hear "Buddy Guy's positive clarion call for brotherhood. If this be diplomacy, sock it to 'em."[103]

The success of these blues and R&B tours eroded the twin ideologies of color-blind liberalism and the commitment to a high-modernist aesthetic that the State Department had earlier pursued, as U.S. officials increasingly recognized the appeal of African diasporic solidarities as well as popular cultural forms. By 1970, the

State Department had abandoned its insistence on representing America through what was deemed "art" rather than through entertainment. But if the commitment to a particular modernist aesthetic had proven untenable, the government continued to rely on African American culture to represent the moral authority of the nation through a range of music and art forms.

Mahalia Jackson toured India for the State Department from April 27 through May 9, 1971 (following a commercial tour of Japan). Just as African Americans had drawn inspiration from the Indian national independence movement in the 1940s and 1950s, and had worked closely with Indian activists in international forums, politically active Indians had long identified with black American struggles. The black American activist, singer, and actor Paul Robeson, deprived of his passport and livelihood by anti-Communist witch-hunts, remained a revered figure in India. His signature song, "Old Man River" had inspired a Bengali song about the Ganges, which, like the Mississippi, was said to be indifferent to the suffering of those who lived on its banks. Martin Luther King Jr.'s philosophy of nonviolent direct action had been deeply influenced by Mahatma Gandhi, and the slain American leader was a hero in India.[104] Jackson was already widely known in India as the gospel singer who had performed "We Shall Overcome" while appearing with King at the 1963 march on Washington. She had also appeared at the march's precursor, the 1957 Pilgrimage for Prayer, a civil rights demonstration at the Lincoln Memorial. Jackson gave five performances in India—in Calcutta, New Delhi, Madras, and Bombay (two)—reaching a total of 6,200 people. By June 17, ninety Indian newspapers and periodicals had published stories on Jackson or reviews of her concerts, and these articles reached an estimated audience of 3.8 million. Her concert in New Delhi was attended by Prime Minister Indira Gandhi, who met Jackson during intermission and, after a ceremonial exit at the end of the concert, returned from her car to hear the encores.[105]

Jackson's popularity with Indian audiences and the prime minister was expected to foster diplomatic goodwill between the two countries, but the crisis in U.S.-Indian relations could not be so easily overcome. America's contempt for the Indian stance of non-alignment and its military alliance with India's rival Pakistan, led to bitter relations between the two countries. Moreover, President Richard Nixon admired Pakistan and despised Indira Gandhi. The historian H. W. Brands has quoted the explanation proposed by Henry Kissinger, Nixon's Secretary of State. According to Kissinger, Gandhi's "assumption of almost hereditary moral superiority and her moody silences brought out all of Nixon's latent insecurities. . . . Nixon's comments after meetings with her were not always printable."[106] Jackson arrived on her goodwill mission just a month after the onset of violence in East Pakistan (now Bangladesh). As West Pakistan invaded the country, its "soldiers incited to mass-rape the women to mutate the Hindi Bengali gene," students and left-wing intellectuals were arrested and shot.[107] The United States had sent $40 million worth of weapons to Islamabad in 1970. U.S. officials in both Dacca and New Delhi worried about the damage done by the U.S. association with what they viewed as a reign of terror in East Pakistan, characterized by the "mass killing of unarmed civilians, the systematic elimination of the intelligentsia, and the annihilation of the Hindu population."[108] Without the knowledge of the White House, the State Department moved to curtail the flow of weapons to West Pakistan. But despite considerable criticism, the pro-Pakistani position of Nixon and Kissinger prevailed.

In the context of the rift between the White House and American officials in New Delhi and Dacca, Jackson's visit was particularly meaningful to the State Department. A U.S. Embassy official in New Delhi proclaimed the visit "more useful to the Embassy's program than many others, since it effectively demonstrated America's great regard for matters of the soul as against purely materialistic pursuits, U.S. regard for peace and joy, U.S. respect for the Negro and the Negro's contribution to America's culture and music."[109] Perhaps not knowing what to make of Indian journalists' politicized readings of Jackson, the embassy report noted that such reviews of Jackson had an "altogether different dimension," with their focus on "Negro emancipation, and . . . religion and peace." Putting the best possible spin on it for the State Department, the report insisted that these "lent useful support to the Embassy's country objectives."[110]

One needn't doubt the sincerity of these officials—in this instance, representatives of policies not of their own making but with horrific consequences—when they embraced the spirit and hope conveyed by Mahalia Jackson. Yet their hope that Jackson, the power of gospel, and African American culture would represent American nationhood for Indian audiences was a fantasy. For many Indian critics, Jackson represented black America and its history of struggle. Jackson's history of involvement in the civil rights movement was invoked by Shanta Serjeet Singh reporting in the Bombay *Economic Times*. Rather than attribute Jackson's success to her Americanness, Singh understood her power as coming from a history distinct from that of white Americans: "'Negro Spirituals' is the white man's patronizing label for songs of the black American, whose contact with Christianity for nearly three centuries has been more meaningful than the white man's two millenniums of carrying the cross." Continuing the moral critique of white America and Europe, Singh spoke of the meaning of Christianity to black Americans. Innocent of the sins of the Inquisition and other Christian errors, they had "plunged into it wholeheartedly"—unlike "Europeans, who to this day have not quite accepted Christianity."[111] The music critic for the *Times of India,* likewise critical of Western Christianity, described Mahalia Jackson's performance at the march on Washington as an occasion on which the Christian spirit was "recovering its profound humanity after epochs of betrayal." For this critic, whose country was facing yet another war with U.S-backed Pakistan, "in a great song like 'Let there be Peace,' Mahalia Jackson and her race exercise all their bruised memories and reveal that Christ's forgiveness of those who martyred him can still be emulated by men."[112]

From the time of the Dakar festival, the U.S. State Department's exposure to gospel and soul music increasingly challenged its idea of modernism and its resistance to forms of popular entertainment. With the embrace of gospel, soul, and the blues, the State Department acknowledged the mainstreaming of African-diasporic styles in American culture, as well as the flowering of a global music economy in which residents of Africa and India were familiar with popular artists in the United States. The pressure to embrace black culture reflected the challenges of reaching African audiences unimpressed by claims of America's political and moral superiority. Jazz, gospel, and soul could not redeem American foreign policy—decisions that had led to the war in Vietnam, the military alliance with Pakistan, and U.S. support of African coups. The State Department's embrace of a once marginalized music to reform and revitalize the image of America shows a misplaced reliance on African American culture to project vitality and optimism on the part of a country that was deep in crisis.

CHAPTER 7

Improvising Détente

Given President Nixon's mean-spirited attempts to undermine civil rights gains and his all-out war on black radicals, it is ironic that he turned to black cultural capital in his effort to build his reputation as a statesman.[1] From Charles Mingus, Thelonious Monk, and Ornette Coleman in Belgrade to Duke Ellington in Moscow and Laos, the relationship between jazz and the State Department thrived during the Nixon administration. The administration's deployment of jazz may have been due in part to the proclivities of Nixon's first Secretary of State, William Rogers. Rogers' support for civil rights—stemming from his days in the Justice Department during the Eisenhower administration—made him something of an exception during the Nixon years.[2] But ultimately it was Nixon the jazz fan and pianist, not Rogers, who showed the greatest interest in the tours. The jazz tours were a perfect fit for the president's diplomatic goals. Indeed, the performing-arts programs appear as a mirror image of political détente, since the United States was striving to achieve leverage in superpower negotiations by opening new avenues of trade and exchange. The popular appeal of jazz in the Soviet Union and Eastern Europe ensured it pride of place in the performing-arts programs, even as the programs continued to broaden the representation of musical forms, including rock and roll, which was sent abroad in 1970 on a tour of Eastern Europe by Blood Sweat and Tears. The opening of trade with the Soviet Union and the liberalization of many Eastern European regimes paved the way for numerous jazz musicians to visit the Eastern bloc under the auspices of the Newport Jazz Festival. This period also saw the triumphant Soviet tours of Alvin Ailey (1970) and Duke Ellington (1971).

Yet the artists' globetrotting also traces the underside of détente. Tours to Southeast Asia seemed to escalate along with Nixon's secret bombings. According to the "Nixon Doctrine," counterinsurgency was to be tempered by placing the "burden for communist containment on regional powers," using "local, not American, manpower to fight battles on the ground."[3] But the Southeast Asian tours by some of America's greatest artists, including Ellington and the choreographer Martha Graham, could not conceal the failure of Nixon-Kissinger foreign policy and its ill-founded assumption that all conflicts throughout the globe could be resolved through improved superpower relations. And despite all of Nixon's attempts to paper over the raging social crises at home, the resonances of the tours changed in tandem with the American political landscape. From Dizzy Gillespie's first State Department jazz tour in 1956 through Duke Ellington's 1963 tour of the Middle East, the jazz tours had been suffused with the spirit and optimism of the civil rights movement. But with the assassinations of John F. Kennedy and Malcolm X and the 120-odd urban rebellions that followed the 1968 assassination of Martin Luther King Jr., many people were in despair over the endemic violence of American society. In view of the widespread youth rebellion, an aggressive government campaign to neutralize black activism, and revelations of U.S. atrocities in Vietnam, to export American culture meant exporting a culture that was (as historian George Herring put it) in the midst of a "national nervous breakdown."[4] That Nixon could trade on America's breakdown and on black militancy to appeal to Eastern European and Soviet audiences restless for change in their own countries attests to the boldness of his diplomatic initiatives. But as domestic protest and international censure of the American war in Vietnam escalated, and as U.S. covert and overt militarism were exposed across the globe, the liberal internationalist idealism and optimism in which the tours had thrived were beginning to fade.

American jazz musicians visiting Eastern Europe in the early

1970s found societies as tumultuous as their own. And jazz had particular resonance for the youthful rebellions sweeping the region. In Europe, as historian Geoff Eley has argued, the prehistories of the 1968 youth rebellion were grounded in "the world of jazz and R&B, poetry in pubs, little magazines and art schools," as much as in the Campaign for Nuclear Disarmament.[5] Growing disaffection with Soviet hegemony throughout the Eastern bloc had crested in the reform-Communist, New Left movement of the Prague Spring, which aimed to replace large bureaucracies and coercive police forces with "a more utopian society based on shared needs."[6] The arrival of the Warsaw Pact armies in Prague on August 20, 1968, reestablished authoritarian rule, in line with the entrenched conservatism of the USSR.[7] As defiant guerilla warfare continued for weeks after the invasion, "public condemnations of the Soviet invasion came from many communist countries," such as Romania and Yugoslavia.[8] Although Brezhnev, like Nixon, moved decisively to put down challenges from below, as Jeremi Suri has argued, "Brezhnev's government never recovered the authority it had possessed before 1968" and defiance remained strong throughout Eastern Europe.[9] Phil Woods captured the shift in Eastern Europe for jazz musicians: he remembered Belgrade as "politically and socially repressed" on his 1956 trip with Gillespie, but "positively loose as a goose in the early 1970s."[10]

The jazz tours to the Eastern bloc were facilitated by the State Department's working relationship with the jazz producer George Wein, founder of the Newport Jazz Festival, and with his colleague Robert Jones. The relationship had begun in 1958, when Wein had organized an international jazz band for the Newport Jazz Festival. He had traveled independently, without government aid, through Hungary, Poland, Yugoslavia, Romania, and Czechoslovakia in search of the finest jazz musicians. Once in Eastern Europe, Wein had contacted the State Department for assistance in obtaining U.S. visas for those foreign musicians. Through his company, Festival Productions, Wein had paid to bring all the European musicians to Newport, successfully obtaining exit visas for all but the Czech trombonist. Wein had thought of calling the band the "Tower of Babel" but settled on the name Newport International Youth Band when friends sharply objected to his proposed name.[11] After a successful performance by the group at Newport, the State Department had become interested and asked Wein to take the band to the 1958 Brussels World's Fair under State Department sponsorship.

The partnership with Wein and his Festival Productions proved to be a great boon to the State Department. Given U.S. officials' early emphasis on collaboration with the private sector, it is curious that such linkages had not materialized over the previous decade. But by 1970, sweeping changes in the cultural-presentations programs had created the incentive for such collaboration. Mark B. Lewis, director of the Bureau of Educational and Cultural Presentations, in an effort to cut government costs, told the music committee that henceforth there had to be greater private-sector involvement and more commercial pickups. Moreover, to trim expenses, the previous "concept of blanketing a continent is out, nor do we have artists touring for six to eight weeks."[12] But if the days of Louis Armstrong's three-month tour of Africa and Duke Ellington's three-month tour of the Middle East were over, Festival Productions could deliver a program the State Department could never, even under the best of circumstances, have offered: a prestigious jazz festival with many renowned acts.

Newport Jazz came with a history of contention that would not have been unknown to ardent underground jazz fans in the Eastern bloc. In 1960, Charles Mingus and drummer Max Roach had organized an alternative "Rebel Festival" at Newport to protest what they viewed as unfair pay for African American artists at jazz festivals. They also believed that festivals such as Newport were no longer presenting quality music. Among the participants in the alternative festival were artists who, like Mingus, would tour throughout the next decade for the State Department under the auspices of Newport, and one of these was Ornette Coleman.[13] The groups presented by Festival Productions were multigenerational and eclectic, but the State Department festivals specifically featured avant-garde jazz whose "genre-challenging" techniques and sensibilities had profound appeal for Eastern European audiences facing repressive bureaucracies. Ornette Coleman and Miles Davis, who were part of "American Jazz Week in Eastern Europe" in 1971, were among a group of artists who "built upon the earlier experiments of Mingus, Monk, and others, reorienting sound and perception by breaking down the structures of established compositional forms and questioning familiar notions of harmony, rhythm, and tonality."[14] Coleman had outlined his vision of "free group improvisation," building on earlier practices of group improvisation in jazz but breaking out of the creative limitations imposed by the jazz tradition. Many avant-garde artists emphasized the spiritual purpose of their music and the role of the artist in "communicating knowledge, experience, and a sense of human connection."[15] And as musicians debated historical, political, and spiritual approaches to the black aesthetic, many shared Anthony Braxton's view that music of the avant-garde was a "tool for global social transformation." For Braxton, the hybrid character of free jazz "points in the direction of erasing the boundaries and labels that are symbolic of racism, sexism, and European and American political domination of people of color throughout the globe."[16] Indeed, in the late 1960s and early '70s, as youth from Eastern Europe, China, France, Brazil, Mexico, South Africa, and the United States revolted against political and social constraints, new developments in jazz were part and parcel of that rebellion.[17] By bringing cutting-edge jazz into cultural exchanges, the State Department helped to elevate such artists as Mingus and Coleman to the status of international icons of rebellion.

The relationship with Festival Productions and the pursuit of local sponsors enabled the State Department to sponsor jazz with minimal expense.[18] In Wein, Jones, and Festival Productions, the State Department was getting experienced impresarios who were accustomed to coping with difficult local logistical arrangements, as well as volatile musicians. In most cases, their professional management made the escort officer superfluous. Multiple artists routinely toured under the banner of the Newport Jazz Festival, and the State Department, Wein later recalled, "was impressed that we were taking a festival."[19] Indeed, the prestige of Newport, along with the ability of Festival Productions to deliver several stars together, was very important to the State Department, especially as restrictions began to be relaxed in several Eastern European countries and in the Soviet Union.

One such commercial pickup began in October 1970, when the State Department picked up two of the Newport acts touring Europe: Dave Brubeck and Earl "Fatha" Hines. Brubeck was delighted to return to Warsaw twelve years after his first State Department tour. The classic quartet that had made the 1958 tour through Poland and the Middle East had disbanded, and his new jazz ensemble, formed in 1968, included the famous baritone saxophonist Gerry Mulligan, bassist Jack Six, and drummer Alan Dawson. The group was usually billed as the "Brubeck Trio with Gerry Mulligan."[20] An official at the American Embassy in Warsaw was thrilled to report that "the concert by Dave Brubeck and his Trio with Gerry Mulligan was the highlight of the Warsaw Jazz Jamboree." Emphasizing the Cold War competition of the jamboree, the official, Stoessel, reported that the ensemble had followed a Swedish group, a Polish modern jazz band, and a Cuban jazz quintet and had "totally overshadowed their predecessors and brought the house down on several occasions."[21] The president of the Polish Jazz Federation, reported Stoessel, had said that "without Brubeck the 1970 Jazz Jamboree would have been a disaster." Building on the relationships that Brubeck had made in 1958 and that he and Iola had maintained over the decade, the pianist gave exclusive interviews to several magazines, including *Jazz* and *Ruch Muzyczny* (Music Movements). As a result of the interview with Josef Balcerak of *Jazz,* Brubeck and Mulligan donated their payment for the recordings of their performance, about 6,000 złotys (approximately $60 on the black market, or slightly more than two months' wages for the average Polish worker), to a fund for the development of jazz music and jazz clubs in Poland. The State Department could not have been more pleased with what they described as Brubeck and Mulligan's "intense interest in making contacts with others at all levels of society." At press conferences and receptions, the State Department praised the musicians "articulate" renderings of "their concepts of jazz, their philosophy of music, and what music means in the general structure of a man's life." Underlining the importance of the State Department's sponsorship in the context of Cold War competition, the embassy in Warsaw celebrated the "impression" the Brubeck group had made: "not only of superb jazz musicians on a State Department–sponsored tour but also of Americans who are superb representatives of the United States in every way."[22]

For many in the State Department, the pinnacle of cultural exchange was reached with the jazz tours of Eastern Europe and the Soviet Union in the 1970s. Unlike the earlier tours, they showed a striking convergence of interest between the State Department, the musicians, and the audiences. And there was a marked difference between that convergence and the tensions that had often emerged (as in the 1963 Middle East trip by the Duke Ellington orchestra) between the musicians' desires to reach new audiences and meet local instrumentalists and the officials' courtship of neocolonial elites. There was little that resembled officials' resistance to Randy Weston's attempt to reach African audiences on his 1967 African tour. This lack of resistance reflected the development of jazz in Eastern Europe, but it also reveals how assumptions about race, culture, and democracy had shifted. To many American officials, the "man in the street" was less significant in countries where the United States was supporting a pro-Western authoritarian government, or even in nonwhite countries with democratically elected governments. But in the Soviet Union and Eastern Europe, the "man in the street" *did* count. It was the Communist elite that U.S. officials were hoping to bypass. They could imagine Soviet and European citizens not only as political agents but as oppressed democrats among whom freedom and democracy would thrive if given the chance.

The State Department's enthusiasm for what an official at the American Embassy in Bucharest termed "roughly dressed working-class people" and "dyed-in-the-wool" jazz fans continued through the Earl Hines Quartet and Brubeck-Mulligan performances during the Romanian "First Festival of Jazz Week."[23] Pianist Earl "Fatha" Hines performed with his quartet on November 4, 1970, as a last-minute substitute for the Bill Evans Trio. The trio's appearance was canceled when Evans was arrested on November 2 at Kennedy Airport and charged with carrying a large quantity of heroin.[24] Hines had made the second cultural-presentations jazz tour of the Soviet Union in 1966, after Benny Goodman. He had been among the eight groups touring Europe with Wein and was thus able to participate at twenty-four hours' notice. The quartet— Haywood Henry on reeds, Richie Goldberg on drums, Larry Richardson on bass, and vocalist Marva Josie—performed on November 4 in the Sala Palatului (Palace Hall). State Department officials praised Hines's "inimitable piano stylings," the "solid professional musicianship of his sidemen," and Marva Josie's "sometimes earthy, sometimes bluesy style," which was "an immediate hit with the audiences." After the concert, the group was greeted by two hundred members of the local Jazz Club for a late-night reception and a jam session with Romanian musicians.[25] But the suspicion of innovation so typical of Eastern bloc governments was still evident; the paper *Romania Libera,* for example, praised Hines for taking "us into a wonderful world of classical jazz, devoid of the impurities which are characteristic to newer trends in jazz."[26] The next day, Hines wrapped up his stand-in gig by giving interviews with the press and radio. Then, less than twenty-four hours after his arrival, he departed for Belgrade to join Charles Mingus and Anita O'Day for a Yugoslavian Newport Festival.[27]

Bassist, composer, and arranger Charles Mingus, however, raised problems for the State Department. Born on April 22, 1922, in Nogales, Arizona, Mingus was acclaimed in the jazz world as an instrumentalist and composer, and represented political militancy as well as innovation. Noted for his struggle against establishment control of his art, he had formed—along with his wife, Sue Mingus

—an independent record label, tellingly named Revenge. Mingus, known for "sometimes deliberately chaotic and provocative social commentary," would annoy the State Department by asserting his antiwar politics while on tour in Romania in 1975.[28] Although George Wein and Bob Jones were given broad discretion in choosing musicians, they were questioned by State Department officials and Music Committee representatives about the behavior and politics of Mingus. Willis Conover, who had joined the committee in 1965 after the death of Marshall Stearns, evaluated Mingus as "Musically, A. Temperamentally, a question mark." He said, "I get along beautifully with Mingus," but warned the chairman, Mark Lewis, that "he would be yelling at you for calling him 'Charlie.' Change it to 'Charles' from here on in."[29] Yet the fact that Mingus appeared under the auspices of the State Department at all (and more than once) is a testament to the importance of the State Department–Newport relationship in encouraging and enabling a broader and more dynamic sampling of the jazz world and a greater flexibility and acceptance of musicians' idiosyncrasies. And despite the State Department's nervousness about certain people's politics, the oppositional and rebellious edge of a figure such as Mingus or Thelonious Monk enhanced their appeal for Eastern European audiences and made these audiences more eager for change. Indeed, the State Department benefited considerably from the new black militancy and pride revealed on tour in Eastern Europe, since fans who may have abhorred American foreign policy sympathized with the innovative and liberating jazz of Mingus, Monk, and Gillespie.

In Belgrade, Mingus, Hines, and O'Day performed before 1,400–1,600 people and reached many more through Radio Belgrade, which broadcast the entire concert in the days following the performance. Belgrade Television broadcast the first program, featuring Mingus, as a half-hour show on November 13. Belgrade TV also helped to finance the project (along with the Associated Banks of Belgrade and the American Embassy) and filmed all of the proceedings. The foremost music critic in Belgrade, B. Dragutinovic, paid tribute to the Newport Jazz Festival as "one of the most important musical accomplishments of modern jazz." *Omladinski Tjednik,* a youth paper in Zagreb, declared that the jazz evening in Belgrade had been "perhaps the most exciting ever to take place among us." In setting up the program, Festival Productions worked with local jazz promoter Aleksandar Zivkovic. The American Embassy had nothing but praise for Zivkovic and urged Wein to encourage him in his future jazz promotions. Officials emphasized once again that letting local promoters pick up local expenses made the Eastern European trips a promising way to spend the cultural-presentations budget.[30]

Meanwhile, Brubeck and Mulligan arrived in Bucharest an hour and half after Hines had departed for Belgrade; they were met by representatives from ARIA, the Romanian cultural agency that was co-sponsoring the concerts with the American Embassy. ARIA took care of the cumbersome logistical details that earlier escort officers had covered: transportation of luggage and instruments, and hotel accommodations. The Romanians also arranged for advertising and outdoor posters, which had hitherto been taken care of by USIS and State Department officials. The USIS Regional Projects Office in Vienna provided displays and photographs of the musicians. The group gave two concerts, a November 6 matinee and an evening concert, which was also televised live and videotaped for later playback. As at Hines's concert, the audiences were "predominantly youthful but with a hard core of knowledgeable and jazz-literate over-forty-year-olds." Thrilled by the "infectious rhythms and dominating piano style of Brubeck," the group was called back for three encores and Brubeck "skillfully ended the show with his well-known 'Take Five.'"[31] As in Poland, American officials in Bucharest were delighted that the performers made themselves so accessible: the "musicians were so open and available to Romanians that the number of contacts they made was almost infinite."[32] *Romania Libera* reported that Brubeck entered "the zone of intellectual jazz," revealing himself to be "an excellent thinker, constructor, and improviser."[33] The embassy in Bucharest concluded that the trip had "paid off handsomely by exposing yet another facet of

American culture to a wide and diverse Romanian audience and by reinforcing America's image as a culturally productive and vigorous nation."[34] By working with Festival Productions and having the performances co-sponsored by the American Embassy and ARIA, the State Department was able to gain enormous mileage with a minimal output of resources.

There was another way in which the State Department made good on its determination to court youth audiences and embrace popular culture: it sent Blood, Sweat, and Tears to Yugoslavia, Romania, and Poland. Although sending a rock 'n' roll group represented a marked change in policy, rock 'n' roll had been circulating throughout Europe for nearly two decades, and, along with jazz, had become an international symbol of rebellion. Much like jazz, it had faced accusations of decadence and race-mixing in Europe and the United States.[35] In 1970, Blood, Sweat and Tears had won three Grammy Awards, including album of the year, and was judged by the State Department music panel to be "of the highest artistic excellence and representative of the direction and development of one of the creative currents of American music of the young people."[36] Casey Anderson, a black American vocalist and guitarist, opened for the nine-person band at each concert. In an episode reminiscent of the outcry over the first Gillespie tour, a syndicated column out of Washington at the start of the tour—"Inside Washington," by Robert S. Allen and John A. Goldsmith—had prompted letters of inquiry from thirty members of Congress, who had received letters from constituents questioning the tour. But for the State Department, "the cultural impact of BS&T was positively meaningful, as their music established immediate contact with the young and the music lovers." In the spirit of the jazz tours, the band jammed with local jazz musicians; one Yugoslav reviewer declared that their appearance was "the event of the decade."[37] Under the heading "Special Factors and Problems," the State Department noted that with an average age of twenty-five, "this group reflected the troubling concerns of American youth or the 'now generation,' which actively questions the established way of life in all levels." A positive outcome of the tour, argued the State Department, was not only the ability of the "now generation" to reach Eastern European youth, but the fact that when the members of the band returned to the United States, they "reflected a positive and constructive change in their attitudes toward their own country." According to the State Department, the group's propensity to question authority had led them to question and "not accept the patterns of life in these countries."[38] Though the administration of Nixon and Vice President Spiro Agnew was notoriously contemptuous of youthful rebellion, the State Department was discovering its positive aspects abroad.

The following year, in April 1971, again through the auspices of Wein, the State Department took advantage of vibraphonist Lionel Hampton's commercial performances in Western Europe and Yugoslavia, picking him up for State Department–sponsored concerts in Warsaw, Budapest, and Bucharest. Hampton, one of the few Republicans among jazz musicians, met with President Nixon at the White House prior to his departure for Europe. Following the tour, Secretary of State William P. Rogers explained in a memo to Nixon that "by combining the financing of the private American organization handling Hampton with partial funding from Eastern European concert bureaus, we were able to extend Hampton's tour into Poland, Hungary, and Romania at a cost to us of only $8,000."[39] U.S. embassy officials were delighted with Hampton's reception, reporting from Warsaw that "the audience would not let Hampton go." When he finally left the stage and reappeared after fifteen minutes, "he was greeted by a spontaneous rendition of 'Stolat!' ('Live a hundred years!') from the audience." Hampton, who had felt slighted by not being included in the first State Department tours, was an enthusiastic ambassador, and his generosity offstage brought immense satisfaction to all parties involved. After a performance in Belgrade, which was praised by Yugoslav officials and embassy officers for the rapport established with the audience, the band returned to its hotel and "found [a] delegation of young Yugoslav musicians awaiting them and became involved in an impromptu session that went on until 5 a.m." In Budapest, Hampton again demonstrated his infectious delight by extending his concerts well beyond midnight. On one occasion, he and his band talked for three hours with "a young group of Hungarian musicians, older musicians to whom Hampton has been a legend, music critics, and members of the press." During their stay in Bucharest, "Hampton and his musicians visited Romanian jazz clubs and sat in with local musicians, playing until six in the morning."[40]

Later that year, from October 29 through November 4, the State Department and the Newport Jazz festival followed up with a spectacular "American Jazz Week in Eastern Europe," during which groups moved among the capitals of Czechoslovakia, Poland, Yugoslavia, Hungary, and Romania. The State Department once again supplemented local sponsorship, and the U.S. government picked up musicians who were touring Europe commercially: the Duke Ellington Orchestra, the Preservation Hall Band, Ornette Coleman, the Giants of Jazz, and Gary Burton. As part of the Giants of Jazz revue, Dizzy Gillespie returned to the State Department circuit with pianist and composer Thelonious Monk, saxophonist Sonny Stitt, drummer Art Blakey, bassist Al McKibbon, and trombonist Kai Winding. It is highly unlikely that Gillespie would have gotten past the congressional radar as an individual, since only a year before he had been still "anathema to John Rooney," the congressman who had targeted Gillespie after his 1956 tours.[41] The Miles Davis Orchestra also appeared commercially in Yugoslavia and Europe. While the State Department took care to note that it was not sponsoring the controversial Davis, its close association with Newport made this point a mere technicality.[42]

For a remarkable seven days, the five groups—representing an astounding number of America's best jazz musicians—rotated among International Jazz Festivals in Warsaw, Prague, Belgrade, and Budapest. At the end of their twenty-one concert schedule, they came together in Bucharest, with two groups playing at each show. Audience response, in the words of one U.S. Embassy official, was "bordering on unbelievable."[43] The Prague newspaper *Lidova*

Demokracio declared that those "legendary jazz musicians" the Giants of Jazz, "led by the outstanding trumpeter Dizzy Gillespie," represented "the world interpretational peak" of jazz. In Belgrade, Ornette Coleman's Quintet "brought gasps of amazement from audiences accustomed to less intense music." In Budapest, "the audience couldn't get enough of Ellington playing Ellington, and well after midnight they were still calling for more."[44] By the end of the year, plans for "Newport '72" were underway and Newport was already being claimed as a "traditional jazz festival" in Eastern Europe.[45] In addition to the modern innovation of Ellington's generation, avant-garde and free jazz were penetrating the Iron Curtain with amazing impact.

But if the State Department's collaboration with Wein and the Newport Jazz Festival brought unprecedented success in Eastern Europe, the situation was far more contentious in the Soviet Union. Earl "Fatha" Hines had scored a spectacular success on his tour of the Soviet Union in 1966, rolling with the punches as the government canceled his Moscow and Leningrad concerts a week into the tour. The cancellations coincided with the Soviet Union's cancellation of a USSR-U.S. track meet and a visit by a U.S. basketball team. The American Embassy in Moscow charged the Soviet Union with making the Cultural Exchange Agreement "the political scapegoat for its opposition to American actions in Vietnam."[46] By the time the cancellations occurred, Hines had received an overwhelmingly enthusiastic reception before 40,000 people in Kiev, with sellout concerts in the Kiev Sports Palace over four nights, and then in Tbilisi, with 3,000–4,000 people attending each concert. State Department officials believed that the "band's obvious appeal and the prospect of even more stormy successes in Leningrad and Moscow had become a matter of concern to Soviet officials."[47] The revised schedule sent the band "in circles around the Caucasus" for the remaining five weeks of the tour. The improvised itinerary proved exhausting—no one knew "in which hotels or theaters the band would be living and performing in each city." Additional chaos was caused by lost luggage, including the drums and Hines's stage costumes. Local drummers came to the aid of the band's drummer, Oliver Jackson, offering to lend him their equipment (though "the quality of the instruments was rarely equal to the generosity in which they were offered").[48] From night to night, Johnson had no idea where his drums would come from, and for ten days Hines performed in one pair of shoes and one suit.[49] Even after the luggage was recovered, the quality of the pianos remained a sore point. Though the band always phoned ahead and were promised concert-quality pianos, they "invariably found upon arrival old, worn-out instruments with missing ivories or broken pedals, many of them exposed to open air year-round, and one of them bearing the ominous trade name 'Red October.'"[50] Beyond this, band members were simply ill-prepared for the USSR's standard of living. The State Department recommended issuing a warning to future performers: "It is just not possible to find in the Soviet stores good cigarettes, film, whiskey, razors, suspenders, soap powder, pens, hair conditioners, and any number of other items the Earl Hines Band thought it could 'pick up along the way.'"[51]

Implicit comparisons to the contentious Goodman on his 1962 tour were unavoidable, and in this context State Department officials praised Hines as "delightful" and "cooperative." Observing that Hines acted as "Fatha" and "confessor to his musicians," officials noted the "respect which Earl engendered in his musicians, his control over them, and his clear understanding of the political-psychological implications of the tour."[52] Hines, like Goodman before him, was associated with "classical" rather than "modern" jazz, and the "very hep," reported the State Department, "inquire why don't we send Charles Mingus or John Coltrane rather than old-timers like Hines." But unlike the more inflexible Goodman, Hines was "clever enough to sense the preferences and comprehension-level of audiences in each city, and continually altered the pace and content of the show to meet local conditions."[53]

For the State Department, the Hines tour underlined the "abysmal ignorance of American Negroes and U.S. racial problems displayed by an astonishing number of educated Soviet people." The band consisted of six black and two white musicians, and "many intermission conversations were devoted to arguments about who the black people were, where they had been hired, and how they got to the Soviet Union." The consensus among Soviets, noted an irritated State Department official, was that the black Americans were Africans, Mexicans, or "perhaps mulattos of some sort." This image of the United States, "comparable to the situation which prevailed fifty or seventy-five years ago," was perhaps not surprising, argued the official, given that people's information came from *Pravda*. In the eyes of the State Department, the musicians' responses "clearly started a lot of people thinking," and U.S. officials credited the band with "correct[ing] many mistaken impressions prevalent in the USSR about American music and Negro Americans." Proud of the professionalism of the musicians and perhaps delighted at the chance to point out the smug racial assumptions of the Russians, American officials were deeply impressed with the diplomatic power of jazz, as seen in the musicians' ability to transform the attitudes of Soviet apparatchiks. Escorts from the Soviet concert agency *Goskontsert* had been at first "haughty and a bit disdainful of their charges," but the administrator, translator, and announcer were won over by the "eight well-dressed Americans." As the band went about "their business in an unpretentious and dignified manner, impervious to the stares which followed them everywhere, courteous, good-humored, and prompt for all appointments," the escorts' attitude changed. The Soviets, reported the State Department, even changed their "way of dress" to reflect their increasing friendliness toward and respect for the musicians.[54]

In the first Soviet tour by an American contemporary dance group, the Alvin Ailey American Dance Theater did thirty-four performances in six Soviet cities from September 24 to November 9, 1970. The company met with wide critical acclaim and, reported the State Department, "intense interest in the experimentation of American dancers." With a repertoire including *The Prodigal Prince, Blues Suite, Revelations,* and the more abstract *Metallics* and *Streams,* the company played to more than 60,000 people, filling auditoriums to capacity "time after time and inspiring prolonged ovations and repeated curtain calls." In Leningrad, theater administrators relented when besieged by "ticketless scores of young people" and permitted fans to stand, tightly packed, in the outer aisles. In Leningrad, after the last performance of the tour, audiences chanted "Thank you!" and "Come back!" in a twenty-three-minute ovation. What the State Department considered Ailey's "special professional and personal talents" were fully in evidence, as Ailey invited Ukrainian dancers in Kiev to participate in all of the group's rehearsals.[55]

But the tour was not free of the tensions endemic to the U.S.-Soviet exchanges or the logistical problems that had plagued earlier tours. The fluctuating supply of electricity in each theater was particularly problematic, given the Ailey company's specialized lighting requirements. The services furnished by *Goskontsert* were inefficient; freight never arrived on time, and setup was frequently delayed. Most notably, Soviet officials insisted that *Masekela Language* be dropped from the program, claiming it was "too grim" and did not fit the rest of the program.[56] The dance had been inspired by the plight of the South African people under apartheid, and was described by Ailey as having "universal application." Judith Jamison, who has called *Masekela* her favorite role, explained that the "people in *Masekela* survive, but you still feel they're trapped, literally, because they end the ballet as confined as they begin it." For Jamison, the dance "was also a reflection of the frustrations you have as an African-American living in the United States."[57] On the one hand, Soviet officials might have welcomed the implied criticism of the United States. But on the other, they may have understood the universal implications of the dance all too well. Ailey's audiences, like Armstrong's, responded to the yearning for freedom that was so evident in Ailey's choreography. For the Soviets, that could be inconvenient, and even dangerous.

The stunning successes of the Newport Jazz Festival in Eastern Europe and Alvin Ailey in the Soviet Union fit perfectly with the Nixon strategy of appearing to take the diplomatic high road to detract attention from the war in Vietnam and from the political and social unrest in America. But protest and violence at home finally jeopardized further cultural exchanges between the United States and the Soviet Union. Just as the Newport artists were enjoying their triumphs in Warsaw and Bucharest and Ailey was being welcomed and celebrated in the Soviet Union, Soviet artists in the United States were meeting with an altogether different kind of reception. A series of incidents targeting visiting Soviet artists and exhibits began in March 1970. Six young persons, identified by the State Department as members of the Jewish Defense League (JDL), entered a Soviet art exhibition in New York and "and sprayed walls and twenty-nine photographs" with red paint; they "slipped out before policemen at the entrance could be alerted." The State Department believed the incident was related to a JDL action on behalf of oppressed Soviet Jewry planned for March 29 at the Soviet UN mission. Apparently, however, they did little to attempt to protect other Soviet cultural presentations.[58] On August 26, during the opening performance of the Soviet Moiseyev Dance Ensemble at the Chicago Opera House, a tear-gas grenade exploded, sending dancers and patrons pell-mell toward the exits and ending the performance.[59] When the State Department responded to furious Soviet protests with "regret over the unfortunate incident," the Soviets reminded the State Department that they had not yet received compensation for an exhibition in New Orleans that had been vandalized earlier that month.[60] Then on December 3 and 5, performers in the Soviet ice-skating show *Circus on Ice* were harassed during and after their appearances in Philadelphia. In response to queries from the American Embassy in Moscow about Soviet reports that "thugs" had surrounded the performers' bus and beaten up the driver, the State Department reported that the JDL had picketed and that "demonstrators attempted to enter the rink but were removed." To the seeming relief of the State Department, the "arena manager declined to prosecute and there was no press, radio, or TV coverage." After the show, two buses carrying the Soviet performers had been blocked by cars and "pelted with eggs." One Soviet troupe member and a bus driver had been "struck with a brief-case." In the view of the Soviets, these were "terrorist acts"; they were continuing despite official protests and were taking on a "more serious character." (Indeed, the attacks continued into January of the next year.)[61]

The American Embassy in Moscow and the State Department expected retaliation for the actions of the JDL extremists, but were taken aback when Moscow canceled appearances by the Bolshoi Ballet that had been scheduled for the following year. Suspecting other motives, the State Department believed that Moscow wanted to "stress lawlessness in the U.S. and the alleged subservience of U.S. officials to Jewish and particularly Zionist pressure."[62] Moreover, the State Department felt that the incidents provided an excuse for the Soviets to exert more control over their own artistic groups abroad, given their concern over the September defections of three ballet stars (including Natalia Makarova), which had caused "increasing malaise in the Soviet cultural community."[63] In canceling the Bolshoi tour, the Soviets—argued the American Embassy in Moscow—had "penalized themselves." The troupe would have been "a good money maker and enhancer of Soviet prestige." The cancellation simply called attention to the JDL's views, which were assumed to be the cause.[64] The State Department was certainly correct in surmising that the Soviets were embarrassed and threatened by the defections of their artists and searching for a way to assert control. Yet given the State Department's repeated assertions that cultural exchange with the Soviets was valuable, it is surprising that the U.S. government did so little to protect visiting Soviet artists from harassment. From the American vantage point, "cultural exchange" was always something of a euphemism. The State Department and other agencies never considered genuine reciprocity to be possible or even desirable: foreign artists would never be brought to the United States in the same numbers that American artists were sent abroad. While the tensions of 1970 are not entirely understood, it is clear that U.S.-Soviet exchange had slipped to another low point. When the United States boycotted a Soviet film festival the following spring, Murrey Marder, staff writer for the *Washington Post* observed that "this is a particularly sensitive time" in U.S.-Soviet cultural relations.[65] It was only fitting that jazz should play a part in the events leading to Nixon's policy of détente.

Nixon's deployment of jazz adds yet another twist to the extensively documented ironies of détente. The "first American President to visit Russia since Franklin D. Roosevelt had conferenced at Yalta in 1945," Nixon was widely hailed for successfully relaxing tensions with the Soviet Union and opening up trade and exchange between the two nations. As the historian Robert Schulzinger has argued, Nixon's trip "was all the more surprising because it came on the heels of another major escalation of the war in Vietnam by the United States," including raids in which "Nixon expected that Soviet ships would be hit."[66] That Soviet president Leonid Brezhnev did not cancel the invitation to Nixon under these circumstances attests to the vulnerability of the Soviet economy and the enormous advantages the Soviets would gain from opening trade.[67] The timing of Duke Ellington's trip to the Soviet Union was critical: the tour followed the announcement of the president's impending visit. Both State Department officials and nongovernmental observers considered Ellington's trip, arranged through George Wein and Festival Productions, to be a diplomatic triumph. In 1969 Ellington had been fêted at the Nixon White House for his seventieth birthday—a celebration at which he received the Presidential Medal of Freedom, the nation's highest civilian honor.[68] "In the royalty of American music," declared Nixon, "no man swings more or stands higher than the Duke." Leonard Garment—formerly a clarinetist with Woody Herman, then an attorney and aide to Nixon—organized the event with Willis Conover, and the star-studded guest list included Dizzy Gillespie, Count Basie, Benny Goodman, Mahalia Jackson, Dave Brubeck, George Wein, and Leonard Feather.[69] For Ellington, this award, along with his role as senior statesman on the Soviet trip and his earlier presence at the Johnson White House launching the Na-

18. *Ellington with President Nixon at the White House, April 29, 1969.* Courtesy of
the Duke Ellington Collection, Archives Center, National Museum of American History,
Smithsonian Institution, Washington, D.C.

tional Endowment for the Humanities with Martha Graham and Dave Brubeck, represented the liberal, integrationist embrace of jazz. Together, these honors constituted fitting acknowledgment of a lifetime spent promoting civil rights for black Americans and fighting for recognition as an artist. They helped to rectify the fact that he had been passed over by the Pulitzer committee in 1965 for an award recognizing distinguished achievement in music.[70] Following the White House birthday party for Ellington, one Bureau of Cultural Presentations officer, discussing upcoming Ellington tours, noted that they "had a White House angle now."[71]

Indeed, playing on Ellington's close association with Nixon, promotions and publicity for the tour presented the Duke as the diplomatic advance man for the president. Joseph Presel, the escort officer for the tour, attributed the Russians' substantial cooperation to Ellington's relationship with Nixon. "The Soviets," argued Presel, "were scared of Ellington, both personally and politically, because they admitted that they knew of his relationship with the President, and because of the Duke's importance in the United States in general."[72] In *Music Is My Mistress,* Ellington wrote: "The anticipation of our tour of Russia is so great that there is a risk of being consumed by it."[73] The Ellington Orchestra played twenty-two concerts in five cities, reaching a combined audience of 126,000.[74] As one U.S. official reported, "Ellington was a mythical figure for the hard-core thousands of truly dedicated Soviet aficionados that waited for his arrival in the USSR with something akin to the anticipation of a Second Coming."[75] For some Soviet fans, it was as if modernity itself had walked through the door with Ellington. Secretary of State Rogers reported to Nixon that one young fan yelled, "We've been waiting for you for centuries!"—a welcome Nixon no doubt envied.[76] Presel described Ellington as "a personage of immense historical importance to the Soviets. . . . He is, for them, composer of 'Take the A Train' [actually composed by Billy Strayhorn], Willis Conover's theme song; he is one of the last survivors of the heroic age of jazz; and he is one of the seminal figures of jazz for the Soviet jazz buffs."[77]

The Ellington Orchestra of 1971 included many of the same musicians who had toured the Middle East in 1963, but there had been critical losses. Billy Strayhorn had died in 1967; lead alto saxophonist Johnny Hodges, in 1970. But although such individuals were irreplaceable and Ellington believed the band "will never sound the same," his "distinctive stylings at the piano" and the imprint of other veteran Ellingtonians "continued to define an unmistakable sound."[78] Leonard Feather, who had been in the USSR during the Goodman tour, contrasted the young fans' skepticism about Goodman with their warm embrace of Ellington. With Goodman, fans had asked: "Why not Louis Armstrong?" and "Why not Duke Ellington?" As Feather said regretfully, "Satchmo never made it"—the original ambassador of jazz had died earlier that year, on July 6. But when Ellington "finally arrived on the scene," he "let nothing stand between him and total triumph."[79]

The orchestra opened in Leningrad on September 13, to tumultuous applause that began even before the curtain went up. Hedrick Smith reported in the *New York Times* that Leningrad jazz fans had staged their own Duke Ellington celebration two years before "without their hero," and "needed no introduction and no warming up."[80] Beginning with "C-Jam Blues" and capping forty-five minutes of encores with "Take the A Train," Ellington moved between "more translucent modern improvisations" with "Fife" (a jazzy flute solo), "Black and Tan Fantasy," an experimental version of "Harlem," and many crowd-pleasing old favorites. The favorites, reported Smith, included "A Train," "Perdido," "I Can't Get Started," "Don't Get Around Much Anymore," and "Satin Doll." And the "ripping, flying drum solo" of Rufus Jones, and the "eyes-rolling duo of trumpeter Cootie Williams and vocalist Nell Brookshire on 'I Got It Bad and That Ain't Good,' sent the crowd hooting and whistling its unrestrained approval."[81] Tenor saxophonist Paul Gonsalves "brought the house down." He and Ellington had "even matrons smiling wistfully" in the ninth encore, with an improvised version of the old Russian love song "Dark Eyes." Aleksei Batashev, the young physicist who had greeted Goodman's band in

1962 as the president of Moscow's largest jazz club, was now identified as a jazz historian and told Smith that "we like the old favorites." Ellington charmed the Russians, telling them, "You're very
beautiful, you're very sweet, you're very generous." With enough of
the audience understanding English to applaud, the crowd "burst
into happy laughter when he rolled out his slogan 'I love you
madly!' in Russian."[82] If the crowds had initially expected the old
favorites, Ellington presented increasing amounts of newer material and several works outside "the normal boundaries of Elling-
tonia.'"Duke," reported Leonard Feather, "had the crowds finger-
snapping on 'La Plus Belle Africaine.'" And in a tribute to Louis
Armstrong, trumpeter Money Johnson "had the crowds in near-
hysteria with his impression of Armstrong playing, singing, and
mugging on 'Hello Dolly!'"[83]

The State Department and the orchestra were both frustrated
with the considerable efforts made by Soviet officials to minimize
and monitor contacts between American and Soviet musicians.
B. H. Klosson explained that discussions with the public were con-
ducted through "the generally stiff and structured 'warm meetings'
which the Soviet officialdom has become so adept at staging over
the years."[84] Paul Gonsalves, ever the diplomat and very much at
home in the convivial atmosphere of flowing vodka, was described
by U.S. officials as "glorious" and was praised for his willingness "to
talk with anyone at anytime." He endeared himself to the escort officer by "cutting off a flow of speeches at an especially boring
House of Friendship reception by simply picking up his saxophone
and, in a brief interval, starting to play."[85]

Clearly seeing jazz as the road to the Soviet heart, State Department officials profited from Ellington's visit to Leningrad as "a
unique opportunity to view the local jazz scene close up." At the
very first "official" Leningrad jam session, as "flowery Russian
speeches floated toward crenelated ceilings and Soviets and Americans alike shifted in their seats," local leading advocates of jazz—described by the State Department as "jazz activists"—had sought
out escort officers to arrange jam sessions and pass on messages.[86]
Later that night, ten Ellington band members joined seven or eight

19. *Paul Gonsalves on sax with Ellington at the piano, Leningrad, September 1971.* The backdrop with its bust of Lenin translates: "Lenin's Directives Live On and Triumph." Courtesy of the Duke Ellington Collection, Archives Center, National Museum of American History, Smithsonian Institution, Washington, D.C.

Soviet musicians for a "highly unofficial" jam session at the Byeliye Nochi (White Nights) café. The "most open secret in Leningrad," the session drew "score upon score of onlookers packed against the ground-floor plate glass windows to catch a glimpse of Johnny Coles blowing hot licks on his flugelhorn and Nell 'Songbird' Brookshire belting out the blues."[87] The local jazz activists "incurred the wrath of the Komsomol when the jam, by all accounts, got out of hand.[88] The band's escort officer, Presel, explained that this jam session was "remarkable for me in many ways, including the fact that I eventually had to leave by diving out the kitchen window." The next day, Presel was "accosted" by the leaders of the jazz club, who took him to another café and "talked at length about the problems they would face as a result of the jam session having gotten out of hand."[89] The State Department later reported that Kamerton (Tuning Fork), the jazz club that had arranged the session, "would be made inactive for a year."[90]

Building on these contacts, the State Department produced a profile on jazz clubs of Leningrad such as Kamerton and Kvadrat (Square), identifying four "prime movers" and attempting to understand the factional disputes in order to augment American intelligence on potentially pro-American Soviet citizens. The reporting official, whose name was Beam, explained that "petty jealousies and apparent feuds" readily surfaced when he "happened to mention one [faction leader] to another." In what may be seen as partly an expression of the genuine importance that American officials placed on jazz in the Soviet Union, and partly the sheer excess of Cold War intelligence gathering, Beam appeared most interested in sorting out their varying degrees of credibility and their level of contacts with and knowledge about America. Beam noted that Vadim Yurchenko "professes to be the Leningrad stringer for *Billboard*," and while "he nurtures the English-gentleman image to the point of being comic" he "is obviously well-known to the Leningrad music world."[91] Vladimir (Volodya) Garfunkel taught English at a technical institute and spoke the language "well and idiomatically with a pronounced American accent." Garfunkel "professed" to know William Dickson, formerly the head of the embassy's cultural staff, and Beam was impressed that although Garfunkel didn't possess the credentials to get backstage, "he managed to maintain close contact with the escort officers." Moreover, he passed on "most of the details about the planned jam session to the escort officers" and provided background on the club Kamerton. Garfunkel denounced another jazz activist, Efim (Fima) Barban as "a bag of wind" but Beam found Barban, the president of the small Kvadrat jazz club, very impressive. The editor of a semi-underground jazz periodical of the same name, Barban "speaks excellent English and dresses suspiciously well for a Soviet." Asked if his periodical qualified for the rubric "samizdat," Barban first said "rather indignantly," that "no, it was not political." But after thinking for a second, he acknowledged: "Well, perhaps. Here, even jazz is political." Barban "very knowledgeably" discussed the works of Saul Bellow, and it was he who stood up in the Byeliye Nochi club and introduced the individual Ellington players as they came out.[92] Finally, Vladimir Khavkin—"twenty-six, Jewish, and sports a full beard and rather wild bushy hair"—told Beam that "he had done most of the work in setting up the jam session." But in contrast to the others, Khavkin described himself as the organization's "expendable man" and stressed that that was why he'd been given the job. In a poignant reminder of the dangers of dissent in the Soviet Union, Khavkin fatalistically explained: "The police all know me, because I am a suspicious person. I have friends in Europe, America and Israel and have therefore been photographed, bugged, and taken in for questioning many times."[93] Finally, whatever the purposes of the jazz intelligence gathering, these reports underline the profoundly cynical side of détente. While superficially characterized as an effort to open relations and cool tensions, détente was primarily intended to manipulate trade and cultural exchange as more potent Cold War weapons.

After the five-night stand in Leningrad, playing to sellout crowds at the 4,200-seat October Theater, the band played Minsk, Kiev, and Rostov-on-the-Don before capping the tour with a Moscow run on October 9–12. Like all of the Soviet tours, this trip had its share of logistical and organizational mixups, ranging from the theft of Mercer Ellington's trumpet to poorly arranged concerts. And there were numerous other problems, which the State Department viewed as endemic to Soviet tours. Ellington was unhappy because he was "always cold." The food was consistently "uninspiring," and (reported Presel) the "genius of Soviet service made it arrive cold, delayed and unattractive." Food problems were compounded by the fact that the band included "two vegetarians, of two separate sorts," and other individuals who were controlling their diabetes through diet. Overall, Soviet "preparations and arrangements were grim."[94]

In Kiev, local authorities injected some levity into the Cold War atmosphere of scarcity and surveillance. Presel was surprised by the number of police in the concert hall, and "asked the *militsioneri* what the trouble was." It turned out that most of the police were members of one of the best local jazz bands. There had been no tickets available, the policemen explained, and "they wouldn't let us in. So we all put our uniforms on, and then there was no trouble getting in to hear the band." That night, there was no trouble about the police wearing the Ellington buttons Presel had given them.[95] But in Minsk, fans who simply wanted to approach the musicians for an autograph were kept at bay by a phalanx of "goons." The Goskontsert escort denied that the "rough-looking customers guarding the entrance" were anything but simple employees of the theater. But "a chagrined bunch of Baltic musicians" who were turned away when they came to Ellington for autographs referred to the head of security as "that KGB major on the door." When Klosson asked how they knew the man's rank, the musicians shrugged at his naïveté. "You can smell them after a while," one replied.[96]

For Presel, the State Department escort, the Ellingtonians "presented certain problems all their own." One such problem was "cheerful orchestral ideas on the subject of 'booze and broads.'"[97] Presel was in awe of the musicians' "abilities in these areas. . . . The band members displayed remarkable ingenuity in contriving to supply themselves with both commodities, despite all the difficult conditions that obtain in the USSR."[98] When the band went broke for a while, Presel remarked: "The Ellington organization appears to share with the State Department the fact that its authority is fragmented." Mercer Ellington, the road manager, had only enough money to meet one of the four payrolls in the USSR; he was told that, in any case, "there was nothing on which the band could spend money."[99] One possible explanation for the lack of funds is that as Ellington was scoring his "diplomatic coup" in the Soviet Union, the Internal Revenue Service was requesting a lien on monies earned by Ellington, who had fallen behind on his tax payments.[100] Mark Lewis, the director of cultural presentations, assured the IRS of the department's full cooperation and informed them of the contract with George Wein for an Ellington performance after the Soviet tour.[101] It is unclear whether the correspondence between the IRS and the State Department caused a temporary bureaucratic glitch, but the matter appears to have been resolved; the files show no further correspondence. But Ellington's tours for the government would accelerate after the Soviet tour.

The band arrived in Moscow on October 8 for the last leg of its trip. The American Embassy reported that "during the band's appearance in Moscow, hundreds of travelers from distant places such as Odessa, Riga, and Yakutsk arrived in Moscow for the concerts. . . . Tickets in Moscow were being scalped for $50.00 each.[102] The State Department was delighted by the Soviets' last-minute request to schedule two extra matinees at the Luzhnili Sports Palace, which seated nearly 10,000. Initially, the Soviets had promised four Moscow concerts at a 2,500-seat theater, but had then cut back to two concerts in the "depressing Estradii Theater," which held only 1,300 and had "a most unsuitable stage." "It was worth a great deal," wrote Presel, "to experience the Soviets coming to us to ask us to perform more, to expose still larger numbers of people to Ellington's art. Obviously, they had so badly miscalculated the pressure for tickets that they had to give in. It was extremely good for our morale." Despite protests from the exhausted and overworked orchestra, Ellington agreed to the additional performances.[103] Evoking the band's 1963 disputes with the State Department over their audience, Mercer Ellington was particularly gratified to be playing in the larger Sports Palace, because "I felt we really got through to the people, to the man in the streets."[104]

Robert O'Meally has discussed the complexity of Ellington's sense of audience, calling Ellington a "master of the fulfillment of wishes."[105] The spell of Ellington's mastery seemed to work on the State Department as well as on Soviet audiences. The State Department saw Ellington as a model gentleman and statesman. No less than their counterparts in smaller posts around the world, who welcomed Ellington as something akin to a victrola in the wilderness, U.S. officials in Moscow were delighted by his charming company. If alternately annoyed and awed by the band, Presel clearly relished the time he spent with Ellington. Referring to the Soviets' alleged fear of Ellington, Presel explained, "I saw no need to enlighten the Soviets who accompanied us to Ellington's true nature: that he is a very thoughtful, seventy-two-year-old gentleman who wants basically to be left alone to compose and play music and have someone—me, in this case—to whom he could bitch for an hour or so every few days."[106] Klosson, the apparently star-struck official in Moscow, took an entire single-spaced page, under the tongue-in-cheek heading "Rare Please," to explain the "famous Ellington steaks."[107] The steaks had been "the subject of numerous newspaper articles, much cable traffic, and no little amount of low humor," causing embarrassment when a "hanger-on" would ardently plead "not to let the Duke practically starve to death as he had in India." "There is absolutely no doubt," reported Klosson, "that the steaks—as well as the blessedly obscure and unpublicized limes for the Duke's cokes—played a role in maintaining the Ellington morale."[108]

Leonard Feather called the tour "the greatest coup in the history of musical diplomacy." Ellington had been "ecstatic"; the State Department and Soviet public had been "overjoyed."[109] For U.S. officials, it was highly significant that the Soviets were acknowledging the accomplishments of an American artist.[110] "Even *Pravda*," which had never before acknowledged the artistry of a visiting American musician, "waxes rapturous with a long glowing review."[111] Though there had been raves in numerous Soviet papers, American officials considered the article in *Pravda*—entitled "Orchestra of Virtuosos"—to be "the real coup." It "gushed praise for Ellington and his men."[112] Following *Pravda's* lead, the conservative paper *Sovietskaya Rossiya* ran a piece two days later entitled: "Duke Ellington, I Love You!" Coming from the organ of the Communist Party's central committee, this piece was welcomed by the State Department as "heady stuff indeed!"[113] Despite all the little glitches, Presel declared the tour an "immense success" for everyone concerned. The Ellington Orchestra had "genuinely enjoyed their stay," and the Soviet Goskontsert agency "made a great deal of money." The U.S. government relished its success, in that the audience reaction was extraordinarily good, and that a top American presentation had performed well as cultural ambassadors. And finally, the tour benefited the 115,000 Soviet citizens who were able to see Ellington perform.[114] The only problem, commented a friend of Ellington's, was that the Soviets would now "expect every visiting entertainer to display the same limitless energy."[115]

Ellington was seventy-two at the time of the Soviet tour. Subsequent to the tour, with only two and a half years of his life remaining, Ellington's activities for the State Department actually increased. He followed up the Soviet tour with performances in Western and Eastern Europe and a mixed commercial—State Department tour of Latin America, Brazil, and Mexico in November and December 1971. Just before leaving for the Soviet tour, Ellington had told reporters for the *Evening Star:* "After the Russian tour, we have our regular European concert tour, and then after that we go to South America, and then we come back to the Rainbow Grill in New York, then to Japan and the Orient, then to Australia, New Zealand, and then we'll come back and probably catch another blizzard in Buffalo." Asked how he could maintain such a pace at seventy-two, Ellington discounted the importance of age. "Anything can be a hardship," he explained. "A man who enjoys chopping down redwood trees in California, if you give him a job in a Fifth Avenue store demonstrating mattresses, he is a dead man." Musicians are unique in that "we're the only people in the world who do something fifty-two weeks a year without a holiday, a weekend, or a vacation. We never leave it. . . . We breathe fresh air through music." And rejecting the category of jazz for the umpteenth time, Ellington concluded, "I live in this music and this is the world."[116]

Though Ellington rejected the relevance of age, he was, according to friends, obsessed with death and keenly feeling the loss of loved ones. And while vindicated by his recent recognition, he was deeply aware of his place in the world and was thinking about his legacy. Ellington had been an international figure long before his first State Department—sponsored tour. But he was still expressing the deep concern "not to understate the world out there" that he had voiced after his 1963 tour. His expansive sense of "the world" had been shaped by his experiences as a goodwill ambassador. The tours had expanded the boundaries of Ellington's world in a remarkable and perhaps unparalleled way, taking him to places that would simply not have been possible—not commercially viable, or politically or logistically negotiable—without government sponsorship. To the end of his life, Ellington was constantly composing and open to the collaborative possibilities he encountered on the tours. But even as Ellington was expanding his sense of the world, American foreign policy was rapidly making that world a far messier and more difficult place to negotiate.

In a tour sponsored by the State Department throughout, the Duke Ellington Orchestra played twenty-one concerts in Brazil, Uruguay, Argentina, Chile, Peru, Costa Rica, Ecuador, Colombia, Venezuela, Puerto Rico, and Mexico from November 16 to December 10, 1971. The State Department and Festival Productions worked with the promoter, A. Szterenfeld of Conciertos Gama, Buenos Aires (Argentina), who handled local arrangements throughout.[117] The tour was a musical triumph from beginning to end. U.S. officials in San José (Costa Rica) celebrated it as a "fine counterpoint" to what they termed a "seeming Russian cultural offensive" amid the "tremendous public furor over the establishment of a Russian embassy here." Ellington's "triumphal appearance" before an audience of 5,000 "served to remind Costa Ricans of America's major contribution to the medium of jazz."[118] The embassy in Managua (Nicaragua) judged the orchestra a "resounding success" at its two sellout concerts at the 1,215-seat Rubén Darío National Theater, and at a 300-person reception given by U.S. ambassador Turner B. Shelton and his wife, with guests of honor President and Mrs. Somoza. "Nicaraguans," said Shelton, "seem to understand a little better what U.S. culture is all about, . . . that we're something 'alive and now.'"[119]

The State Department dramatically shifted its presentation in Central and South America, as the tour moved from areas such as Nicaragua, with American-supported dictators, to areas where audiences might be more openly critical of the United States. The State Department was eager to be closely associated with jazz in Managua, in Eastern Europe, and in the Soviet Union; but in several cities on this tour, it actually *withheld* the fact that it was the sponsor. In Buenos Aires, Caracas, Guadalajara, Monterrey, Rio de Janeiro, and São Paulo—perhaps judging that the raging critiques of the American war in Vietnam, on top of resentment of the ubiquitous American imperial presence, would make the State Department association a liability—the Bureau of Cultural Presentations directed that "*all* advance publicity will be handled by . . . local sponsors . . . and will *not* feature any *advance* notice that the tour is under Department auspices."[120] Posts were "requested to alert local UPI, AP, and other U.S. media representatives to the orchestra's appearance and encourage them to cover the visit."[121] Picking up on the ensuing ambiguities and confusions, Mercer Ellington later explained that their commercial appearances were "in a sense . . . a goodwill tour. . . . Even when we were not appearing under the auspices of the State Department, it was good to go to the embassies."[122] Yet while publicly sanguine about the State Department relationship, Mercer Ellington confided to Iola Brubeck that on this particular tour, he and other band members had concerns about being used by the State Department.[123] Clearly affected by the political tensions and perhaps wondering about the less than transparent American role, Mercer Ellington described the stop in Montevideo as being openly for the State Department. With the Uruguayan elections only days away, Mercer explained in a *Down Beat* interview: "The chief of police provided Duke Ellington with a bodyguard, which never left his side until he flew out for Buenos Aires the next day."[124] Determined to assert their own egalitarian politics, the band continued to raise the theme of "playing for the people," noting that—as at the Sports Palace in Moscow—the performance in Uruguay had been especially rewarding because they had reached "the man in the street."[125]

The cultural-presentations programs not only strove to maintain the support of strategic allies in Latin America and the oil-rich Middle East, win over potential dissidents in the Eastern bloc, and court new African nations. They also targeted elites in Southeast Asia. After Benny Goodman played for and with the jazz-loving king of Thailand in 1957, Stan Getz made another trip to Thailand in 1967 to smooth over relations after Lyndon Johnson had offended the king at a White House dinner. Following Johnson's various faux pas (sitting cross-legged with his feet facing the king's face; being taller sitting down than the king was standing up), Dave Brubeck had received an urgent call from a White House staff member. Explaining that things were not going well between Johnson and King Bhumibol Adulyadej, the staffer had asked Brubeck to travel to Thailand. Brubeck had been unable to make the trip and had recommended Getz.[126] And with the escalation in the Vietnam War, as well as in global criticism of America, U.S. officials were desperate for any support they could muster in the region.

In the midst of Ellington's Latin American tours, Wein and the State Department had been busy arranging pickups in Asia, most notably in Rangoon (Burma) and Vientiane (Laos) with Duke Ellington in 1970, and in Rangoon with Count Basie in 1971. In the 1970 Rangoon appearance, Ellington had been picked up by the State Department as he was making a commercial tour of the Far East. For the State Department, Ellington's performances constituted a considerable breakthrough in relations: they were the first American cultural presentations in Burma in eight years. Jazz, American officials argued, was "of central importance to our mission because it permits" communication with "a significant priority group, the university students, as well as with the young community leaders and emergent political figures."[127] Then, according to the *Bangkok Post,* Ellington "lost a packet" of money by agreeing, at the State Department's urging, to cancel scheduled commercial appearances in Hong Kong and play instead in Vientiane. With a program closely resembling that of the Soviet and Latin American tours, the Ellington orchestra played before nearly 2,000 in the National Stadium. From there, "they were whisked off to play for a black-tie audience, including the prime minister."[128] The *Bangkok Post* reported that "American foreign policy, in this case, was right. The out-of-the-way places need to experience the music of the de luxe class once in a while. . . . Duke was the perfect diplomat musician."[129]

In January of the following year, 1971, Festival Productions delivered another tour through Burma and Laos for the State Department, this time with Count Basie—a pickup from a commercial tour of Europe and Asia. "We had arranged to penetrate this territory on behalf of the U.S. State Department," remembered George Wein, "in spite of the fact that it was a danger zone." Terrified by the prospect of flying through a war zone, Basie nearly backed out of the Laos leg. More than a decade later, Basie recalled that the trip into Laos on a chartered U.S. army plane "was no sight-seeing trip for me. All I was concerned about was when we were going to get the hell out of there."[130] In May 1971, just months after Basie's Vientiane performance, the United States helped South Vietnamese troops move into neutral Laos. (Though they were quickly put to rout, in a visible mockery of Nixon's "Vietnamization," war continued to plague Laos until 1975.)[131]

On Ellington's extensive 1972 tour of Asia, which began as a commercial pickup out of Japan and then continued under State Department auspices in Manila, the pendulum swung wildly between an all-too-American mix of militarism and political intrigue on the one hand, and tourism and shopping on the other. From Manila, the orchestra flew through Hong Kong and then to Bangkok, where—breaking the usual distinction between cultural-presentation and USO tours—they performed before American troops on rest-and-recreation break from Vietnam. Ellington, accompanied by Bob Jones of Festival Productions, then boarded a plane for Laos, this time surreptitiously on the CIA airline, Air America. In Vientiane, the band played while guarded by three different governments. With Vientiane now a recreation spot for the Viet Cong, Ellington played first in a public park and then gave a second concert for the American community.[132] In Bangkok again, Ellington played for the king of Thailand, then continued on to Rangoon, then caught a charter flight to Mandalay and gave an outdoor concert for 15,000. From Rangoon, the band flew to India; but when they arrived in Calcutta they found that their concerts had been canceled because of U.S. support of Pakistan in the Indian-Pakistani war. Waiting in a hotel in Calcutta for their next move, Bob Jones, whose wife was from Calcutta, met his wife's uncle, "Uncle Sonny," who happened to manage Indian defense accounts. Jones quickly received a nervous inquiry from the State Department—"How do you know this guy?"—and then a terse memo: "Please advise us of any other uncles you have." In a rare dispute between the State Department and Festival Productions, George Wein was furious about the canceled dates. Festival never made more than three or four hundred dollars on a tour, and Wein wanted the money recovered from the canceled concerts. The State Department somehow quickly arranged makeup dates in Ceylon (where stores in the capital, Colombo, were opened on a Buddhist holiday so the musicians could shop for sapphires), Jakarta (Indonesia), and Kuala Lumpur (Malaysia), en route to final scheduled appearances in Perth (Australia) and New Zealand.[133]

The tour had not included Vietnam, but Ellington had volunteered to perform in Vietnam in 1971.[134] Although the State Department was unable to arrange local sponsorship, officials were in fact interested in bringing cultural presentations to Saigon. As testimony to the government's capacity for self-delusion about the omnipotence of American culture, a 1968 report from the Saigon cultural attaché described the year as one of "unexpected problems" brought on by the Tet Offensive. Yet, he concluded, this made the programs all the more important. Cultural and educational programs would "give some balance to the overwhelming military presence."[135] While initial requests for a major act were delayed, the program officers were able to deliver one in 1974, when the Martha Graham Company performed in Saigon—to sighs of relief from State Department officials and the media. In an eerie echo of the State Department's desire to balance bombing with culture, a *New York Times* correspondent wrote: "For the first time in Vietnam, I felt proud of the U.S. . . . . For two fleeting days, the U.S. showed a new face in Vietnam."[136]

In the early 1970s, Graham, along with Ellington, seemed to share the assumption of many patriots of their generation that the U.S. was fighting a war for freedom and against Communism in Vietnam. But if détente was intended to diffuse tensions between superpowers, the Cold War remained deadly hot for many of the world's peoples.[137] Nixon and Kissinger had hoped that détente with the Soviets and the opening to China would produce Soviet and Chinese pressure on the North Vietnamese and the National Liberation Front and encourage a quicker exit for the United States from Vietnam. But as measured in the tonnage of bombs dropped and the staggering number of dead in the region, their theory that all global conflicts could be resolved through greater superpower cooperation simply didn't apply in the Vietnamese war for national liberation. Like earlier American policymakers, Nixon and Kissinger continued to confuse nationalism and Communism, and their attempts to shift U.S. policy away from its earlier reliance on counterinsurgency proved too little too late. Despite the faith in

American policy displayed by such artists as Ellington and Graham, covert and overt militarism was rapidly undermining the liberal internationalism in which the tours had thrived. And by featuring avant-garde artists who represented for Eastern European audiences a challenge to repressive state structures, the jazz tours themselves had, ironically, facilitated a mood of international rebellion which could be turned on American liberalism as well as on the Soviet bureaucracy.[138] The artists still dreamed of pulling out of the contradictions of Cold War America a more democratic foreign relations that foregrounded America's art and culture. But even as the tours were enjoying their greatest successes, the seeds of the destruction of that dream were taking root.

CHAPTER 8

Playing the International Changes

Jazz "is really an international music," said saxophonist Sonny Rollins to reporter Meher Pestonji during the 1978 Bombay Jazz Yatra Festival. From Rollins' jazz calypso piece "St. Thomas" to his investigations of Rosicrucianism and his visits to Japan and India in 1969–1971, his sensibility reflected the complex influences permeating the jazz world. The MC for the festival, Voice of America's Willis Conover, emphasized that the tributaries and heritage of jazz "extend beyond the confines of America"; others stressed "the influences it had absorbed over the years from many places, including India."[1] Indeed, Rollins had been drawn to Jazz Yatra by his admiration for classical Indian music. Much like Duke Ellington after his 1963 tour, Rollins explained: "I am affected by the music at a deep, subconscious level. I just absorb it all, let the impressions sink in. Later, after I go, the music will just play itself through me."[2] It is fitting that the global character of jazz should have been the central topic of conversation at the first international jazz festival in India, a festival held in the final year of State Department–sponsored jazz tours and one of the last jazz events with State Department participation. Momentous changes in music and politics—in the United States and throughout the globe—had led up to the point, in 1978, when the cultural-presentation programs slipped quietly out of the tainted political realm of the State Department and into the purview of the U.S. Information Service. The withdrawal of American troops from Vietnam and the resignation of President Nixon in August 1974 left a disoriented and confused group of policymakers. Given the wide opposition to the war and congressional investigations into CIA covert operations, many in Congress tried to curtail the foreign-policy adventurism that had characterized the 1950s and 1960s. Further chastened by the oil crisis of 1973, policymakers could not easily maintain the fantasy of shaping the world to their liking. This loss of mastery was immediately reflected in the cultural-presentations programs. The State Department's music panel, which had evolved into the Advisory Panel on Folk Music and Jazz, simply stopped meeting for two years, acknowledging when they finally reconvened in 1975, that "we've been through a period of bureaucratic stuttering." The overt cause of the stuttering was the need to comply with the new Freedom of Information Act. How, then, could the department "take advantage of the expertise" brought by the panel while "preserving the individual privacy . . . of individuals or groups who are being evaluated?" But more broadly, having been so closely associated with Cold War politics, the panel, like so many American organizations and individuals, experienced considerable political disorientation.

The crisis in U.S. foreign policy had its counterpart in domestic politics. By the mid-1970s, the worst moments of social and political crisis—widespread antiwar protest, urban rebellions—seemed to have passed. But for much of black America, as the country settled into a general political malaise marked by cynicism and disengagement, the 1970s brought the shock of urban crisis.[3] Industrial and manufacturing jobs, to which African Americans had only recently gained access through civil rights victories, moved overseas or to the suburbs or simply evaporated.[4] The number of black people living in poverty grew dramatically as the country appeared to slide into permanent economic crisis.[5] Jazz poet Gil Scott-Heron's 1976 spoken-word piece "Bicentennial Blues" commented on the indifference of politicians to the widespread unemployment and poverty in urban black neighborhoods. Juxtaposing such poverty with the global recognition and acceptance of black music, Scott-Heron argued that it was at once a paradox and an indictment of America to note that "the bluesicians have gone all over the world." For Scott-Heron, like Louis Armstrong and the Brubecks in *The*

Real Ambassadors, jazz carried the gift—and burden—of memory. It bore the responsibility for representing history and (in Ellington's words) "the world out there." Scott-Heron invoked Armstrong and Ellington when he observed, "the blues was born at the shores where the slave ships docked." Then the blues "grew up in Satchmo's horn and on Duke's piano. . . . The blues has grown but the country has not, the blues remembers everything the country forgot."[6]

Amid widespread confusion and political disorientation, sheer institutional momentum—provided by the relationship between the State Department, Newport, and Festival Productions—carried the jazz programs through a final and often remarkable series of tours, including more Newport Jazz Festivals in Eastern Europe. From Eastern Europe, Festival Productions arranged pickup tours of Africa for Duke Ellington, B. B. King, and Dizzy Gillespie in the last months of 1973. There was also an Eastern European tour for the pop group Fifth Dimension and a 1975 program in the Soviet Union celebrating the work of Louis Armstrong. If official ideology remained color-blind, the government's dependence on African American artists to represent the nation often meant presenting a culture that had been transformed by the civil rights movement, and enabling black artists to represent their history and make connections to Africans and black people in the African diaspora. The State Department had been a critical catalyst in enabling Afro-diasporic musical connections, but as we shall see from the experiences of Duke Ellington, B. B. King, and Dizzy Gillespie in Africa, by the early 1970s those connections had taken on a momentum of their own. James Brown's tour of West Africa in 1970 and the 1970 "Soul to Soul" festival in Accra, featuring Wilson Pickett, Ike and Tina Turner, and the Staples Singers, announced that black music was commercially viable outside the sponsorship of the State Department. In the post–civil rights era, for many musicians and other Americans, the center of optimism had shifted outside the United States. As the tours were marking a new moment of black cultural production, tied not just to civil rights but to urban crisis, they allowed musicians to find inspiration by connecting to innovative cultural developments in an international scene.

In the context of the multiple crises of the early 1970s, the Fifth Dimension's tour of Turkey, Romania, Poland, and Czechoslovakia in April 1973, appears as something of a throwback. In one sense, the group fit the mold of what the State Department had envisioned in the early 1950s: they were successful and apolitical black Americans. Presenting such hits as "Aquarius," "Up, Up and Away," and "Wedding Bell Blues," their tour had more of a people-to-people quality than the typical cultural-presentations tour. The State Department had overcome skepticism about sponsoring the highly successful California pop group when the artists volunteered to waive their salaries and do the trip as "a national public service."[7] They also expressed interest in visiting schools and hospitals. The group envisioned the tour as an exchange of cultures. Florence Gordon, a teacher by profession, was particularly interested in visiting schools. Yet if the Fifth Dimension represented the mainstream of American culture, their tour demonstrates how much that culture had been transformed by the black freedom movement and the antiwar and feminist movements. The lyrics of their Laura Nyro hit (and their only antiwar song) "Save the Country" incorporate utopian and civil rights themes into the acknowledgment of a national crisis. "We felt very strongly," explained lead singer Marilyn McCoo, "about saving the children."[8] In advance publicity for the State Department, McCoo explained that "some of the greatest audience reaction comes when we perform songs with social and political messages," like "Save the Country" and their musical arrangement of the Declaration of Independence. While "we don't want to make our evening into social protest, . . . songs discuss all other aspects of life, so why not the problems we're having?" Once overseas, McCoo voiced her advocacy of "women's liberation." She put out a special press release on her views, joking that when the Fifth Dimension slowed down, her husband would have to get her out of jail because of her interest in politics and "especially women's liberation."[9] Lamonte McLemore

—noted for his interest in fashion and fun, expressed in his designs for the group's stage costumes—commented on the fact that the group got a standing ovation when they performed the song "Declaration of Independence" at the White House, though the song was banned on several radio stations, including Armed Services Radio. "They just couldn't live up to the fact that our own Declaration talked about things like overthrowing governments."[10]

It's impossible to judge how aware the State Department may have been of the potential resonances of the Fifth Dimension's mix of mainstream and protest for Eastern European audiences. The tour came just five years after the uprising in Prague. In an extremely rare if not unprecedented move, the music panel went off the record to discuss the "importance" of the tour. What was clear was the overwhelming enthusiasm of the American embassies once the tour began. Calling the Fifth Dimension's "invasion of the Ottoman Empire" a "roaring success," the USIS in Istanbul reported that all four concerts in Istanbul and Ankara were played before a "highly receptive audience which departed the theaters reluctantly wishing there could have been more of the highly moving and brilliantly executed music."[11] For the embassy in Warsaw, "the thickness of the cable file on the Fifth Dimension could easily suggest that it held the history of a cataclysmic event in our foreign relations. If it was not quite that, the appearance of this superb group of singers and musicians did provoke extremes of enthusiasm among Polish audiences that shook the rafters of the huge Sala Kongresowa in Warsaw and in the tremendous flying-saucer-shaped Hala Widowiskowo-Sportowa in Katowice."[12] American officials' delight with the group's overseas reception contrasted with the probing questions from ABC News correspondent Ted Koppel, in an interview upon their return. Asked about foreign impressions of U.S. politics, McLemore claimed that of all the posters and newspapers he had seen, "the only thing I could make out in a foreign language was 'Watergate.'"[13] Throughout the tour, the State Department was continuing to rely on African American artists to "save the country" by presenting an image of America more inclusive than the reality, and by projecting optimism and vitality from a country edging into deep political malaise.

Jazz remained at the heart of the Eastern European cultural-presentation programs. In November 1973, the New Jazz Festival brought yet another strong lineup to the fourth annual festival in Belgrade. The artists included Sarah Vaughan, B. B. King, Miles Davis, the Stars of Faith, the Oscar Peterson Trio, the Young Giants of Jazz, and Duke Ellington. Some of these acts also performed in Zagreb and Ljubljana. Embassy officials once again celebrated the appearance of American artists serving to "boost the American cultural image," and relished the fact that they were reaping the fruits of previous years' labors. Not only were all concerts in each city televised and filmed for future broadcast, but after three years of this practice, stations such as Belgrade TV had accumulated an enviable stock of jazz programs for rebroadcast. The embassy was pleased to note that "American jazz has become a staple on Yugo-slav television."[14]

The festival consisted of eight concerts over four days. The Stars of Faith opened, followed by the trio of Canadian jazz pianist Oscar Peterson. Sarah Vaughan started off the second day and was judged by many critics to be, along with the Miles Davis performance that opened the final day, "undoubtedly the best concert of the festival." The paper *Borba,* in Belgrade, praised Vaughan for her "masterly vocal technique."[15] *Politika* enthused: "Leonard Feather did not ex-aggerate that Sarah was a singer of Ella's spontaneity and Aretha Franklin's soul, Peggy Lee's warmth and Carmen MacRae's perfect phras[ing]." Critics and Vaughan alike were delighted that the tech-nical difficulties she had encountered with the sound system two years before in Belgrade had not been repeated.[16] And as Vaughan told a reporter for *Vecernje Novosti* in Belgrade, she was delighted that the audiences "were mostly young"—a change from the older crowd of 1971.[17] B. B. King also received uniformly enthusiastic re-views for thrilling the young audience with what one critic de-scribed as his "pop-rock-blues."[18] For *Politika,* Davis and his group (called Yamaha) "left a controversial impression and disturbed the spirits. . . . Being always dissatisfied, he keeps 'jumping' into new temptations." Here, he "presented the tendency of breaking melodic and harmonious structures and used extremely unusual syncopes and new colors of sound." The same review praised Roland Kirk, a multitalented instrumentalist famous for playing two saxophones simultaneously, as "one of the most bizarre and the most brilliant artist in the field of jazz."[19] Critic Vojislav Simic agreed, judging Kirk to be "on the edge of unbelievable."[20] Musicians faced devoted, knowledgeable, and highly discerning audiences and critics, many of whom were seeing their heroes in repeat performances from the first three Belgrade festivals. Several critics thought that the performance of Oscar Peterson—whom they had experienced first-hand as "a pianist of phenomenal technique and rich improvisations, a pianist who plays like an entire orchestra"— was not up to expectations, and certainly did not match command performances of earlier years.[21] And in an otherwise celebratory piece titled "The Unique Duke Ellington," a critic in *Dnevnil* acknowledged that "the living legend of jazz" had "disappointed a part of the audience in Trivoi Hall"; he was no longer "the musician they know from the numerous records so well." Though citing the considerable changes in Ellington's orchestra, this critic surely didn't know that Ellington had been diagnosed with lung cancer in January of that year, and that the disease was rapidly spreading throughout his body.[22]

Ellington nonetheless welcomed the opportunity, following the Belgrade Newport appearance, for a pickup tour to Ethiopia and Zambia, arranged through Festival Productions. George Wein was unaware of Ellington's condition, but sensed his vulnerability; he wrote to the Bureau of Cultural Presentations that he was "very concerned" about the Ellington itinerary planned for Ethiopia. The band was scheduled to be up at 6:00 a.m. two days in a row, after flying all night from Europe. "That band will be whipped if we are not careful," Wein objected. "Let's not forget that Duke Ellington is seventy-four years old, although don't tell him I said so."[23]

The twenty-two members of the orchestra arrived in Addis

Ababa on November 23. For the State Department, the tour was magical—it made an "unforgettable" impact on USIS staff, Ethiopian youth, Third World nationals, and the performing-arts world. Publicity and media coverage were superb, drawing on two USIA films about Ellington on the road and at the White House. U.S. officials ran newspaper ads and produced TV and radio commercials, which the Ethiopia television service and Radio Ethiopia ran before and after the visit. At a critical moment in U.S.—Ethiopian relations, the State Department considered the concerts not only an artistic success, but a great cooperative venture between U.S. officials and Ethiopians "from all professions and all walks of life." Since there was no local impresario, the State Department worked closely with a variety of individuals and groups, ranging from the YMCA, students from the university, the minister of communications, and the chairman of the board of Ethiopian Airlines. Challenging the "truism" that in such co-sponsored ventures the "USIS still does all the work," U.S. officials reported that "it was our Ethiopian contacts who did a great deal of the substantial and detailed work."[24] And the visit appeared to work wonders on USIS staff morale. "USIS Addis Ababa may never be the same after this lesson it taught itself. We hope so."[25]

Emperor Haile Selassie I attended the opening "command performance," and at a special palace reception awarded Ellington the rank of Commander in the Imperial Order of Ethiopia. "We reaped an unexpected dividend," noted the State Department, "in the unexpected calling of the eighth extraordinary session of the Organization of African Unity's Council of Ministers." The visiting dignitaries were invited to the opening concert and to the VIP reception with the Ethiopian prime minister. American officials were impressed and grateful that Ellington insisted on being present at the reception, though it was clear he was suffering excruciating pain from arthritis.[26] USIS officials thought it "remarkable" that his music had been received with such enthusiasm by the young people. This had been unexpected, because "our air waves here are almost dominated with recent contemporary American music." Yet an afternoon concert that admitted students at reduced prices had the "most excitedly responsive audience" of all, and as a result Ellington "played his best music. In effect, they metaphorically tore the theater apart with their enthusiasm and cheers."[27]

Ellington became "fast friends" with Mulatu Astatqé, Ethiopia's leading contemporary composer, arranger, conductor, and musician, "who was the Duke's constant companion and friend from the moment of arrival to departure."[28] Astatqé, a pioneer of Ethio-jazz, fused traditional Ethiopian music with a wide range of musical influences he had encountered while studying abroad in England from the age of seventeen. In England, he had been "immediately taken with the Caribbean and Latin music present on the London scene, just before the onset of Beatlemania." He had played with Frank Holder, a calypso musician from the Caribbean, and in Edmundo Ross's Latino band. He had then studied at Harnett National Musical Studies in New York, where he had founded the Ethiopian Quintet. He had released two "Afro-Latin soul" albums with them in 1966, the same year that Ellington had released *Soul Call*.[29] It was no wonder the two modern innovators got on famously. The State Department got a room for Astatqé next door to Ellington at the Addis Ababa Hilton, where the band was staying. Astatqé brought "every available musician of note" to meet Ellington, and gathered a band to play arrangements of Ethiopian music that were composed especially for Ellington's visit.[30] Six Ellington musicians joined artists from the famous traditional Orchestra Ethiopia and modern musicians invited by Astatqé participated "in a jam session that the Ellingtonians will long remember." Within a few minutes, reported the delighted USIS, the American jazz stars were playing along (in the words of an Ellington band member) "as if they were born here." A USIS press release reported that "the saxophone, trumpet, and trombone met the traditional Ethiopian *masinko* and *washint* musical instruments, and according to one Ellington bandsman, 'music may never be the same again.'"[31] When Ellington had first visited the continent of Africa for the Dakar festival in 1966, he had commented that after writing

African music for thirty-five years, he was at last in Africa. It seems fitting that even in the last months of his life and on his final State Department tour, he should contribute to yet another fusion in the seemingly infinite routes of Afro-diasporic innovation.

The Ellington Orchestra's next and final stop on the African tour was Lusaka (Zambia). In a sobering reminder of the mineral wealth that had motivated U.S. interest in the region during the Congo crisis, public affairs officer Arthur W. Lewis had apprised the Bureau of Cultural Presentations that "the copper companies and the Zambian government are terribly interested" in a visit by Duke Ellington as part of the national independence celebrations.[32] The orchestra gave three concerts in two and a half days. In an "arrival-day performance in Lusaka's famed Mulungushi Hall, well over 2,000 cheering, stamping fans welcomed the Duke and his orchestra." "The crowds," reported an official named Wilkowski at the American Embassy, "were absolutely in love with the ageless Duke, who performed many of his old, familiar tunes to thunderous applause and whistles."[33] Early the next morning the orchestra flew to the copper-belt city of Ndola for a luncheon and afternoon performance at a venue called the Broadway Cinema. Returning to Lusaka for an evening reception sponsored by the American ambassador and the Zambian minister of education and culture, they played a Sunday afternoon concert at the State House.[34] Wilkowski judged the value of the visit "immeasurable" and was "extraordinarily satisfied," calling Ellington "an unparalleled representative of the U.S., both personally and professionally." The embassy was clearly pleased with the visit and the "untold opportunities" it afforded for personal contacts with government officials. Ellington's reception belied the notion that, as Wilkowski put it, "American music, particularly jazz, is unknown to Zambians."[35] But many Zambians and the performing-arts community might have taken issue with Wilkowski's emphasis on "American music." Ellington's music, said the *Zambia Daily Mail*, "spans almost every style and mood of the world-wide music that has its roots in Africa."[36] Even more pointedly, the critic Valerie Wilmer argued in the *Zambia*

Daily Mail: "The Western world deceives itself when they talk of Jazz—the only original American art form. What they should be saying and saying loud—is that Black Music is the beat to which the whole world is dancing."[37] And Ellington, who insisted that "the music of my race is more than the American idiom," would surely have agreed.

While the Ellington Orchestra was playing in Ethiopia and Zambia, B. B. King—the "King of Blues"—was picked up by the State Department from his Newport engagement and sent to Dakar, Accra, and Lagos. For the State Department, the highlight of the Lagos visit was a concert on November 25 where King "appeared with Nigeria's Afro-Beat 'superstar,' Fela Ransome-Kuti." Fela was not only a superstar, but was the "founder of Nigeria's radical Afro-Beat subculture." Fela's mother was an activist who had been a founder of the Nigerian Women's Union; but he had also acquired some of his political beliefs in Los Angeles, where he had been influenced by black American activists. His companion, a former Black Panther member named Sandra Smith, introduced him to the political ideas of the Panthers and political and cultural figures such as Kwame Touré (Stokely Carmichael), Angela Davis, Martin Luther King Jr., and Malcolm X.[38] As Fela's biographer Michael E. Veal argues, his Afrobeat music, which Fela proclaimed "the progressive music of the future," had grown out of a jazz–soul–highlife fusion, "reconciled through modal harmonies found in traditional Yoruba genres" and "heavily inflected by African-American culture." [39] Having worked in the United States in 1969 and 1970 with his band Koola Lobitos, which had evolved into Nigeria 70, Fela spoke of the musical affinities between the modal jazz of Miles Davis, John Coltrane, and Archie Shepp and the sounds "common among people in the bush."[40] Returning to Nigeria in 1970 during a period of optimism after the civil war, and when Lagos was the center of the West African music industry, Fela's Afrobeat style got a further spark from the 1970 James Brown tour of West Africa. The anticipation for Brown's Nigerian appearances, says Veal, had "equaled that usually reserved for political or religious leaders"; there had been a three-month buildup in the lively Nigerian press. Most important, for Veal, the "process of cross-cultural influence between West African and African-American musicians had come full circle. The influence of Brown's style on Fela was undeniable, yet the process of creative inspiration clearly was becoming mutual."[41] By the time King arrived in Nigeria three years later, Fela's distinctive Afrobeat was transforming the region and gaining an audience around the world.

That the State Department was willing to have its musical ambassadors sharing the stage with such African superstars attests to the dynamic cross-fertilization of African and Afro-diasporic cultures. Whether or not U.S. officials consciously embraced the idea, posing as the "unique American" would not be effective in the vibrant West African music scene. After the concert with Fela, King conversed at length with reporters, not fielding questions but "deeply engaged in dialogue." "Don't stop us," King said, "I'm enjoying this because I'm learning."[42] The appearance with Fela was the highlight of a tour that featured stages shared by Americans and Africans. In Accra, two Ghanaian groups, the Basabasa Soundz and the Hedzoleh Soundz, had opened for King with what the State Department described as their "tradition-inspired music." Referring to the backlash against the prominence of Caribbean and African American expatriates in Nkrumah's Ghana, officials at the American Embassy cited "the current stress on promoting Ghanaian culture and on minimizing the impact on Ghanaian life of outside influences."[43] U.S. officials appeared delighted that King had been presented along with Ghanaian musicians and they enjoyed the "comic banter by master of ceremonies and disc jockey Mike Eghan."[44] Prior to the Lagos concert, King had jammed with Lagos musicians, including the band Sonny Freeman and the Unusuals, proclaiming the session "the best part of my whole tour, fantastic." Following the concert, a reception was held at the Caban Bamboo Hotel, owned by "the Father of Nigerian Musicians," Bobby Benson. King hit it off with Benson "and joined Art Alade and Bobby Benson's band in a jam session."[45] Back in the United

States, King told *New York Times* reporter Les Ledbetter that "I learned lots listening to the concerts the local musicians played for us. When we played together, the traditional musicians met us head on, even on the up-tempo things. They seemed to feel us, and I know we could feel them."[46]

King's experiences in West Africa were surely ones that Dizzy Gillespie would have envied, for when Gillespie arrived in Kenya just three weeks after King and Ellington had left the continent, he had upped the ante on his earlier resolve to "play for the people." Indeed, Gillespie was now determined to play "with the people." The U.S. Embassy in Nairobi had been determined to bring a "U.S. Soul Group" to celebrations of the tenth anniversary of Kenyan independence on December 12, 1973, and especially wanted the Jackson Five. The State Department explained that it could no longer sponsor groups originating in the United States (with the exception of tours to the Soviet Union) and suggested arranging a November pickup appearance by Duke Ellington in lieu of sending a group to the independence celebration. The Bureau of Cultural Presentations received a sharp rebuff and a lesson in diplomacy from a U.S. Embassy official in Nairobi named Lindstrom. He stated that the embassy "normally would welcome a visit to Kenya by the Duke Ellington Orchestra," but any date other than the actual independence celebration would be an insult to the Kenyans and "could give rise to feeling that [the] U.S.—unlike other cooperative countries—prefers to 'go it alone' in order to maximize public relations impact."[47] Though U.S. officials couldn't book the Jackson Five, or any of the dozen "Soul Groups" they contacted, Dizzy Gillespie was quite a consolation prize.[48]

Kenyan and U.S. officials were delighted to have Gillespie representing the United States. Gillespie, explained the embassy in Nairobi, was "the legendary pioneer of modern jazz, . . . considered by many experts the greatest living jazz trumpet player."[49] The Dizzy Gillespie Quartet—including Mickey Roker on drums, Earl May on bass, and Al Gafa on guitar—played two concerts in Nairobi to a combined audience of 7,000, and then traveled to Dar es Salaam.

Gillespie's arrival had been much anticipated—a headline in the Kenyan *Evening News* had proclaimed, "Dizzy's Trip Like Coming Home." Gillespie explained that bop, the music he had helped to create, "really comes from Africa." The Nairobi *Daily Nation* noted the composition Gillespie had written specifically for the Uhuru (freedom) celebrations, and reported a week later that Gillespie had "thrilled an audience of over 3,000 at a concert in the Plenary Hall of the Kenyatta Conference Center." Fans had applauded the "tremendous" performance of the "tireless Dizzy," despite having arrived just hours earlier on a nonstop flight from New York.[50]

Since his 1956 tours for the State Department, Gillespie had traded in his signature beret for a fez and had become a devout practitioner of the Baha'i faith. In Kenya, he linked the internationalism of his faith to that of his music and politics. "I've always been inspired by your President Mzee Jomo Kenyatta," Gillespie told a reporter. He composed the suite *Burning Spear* (Kenyatta's nickname of old) and explained that the piece was a mélange of Indian, South American, African, and American influences, "with a touch of the blues for good measure."[51] "It's an international piece," Gillespie explained, "because the inspiration, President Kenyatta, is an international figure."[52] And as a "self-appointed duty in his diplomatic role," Gillespie took it upon himself to address the audience in Swahili: "I want to say to all of you—the people of Kenya—that you have been my inspiration since way before independence, . . . and also to say that this is the culmination not only of my professional activities but of my human relationships, to come to Kenya, to perform for you, because I think of you as my people."[53]

In discussing his music and playing in Kenya, Gillespie pointed to the hybrid character of his music and of African American culture, and to that culture's openness to new influences and routes of improvisation. Gillespie thought the music in Kenya sounded like calypso, but "when I said this to an African musician his answer was, 'Wait a minute, man. It's the West Indians who sound like *us*—don't forget it all originated here.'" Gillespie told Leonard Feather that he had agreed to the gig, "provided they would find me a couple of the best local drummers. So I get there, man, and they haven't found me no drummers. I said, 'This is Africa and there aren't any drummers? Wait till I tell the cats back home about this.' Then I ran into an African conga player I'd met at Ronnie Scott's Club in London. He agreed to come to a rehearsal and he brought a friend. They both played on my own conga drums."[54]

Ever the jazz educator, and missing no opportunity to explain the importance of jazz to presidents, fans, and critics alike, Gillespie explained that his determination to play with the Kenyan drummer "goes back to a conversation I had with President Nixon in 1969, when I was a guest at Duke Ellington's birthday party at the White House." Nixon, Gillespie reported, had complimented him on the fine job he had done as jazz ambassador and suggested that it was time for him to go again. Gillespie, however, invoking the same spirit and agenda that had earned him the wrath of Congress after his early tours, had told Nixon, "I ain't too interested in playing for those people; I'm more interested in playing *with* them." According to Gillespie, Nixon had expressed skepticism and asked, "Do they have that caliber of musician over there?" Gillespie had replied: "You don't realize the worldwide extent and breadth of our music. I'm liable to walk into a nightclub in Afghanistan and hear a guy playing a solo he took off one of my records note for note. Sometimes you can find a better musician for a certain job in a place like Osaka than you can get in Philadelphia."[55] Jazz may have been created in America, but Gillespie could find the essential elements of jazz in Afghanistan, Nairobi, or Belgrade. While in Kenya, Gillespie sought out local musicians. In Nairobi, he and his group visited the Starlight Club, where they accompanied a local soul band, "much to the delight of the nearly 100 percent African audience," reported an equally delighted State Department official.[56] Gillespie had wanted to pull together an open-air concert in Jamhuri Park, but time ran out prior to the quartet's departure for Dar es Salaam. "We could have had a local band in attendance and I'd play with them," explained Gillespie. "I'd like that—to play *with* them and not *for* them."[57]

20. *Dizzy Gillespie, in the 1980s.* Courtesy of the Institute for Jazz Studies, Rutgers University.

Gillespie's sense of the international possibilities of jazz was imbued with his sense of black modernity. Gillespie called bebop "modern music" and employed "modern" as a term of praise. And after living and working for decades in a segregated society and then becoming the object of attacks by antimodernists in Congress, he certainly didn't see "the modern" as synonymous with America. He did find the terrain of the modern in the American jazz world but, as he told Nixon, he also found it in Afghanistan, Brazil, Turkey, Yugoslavia, and Kenya. For Gillespie, jazz had evolved through encounters with Afro-Latin rhythms, and it would continue to evolve wherever it traveled. Just as he had on his triumphant 1956 tours, Gillespie continued to espouse his staunch egalitarianism and take it beyond the brother-sisterhood of musicians. He embraced openness, innovation, change, and freedom from racial, social, and economic hierarchies. He told reporters in Nairobi that he hoped socialism would take hold, "so that everyone can know what it's like to wear shoes."[58] And he replied to questions about how his life revolved around music: "I dig it. Besides, I'm too nervous to steal."[59]

In Nairobi, the State Department thought that followers of "rapid modern jazz" were mainly Americans and Europeans and that the Kenyans were milder in their response.[60] Both Gillespie and the State Department cited bad acoustics and the mass audiences of Kenya to be a less than ideal venue for Gillespie's style of jazz. Officials noted a far more uniformly enthusiastic reception in Dar es Salaam, where Gillespie, playing in smaller venues, had fans "dancing in the aisles."[61] He played two concerts and held a standing-room-only clinic and informal jam session for local musicians. The quartet was "extremely well received."[62] George Haven, the public affairs officer in Dar es Salaam, noted that "the group wins friends everywhere, both on and off-stage. Their openness, sincerity, friendliness, and 'approachability' were outstanding."[63]

Overall, the Gillespie visit was judged a tremendous diplomatic success, but Lindstrom in Nairobi mused over the various reactions to Gillespie. One "high Kenyan" official said: "As a group, we do not understand modern jazz. We understand the Louis Armstrong type of jazz." Lindstrom also quoted a University of Nairobi student: "Man, Gillespie is all right, but we dig soul, man, soul." The student, explained Lindstrom, was "obviously alluding to the music of James Brown, Aretha Franklin, and the Jackson Five, which is most often heard in Kenya." Like Harry Hirsch, the escort officer on Randy Weston's 1967 tour, Lindstrom speculated that "modern jazz might be too sophisticated for mass Kenyan ears."[64] But unlike Hirsch, who had worried that Africans were getting "pheasant under glass and cherries jubilee" when hamburgers and shakes would have been more appropriate, Lindstrom seemed to make a genuine attempt to understand the multiplicity of a changing African American culture. Despite noting the preferences of officials and students for styles other than the modern jazz of Gillespie, Lindstrom claimed, the visit of the Gillespie Quartet was a success because "it showed the creativity and diversity of the American cultural scene."[65] As seen by the appeal of James Brown, Aretha Franklin, and the Jackson Five, along with that of jazz, by the early 1970s African American culture had taken on a momentum of its own and didn't need to be promoted by the State Department. A burgeoning African and international record industry and the privately organized concerts of artists such as James Brown and Wilson Pickett created demands the State Department had never anticipated.[66] From the beginning of the tours, the State Department had embraced jazz as a uniquely American art form. But at least in some instances, officials sensed that "America" worked best when it acknowledged connections that couldn't be contained or owned by the *nation*. Gillespie embodied the best of the jazz ambassadors, who, as vibrant representatives of the nation, refused to be exclusively defined by it.

As political disorientation due to Nixon's resignation settled in with a vengeance in 1974, the death of several of the great jazz ambassadors seemed to foreshadow the close of an era. En route to London for a concert following the Zambia concerts, the Ellington Orchestra stopped in Athens, where veteran saxophonist-diplomat Paul Gonsalves suffered a massive stroke.[67] While Ellington had been in Zambia, his close friend and personal physician, Arthur Logan, had died. The distraught Ellington had already endured the deaths of many band members and many friends, and told Logan's widow Marion, "I'll never get over this. I won't last six months."[68] He died of pneumonia six months later, on May 24, 1974, just weeks after his seventy-fifth birthday and nine days after Gonsalves had passed away.

Louis Armstrong too had died, in July 1971, and was proclaimed the ambassador of love by people the world over. In 1975, through the auspices of George Wein and Festival Productions, the State Department arranged a posthumous "Armstrong tour" of the Soviet Union, where the New York Jazz Repertory performed a program of Armstrong music from June 13 through July 9. The multimedia tribute to his musical contributions featured New York Jazz

Repertory renditions of Armstrong's music, along with films clips of Armstrong himself. The narrative moved through Armstrong's music-saturated childhood and his collaborations with King Oliver in Chicago in 1922. For Armstrong's period in New York with Fletcher Henderson, the band played "Cake-Walkin' Babies from Home." The return to Chicago, the birth of Louis Armstrong and His Hot Fives, and the development of scat were portrayed through "Heebie Jeebies." One program focused primarily on Armstrong's earlier career, and included such numbers as "Struttin' with Some Barbecue" and "St. Louis Blues." A script for the program ended with Armstrong discussing and performing what many considered his signature piece, "When It's Sleepy Time Down South." But the Soviet program ended differently, alluding to Armstrong's State Department tours: "Wherever he went in the world, [he made] friends, literally in the millions. In Africa, in Europe, and behind the Iron Curtain, people loved him. . . . His warmth and sincerity communicated with rich and poor alike." The final number had a clip from a 1970 Newport Festival showing Armstrong and Mahalia Jackson singing "Mack the Knife"; the clip was then joined by the live band.[69] The State Department was delighted with the program and sent it to the 1975 Warsaw Jamboree for a performance on October 26, 1975, which was broadcast on Polish television.[70]

The State Department missed no opportunity to promote jazz in Eastern Europe and the Soviet Union. But by the mid 1970s, in the wake of the Vietnam pullout, the Watergate crisis, and the energy crisis, some officials were calling for a more modest foreign policy. Congressional investigations of CIA covert operations had deeply disturbed many lawmakers, who were now determined to "restrict further foreign adventures."[71] In Africa, as evidenced in the music tours, many officials preferred to make connections and embrace African American culture as part of a shifting international scene, rather than espouse the uniqueness and superiority of America.

But some policymakers were reluctant to give up cultural outreach and influence. Despite the new constraints on foreign policy, Secretary of State Kissinger pulled off one last "culture as damage control" tour of Africa by the Buddy Guy—Junior Wells Band during the Angolan crisis of 1975. Kissinger and President Gerald Ford were determined to demonstrate to the Soviets that the U.S. would still oppose leftist revolutions in the Third World, despite America's failure in Vietnam. By 1975, any goodwill won through the Ellington, King, and Gillespie visits to Africa was in danger of being squandered by "Kissinger's War" in Angola. The United States had long been implicated in Angolan white rule through its support of Portugal's right-wing dictatorships. Such governments maintained colonial control of Angola through extreme brutality and the use of U.S. supplied arms. In 1961, President Kennedy had cringed (but had not changed his policy) "when a bomb dropped on an Angolan village carried the clearly visible insignia 'Made in America.'"[72] Following years of armed nationalist struggle for independence in Angola, a 1974 coup overthrew the dictatorial rule of Marcello Caetano in Lisbon. Nixon had supported Portuguese rule in Africa. After the outbreak of civil war in Angola in 1975, the United States had assisted both the União National para a Indepêndencia Total de Angola (UNITA), and the Frente Nacional de Libertação de Angola (FNLA). Though all parties in the civil war were Angolan, the United States had sided with the factions aided by the apartheid government of South Africa—those that accommodated white settler privilege in Angola and throughout southern Africa. Since Cuba and the Soviet Union were aiding the Marxist Movimento Popular de Libertação de Angola (MPLA), which had come to power at the end of 1975, Kissinger "feared the creation of a whole string of radical pro-Soviet regimes in Africa."[73] Although Congress, in an unprecedented move, ended U.S. aid to any faction in Angola and specifically banned American covert operations there, the Kissinger alliance with South African forces had done extensive damage. As criticism of Kissinger within the United States mounted (Scott-Heron's "Bicentennial Blues" sarcastically proclaimed him "International Godfather of 'Peace'—a piece of Vietnam, a piece of Laos, a piece of Angola"), many Africans watched in horror as decades of struggle for independence seemed to unravel.[74] "For people newly freed from white domination," Thomas Borstelmann has written, "the sight of white South African troops pouring across the border from Namibia into Angola was analogous to Americans viewing Soviet troops invading West Germany."[75] Urgent requests from American posts in Africa, asking for help in responding to the vehement criticism of U.S. Angolan policy, lent a sense of emergency to the African tour by the Buddy Guy-Junior Wells Band in late 1975 and early 1976.

The Guy-Wells Blues Band toured West and central Africa from November 25, 1975, to January 13, 1976. They performed in Cameroon, Chad, the Central African Republic, Zaïre, Ghana, Benin, Togo, Upper Volta, Niger, Ivory Coast, Mali, Senegal, Guinea, and Sierra Leone. Outlining the context for the Guy-Wells visit to Accra, the USIS office there reported that December, the month of the Guy-Wells visit, "was open season on the United States." The "immediate occasion was Angola"; in fact, all of the embassies were talking about Angola. In the eyes of the Ghanaian press, America's Angolan policy "was a deep disappointment. It seemed to sacrifice security for hard-won African liberties in favor of Cold War obsessions."[76] Emphasizing the "deep frustration and anger" of Ghanaians, a USIS official warned that "it would be a mistake to dismiss the spate of criticism which Angola has occasioned as either temporary of superficial. Many highly respected and normally moderate Ghanaian leaders . . . are convinced America is siding with the more dangerous enemies of African freedom."[77] The Guy-Wells trip took place during the final stages of the civil war; by the end of the year, the MPLA had come to power. Kissinger was planning a spring 1976 tour of Africa—part of what he termed a "preemptive strategy" to take momentum away from the Soviets and Cubans.[78] If Ellington had been presented as the front man for Nixon in the Soviet Union, in a sense the Guy-Wells Band were front men for Kissinger's April 1976 tour. The State Department had declared in 1970 that there would be no more "blanketing" of continents. But in a throwback to the early days of the tours, the Guy-Wells itinerary went out to posts under Kissinger's name, and the original eight countries expanded to fourteen in response to urgent requests for damage control.[79]

While the tour demonstrated once again that an appreciation of American music could exist alongside disdain for American policies, the posts were uniformly appreciative of the impact of a successful tour. In Accra, the embassy was under no illusions that the criticism had been quelled, but reported that the Guy-Wells Band had "exceeded the Post's best expectations," performing before a "screaming crowd of more than 800."[80] The USIS in Chad breathed a sigh of relief that, given the recent "stresses and strains," the "big flashy event" of the Guy-Wells Blues Band "helped us slide past what could otherwise have been a rough period."[81] The public affairs officer in Chad, E. David Seal, said that the tour proved "we possess a most potent weapon in our culture—our music and art—that can touch profound and deep feelings of community with the American people that exist throughout the young people of the Third World."[82]

That "potent weapon" was a mix of the blues, "from Georgia country Blues to Chicago thumping Blues," with "the whole spectrum of American soul music in the Seventies as well."[83] Along with Buddy Guy's "lightening riffs on the guitar" and Junior Wells's vocals and harmonica, which "wails the plaintive cries of loneliness and heartbreak," Phil Guy's renditions of James Brown hits made the concerts deeply memorable "happenings."[84] In Accra, at a concert at the University of Science and Technology, the "climax of the action-packed show" was Phil Guy's "Sex Machine." "When Phil Guy," reported the USIS in Accra, "invited the wife of the U.S.T. vice-chancellor to join him on stage for a few 'bumps,' the students' roar drowned out the 1300 watts of dynamite sounds." With even the "front row of VIP's bouncing to the solid rhythms," the vice-chancellor remarked that "after a great concert like this, I shouldn't have any trouble with the students for three weeks or more."[85] And in what Seal described as "protocol-conscious Chad," the concert produced a "totally egalitarian evening, . . . with high government officials packed in along with students and music lovers of all sorts."[86]

During four days in Kinshasa, highlights of the stay included an impromptu concert following Guy and Wells's talk on the origin of the blues and a "late-evening visit to the home of Tabu Ley," described by the State Department as "perhaps the most popular vocalist in Zaïre." After a prodigious meal offered by the host, Ley, Guy, and Wells jammed with "vocal and instrumental improvisation" far into the night.[87] Audiences in Senegal were far more conversant with African American culture than those in most of the other countries on the tour. The band met with much enthusiasm, but some officials wondered why, with so few American cultural presentations, Guy-Wells should have been given a repeat act. In a discerning international scene, the group's music was neither new nor "sufficiently bluesy."[88] But most embassies agreed with the public affairs officer in Chad, who saw the tour as reinforcing a significant and welcome development: "There is now substantially more American music played on Radio Chad than on Voice of America." For David Seal, this "sudden infusion" of American music was significant, since Radio Chad had a "considerable" impact on national consciousness. "Without question," argued Seal, "the culture heroes for a whole generation of young Chadians are people like James Brown, the late Otis Redding, Wilson Pickett, Percy Sledge, and now Buddy Guy and Junior Wells."[89]

In the meantime, the Newport Jazz Festival and the State Department continued to bring jazz innovators to Eastern Europe. Given the nation's fatigue over issues of racial injustice, it was ironic that the State Department was trading on audience identification with oppositional African American culture. In 1974, another roving Newport Festival brought the Sonny Rollins Quintet, the Stan Getz Quartet, the McCoy Tyner Quintet, and a program entitled "The Musical Life of Charlie Parker." From October 23 through November 16, the groups gave fifteen concerts and rotated among six cities, including Warsaw (the Jazz Jamboree), Bucharest, Budapest, and Belgrade. The Charlie Parker program had been put together by Dan Morgenstern and Willis Conover and featured twenty-two musicians, including Dizzy Gillespie, Billy Eckstine, Sonny Stitt, and Charles McPherson. The three-hour program featured one segment where local musicians from each country formed the string section of the band.[90]

The following year, the State Department and Newport sponsored the Charles Mingus Sextet in Hungary and Romania, Sarah Vaughan and Trio in Poland, and the New York Jazz Repertory playing the Louis Armstrong homage program. Mingus had been added to the roster in Bucharest at the encouragement of George Wein, who had visited the city the previous May to meet with U.S. officials and ARIA to discuss jazz programming.[91] U.S. officials in Eastern Europe had considered Wein's 1975 visit a great success; it "has given a new impetus to the selective use of jazz as a controlled program tool."[92] Wein also helped the State Department set up more direct communications with ARIA and other Eastern European agencies, suggesting that in the future the embassies could communicate directly with the local agencies.[93] American officials in Bucharest reported that the Mingus concert was a "great artistic success." Local jazz buffs traveled long distances to hear "one of America's best-known performers and most imaginative composers." But U.S. officials in Romania accused Mingus of attempting to project his political views in song titles: "Other posts should be forewarned that Mingus projects his political views into song titles in a way which could prove to be embarrassing." The solution was to change the titles in the Romanian program book. Mingus, officials explained, didn't speak Romanian and he'd never know.[94]

Festival Productions followed up in 1976 with a Newport program in Romania, Poland, Czechoslovakia, and Portugal. The lineup featured the McCoy Tyner Sextet, the Gil Evans Orchestra, the Muddy Waters Sextet, the Sonny Rollins Quintet, and vocalist Betty Carter and Trio. The festival was praised once again for its ability to deliver a wide range of music, including many artists in the prime of their careers, but it was to be among the last of the Newport–State Department gigs.[95] After 1978, and a decade of a remarkably productive working relationship using commercial pickups out of Western Europe, Wein and Festival Productions never heard from the State Department again. Nor did Festival Productions work with USIS after cultural-presentation tours were officially moved out of the State Department and put under the administration of the United States Information Agency.[96] Wein's success as a jazz impresario in Eastern Europe and Festival Productions' role in nurturing local jazz entrepreneurs had made the company superfluous as a conduit. Like black American music throughout Africa, jazz in Eastern Europe had taken on a life of its own.

The last scheduled State Department jazz tour was by the trumpeter Clark Terry and his Jolly Giants. Terry, a native of St. Louis, had played with Count Basie in the 1940s and with the Duke Ellington Orchestra in the 1950s. While with Basie, Terry had performed with vocalist Joe Williams, who now joined him for the tour, along with Ed Soph on percussion, Chris Woods on saxophone, and Victor Sproles on bass.[97] Terry was deeply involved in jazz education, bringing the "Big Band Movement" into high schools through his music clinics.[98] The tour's itinerary had a remarkable overlap with the first Middle Eastern and Asian tours of Gillespie in 1956 and Dave Brubeck in 1958, serving as an eerie reminder that encircling oil fields and shoring up military alliances was a fundamental and abiding feature of American foreign policy. The impetus for the tour had been the State Department's desire to contribute to the Bombay Jazz Yatra Festival, but the department was able to arrange a number of concerts in short stops en route to the festival. The tour lasted from January 23 through February 26, and began in Cairo and Alexandria. The group then moved through Athens, Istanbul, Ankara, Kabul, Peshawar, Rawalpindi, Lahore, and Karachi, winding up in India. The group spent more than a week at Jazz Yatra, before continuing to Calcutta and New Delhi.[99]

Almost two decades after the tour, Terry was still troubled by the startling juxtaposition of goodwill from audiences and the extraordinarily tense, heavily militarized reception from the Pakistani government. The priority of the American-Pakistan alliance was so overwhelming that Terry felt the U.S. officials "didn't care about music. They just wanted to get rid of us so they could go back to their evil deeds."[100] Yet Terry and his band took advantage of every possible opportunity to play with Pakistani musicians and connect with the Pakistani people. He remembered a serendipitous moment in Karachi, when, just as he started to sing Don Redman's "I Want a Little Girl," a "beautiful little five-year-old Pakistani girl wandered onto the stage, almost as if the act had been prearranged."[101] In Lahore, audiences attended concerts on an "exclusively invitational basis"; for the band, this was a far cry from playing for the people. But Terry put his own stamp on this highly controlled event when, "without prior announcement," he "invited three well-known Pakistani musicians"—a clarinetist, an accordionist, and a tabla player—onstage for an impromptu jam session with the Jolly Giants. "They played a traditional Punjabi number," reported the State Department, "to the beats of American jazz." Terry explained: "I thought it would be quite interesting to these Pakistanis to merge their ethnic musical expressions with an American jazz group (and vice-versa)." The concert was recorded for a fifty- minute TV show which, the State Department reported, would be the first "TV Studio One" program to use English instead of Urdu.[102] Terry was still bothered that "the ordinary townspeople had been excluded from attending our concerts," so on the band's night off in Lahore, they did a "'freebie' for the hotel personnel and the 'common people'" at the Lahore Hilton.[103]

The most striking feature of the tour was the way jazz mediated between many musical traditions. Reporting on Jazz Yatra, Meher Pestonji wrote: "Most jazz musicians emphasize that jazz is not a particular kind of music—rather, it is a way of playing and interpreting any kind of music."[104] In the *Pakistan Times,* Saeed Malik invoked Louis Armstrong's famous reply to a reporter who asked, "What is jazz?" Armstrong had replied: "If they gotta ask, they ain't goin to know." But for Malik, the fact that "this unique American contribution to the arts" has "spread worldwide" was worthy of further analysis. Armstrong's art "has evolved through a creative interchange of ideas among its players." If New Orleans was the "earliest center" of jazz, "today, jazz continues to move along—a deepening and many-sided art—reaching out and 'calling its children home' from all over the world, just as Buddy Bolden used to call them home in New Orleans more than seventy years ago."[105] For

Malik—as for Dizzy Gillespie playing in Brazil, Duke Ellington playing with Astatqé in Ethiopia, and Sonny Rollins and Clark Terry performing at Jazz Yatra—jazz was an international music.

At Jazz Yatra, Terry put together a group called the Festival Big Band for the closing three-and-a-half-hour performance. In his trip diary, published in *Jazz Journal International,* Terry celebrated the internationalization of jazz as he thanked the band: Saxes: Chris Woods, United States; Zbigniew Namyslowski, Poland; Rao Kyao, Portugal; Lennert Aberg, Sweden; Sadao Watanabe, Japan. Trombones: Albert Mangelsdorff, West Germany; Hiroshi Fukumura, Japan; Hannibal Castro, India. Trumpets: Palle Mikkelborg, Denmark; Ian Carr, U.K.; Bosco Monsorate, India; Joe Monsorate, India. Drums: Ed Soph, Texas. Piano: Hilton Ruiz, Puerto Rico. Bass: Victor Sproles, United States. Vocals: Joe Williams, United States; Karm Krog, Norway. For Terry, "when people from ten different countries can get together for three and a half hours and the results turn out to be pure harmony and 'good vibes,' it should prove that the heads of state could learn something from jazz people. You dig!!"[106]

When the jazz tours, along with the rest of cultural presentations programs, were removed from the purview of the State Department in 1978 and put under the auspices of the newly created United States International Communication Agency, an era had come to a close.[107] In part, the relationship between the State Department and jazz was a victim of its own success. The success of jazz in Eastern Europe and Asia, and the deepening commercial viability of jazz and other forms of black diasporic music in Africa, made it far more difficult to advocate for state sponsorship of tours. At the same time, dramatic shifts in American politics—due to the Vietnam War, Watergate, and the energy crisis—were undermining American policymakers' confidence in their ability to shape the world. But part of the reason the era ended lies in the very character of jazz itself. An art form born of transnational upheaval and grounded in innovation and improvisation could not be contained by one nation.

CHAPTER 9

Epilogue

The goodwill ambassadors' understanding of jazz as an international music complicates the characterization of jazz as "America's music"—a label used by Willis Conover and others who have subscribed to the view that jazz won the Cold War. In the State Department tours, jazz did not operate as a "music of freedom," in the sense that jazz is the expression of a free country. Nor did jazz simply herald the American Century, as Frantz Fanon suggested; nor, in a more contemporary formulation, did it act as the "soundtrack of American Empire."[1] Both of these views are limited in their focus on the nation. We need to follow the jazz musicians into a more expansive and global way of thinking.[2] To be sure, musicians such as Louis Armstrong, Dizzy Gillespie, and Duke Ellington embraced the tours as opportunities to make claims on a nation that had long denied them recognition as artists, and human and civil rights as African Americans. But jazz was never solely an expression of the nation. For these musicians, jazz was an international and hybrid music combining not just African and European forms, but forms that had developed out of an earlier mode of cultural exchange, through the circuitous routes of the Atlantic slave trade and the "overlapping diasporas" created by migrations throughout the Americas.[3] And if the U.S. State Department had facilitated the music's transnational routes of innovation and improvisation, for many musicians there was a certain poetic justice in that.

In 1992, during the last year of his life, Dizzy Gillespie flew with Secretary of State James Baker to Namibia to attend ceremonies

honoring Namibian independence. The trumpeter had most recently been touring with his United Nations Orchestra, the latest
incarnation of his commitment to international peace and cooperation and ongoing innovation in jazz. In Namibia, Gillespie met
Nelson Mandela, the anti-apartheid leader who would soon become the first democratically elected president of South Africa.
Mandela told Gillespie how his music had sustained him during his
twenty-six years in prison.[4] The meeting of Gillespie and Mandela,
more than two decades after the height of the jazz tours, speaks to
the power of the international movements of jazz and the abiding
power of a democratic vision with roots in an earlier moment.

Jazz and performing-arts tours continued under a reorganized
USIA after the cultural presentations moved out of the State Department in 1978, but they were not as high-profile, and with the
exception of jazz tours to the Soviet Union, they lacked the ambition and urgency of the earlier tours.[5] They also lacked the sharp
contradictions of the early Cold War years, when the State Department had relied so heavily on African American musicians denied
citizenship in their own country on the basis of race. Though cultural presentations had been radically novel in the 1950s and 1960s,
after the fall of the Soviet Union, as Radio Free Europe constricted
and USIA staff was trimmed nearly in half, they became more rou-
tine and less tied to politics. Since considerably less was at stake,
funding for such programs plummeted.[6]

The jazz ambassadors represented America at a unique historical
juncture. The Cold War, the African American civil rights movement, and the emergence of forty new African and Asian nations
created the context in which the jazz ambassadors projected the
optimism and vitality of black American culture throughout the
globe. Through the tours and through the Voice of America, the
music of the jazz ambassadors reached from Kabul, Leningrad,
Damascus, and Tehran to Baghdad, Bombay, Karachi, Accra, and
Kinshasa. The music even reached into the prisons of apartheid.
For all the contradictions of Cold War liberal internationalism, the
global freedom movements of the post-1945 years helped to forge

an alliance of musicians, supporters of the arts, and liberals in the State Department. Out of an improvised and at times highly chaotic policy, these policymakers and musicians created the egalitarian edge in America's international relations and image. For more than two decades, all over the globe, America was associated with jazz, civil rights, African American culture, and egalitarianism—not because the jazz ambassadors claimed to represent a free country, but because they identified so deeply with global struggles for freedom. Musicians were not simply tools or followers of this policy. In the most fundamental sense, they were cultural translators who inspired the vision and shaped its contours, constituting themselves as international ambassadors by taking on the contradictions of Cold War internationalism. They called for increased government support of the arts; they spoke freely about their struggles for civil rights; and they challenged the State Department's priorities. They asserted their right to "play for the people."

Historians have traced the precipitous ending to the historical moment during which the tours had thrived. The questioning of America's global ambitions in the wake of the Vietnam War yielded to the reassertion of imperial might and a revived Cold War with the Soviet Union under the administration of President Ronald Reagan. But unlike the concern for America's global image that mediated the militarism and brinkmanship of the 1950s, Reagan's empire struck back with barely a rhetorical nod to the civil rights movement and only grudging alliance with African and Asian nations. The U.S. invasion of the black Caribbean nation of Grenada in 1983, and the imposition of IMF–World Bank structural adjustment policies throughout the underdeveloped world, marked a departure in America's relationship with the new nations to which American policymakers had made democratic overtures in the late 1950s and 1960s. Future jazz ambassadors no longer represented an America that, at least rhetorically, addressed African and Asian nations in the language of brotherhood and equality. From the Reagan era onward, American leadership was determined to reassert political and economic hierarchies. And when America finally got its own jazz-playing president in Bill Clinton (forty years after Thailand's King Bhumibol Adulyadej had held nightly jam sessions at the palace), he did not reverse the new directions in economic liberalization and global regulation of trade.

But however distinct the historical moment that gave rise to the jazz ambassadors, the fact that they still represented the potential of America well into the 1990s—for Nelson Mandela and others— speaks to the power of jazz as symbolic of the black struggle for equality. To appreciate the impact and the legacy of the State Department jazz tours, we must return to the abiding power of that vision, recover the sense of democratic possibility embodied by the tours, and distinguish it from a post–Cold War triumphalism that has told a very different story about jazz in that era.

Since the early 1990s, there has been an outpouring of interest— popular as well as scholarly—in the role of "culture" during the Cold War. Paralleling the claims made about Willis Conover's singular role in the U.S. triumph over the Soviet Union, claims that the Cold War was won by "blue jeans and jazz" have become commonplace.[7] The appeal of American consumer culture could be held at bay for only so long (goes the account), and consumer capitalism ultimately triumphed over state socialism. There are grains of truth in this view. Conover *was* important for the internationalization of jazz, and no doubt helped to shape the contours of the Cold War and hastened its collapse. And aspects of American culture were demonstrably attractive, if not seductive, for many of the world's people. But the actual history of the jazz ambassadors and the jazz tours belies the American exceptionalism implicit in this nostalgic notion of the effectiveness of American culture as a Cold War weapon.

The story of jazz and the State Department is not the story of a nation standing apart from and unsullied by the exercise of imperial power. It is the story of an America deeply implicated in the machinations and violence of global modernization: the slave trade that forced millions of Africans to the Americas; the U.S. involvement in coups, in countries ranging from Iran and Iraq to the Congo and

Ghana; and the arming of such military states as Pakistan. These events set the context for the tours. The account of the relationship between jazz and the State Department reveals a Janus-faced power, at once unprecedented in its world-ordering ambitions and, in the words of the historian Michael H. Hunt, "too self-absorbed even to grasp the dimensions of those gargantuan ambitions."[8] The view that culture was decisive in winning the Cold War assumes an illusory separation of the categories "culture" and "militarism." But tracing the steps of the jazz ambassadors forces us to contend with the tangled relations between culture and the military. Not only were artists deployed in proximity to covert and overt military campaigns; but in the broader sense of "culture" as structures of feeling and material life, this separation of the cultural from the military ignores the extent to which the awesome material affluence of the United States in the post-1945 era was dependent on the domination of global resources. And in the face of persistent attempts on the part of formerly colonized peoples to reclaim control of their resources, U.S. domination of resources abroad was, in turn, necessarily dependent on militarism.[9]

As we travel with Louis Armstrong, Alvin Ailey, and Buddy Guy to the Congo or with Dave Brubeck and Duke Ellington to Iraq, the jazz tours take us into foreign policy crises. As the Brubecks so astutely pointed out in *The Real Ambassadors,* "No commodity is quite so strange / As this thing called cultural exchange." One thing that was so strange about cultural exchange was that it traced the geographic patterns of those quintessential Cold War commodities oil and uranium, along with many others critical to America's material abundance—the wealth that was so seductive for overseas audiences.[10] The jazz ambassadors were not privy to these highly opaque and often covert political and economic agendas. Nor, as Americans, were they entirely innocent of them. But there is no doubt what side most of the musicians were on. From Gillespie's demand that the "ragamuffin" children be allowed into his concerts, to the surreptitious meetings of members of Benny Goodman's band with Soviet jazz fans, to Randy Weston's insistence on wearing dashikis in West Africa as a symbol of modern African diasporic solidarity, the jazz ambassadors sided with the forces of change and innovation and created new ways of supporting movements for equality and liberation wherever they went.

By suggesting that the United States prevailed through the example of material success and democratic values, historians downplay the fundamental conflicts within the United States, suggesting that a shared, core adherence to material abundance ultimately transcended differences. Yet the story of the cultural-presentations programs shows that there were often pronounced disparities between the aims of artists and those of government officials, and between their respective views of American culture. Indeed, the export of America's conflicts and fissures was critical to the success of cultural exchange. It was often the oppositional elements in American culture—particularly those in African American culture—that proved appealing to groups in various parts of the globe.[11] If jazz fostered an anti-Communist counterculture in the Eastern bloc, elevating musicians such as Duke Ellington and Ornette Coleman to symbols of international rebellion, it was a counterculture that identified as much with black oppositional culture as with the government's ideas of democracy. In Africa and its diaspora, this dynamic was perhaps even more pronounced as jazz, soul, and R&B connected with emerging African popular forms, which in turn inspired American musicians.

While the performing-arts tours accompanied America's post–World War II pursuit of political and economic control through policies of modernization and development, control over the export of culture remained elusive. The State Department failed to anticipate that people would interact in unforeseen ways—that artists would bring their own perceptions, agendas, and aspirations to the tours and become transformed in the process. The role of cultural ambassador lent the musicians, who had previously been circumscribed by racial prejudice in Jim Crow America, an unprecedented authority to speak and act as political subjects. In an ongoing battle over the politics of representation, Armstrong, Gillespie,

Ellington, Ailey, and their allies used the State Department jazz tours as a global platform from which to promote the dignity of black people and their culture in the United States and abroad.

What began as a somewhat accidental harmony of interests among cultural entrepreneurs, U.S. government officials, musicians, and civil rights activists took on cultural, economic, and political dimensions the State Department had never imagined. For the State Department, the tours were a legitimizing and humanizing force, attempting through the affective power of music to make critics of U.S. policy identify with America independently of American policies. But this exported vision of America was often as contested and embattled within America as the nation it attempted to represent, as the more spiritual vision of America—represented by artists ranging from Armstrong to Mahalia Jackson—vied with consumerism as a Cold War weapon abroad. The battles over representation as well as the relationships forged through the tours point to ways in which the dynamic realities of cultural production were not so easily amenable to the objectives of the state's Cold War agenda.

Intended as a color-blind promotion of American democracy, the tours underscored the importance of African American culture in the Cold War redefinition of America. At that awkward moment of racial upheaval within the United States, blackness and race operated culturally to redefine an image of American nationhood more inclusive and integrated than the reality. Yet the promotion of American culture abroad led just as often to the fostering of collaboration and solidarity throughout the African diaspora. The tours, designed to showcase American art, freedom, and democracy as unique and exceptional, also served to promote diasporic and transnational relationships. As the government recognized the power of African American culture and tried to harness it to project an image of U.S. racial progress abroad, the State Department's cultural programs and tours in fact helped to nurture the development of oppositional transnational and Afro-diasporic sensibilities. From Gillespie's meeting with the pianist Lalo Schifrin in Buenos

Aires, to Brubeck's incorporation of the sitar sounds of Abdul Jafar Khan during his tour in Bombay, to Ellington's collaboration with Ethiopian jazz-fusionist Mulatu Astatqé, African American artists and musicians used their status as goodwill ambassadors to establish relationships with musicians in Africa and the Third World. The tours took artists to places that would have been beyond reach without government sponsorship, and enabled transnational musical crossings and collaborations. They acted as a catalyst for the internationalization of jazz. And as tours sent R&B artists throughout Africa and put blues artist B. B. King on a stage in Lagos with Nigerian superstar Fela Kuti, they helped to transform popular music.

In considering the legacies of the jazz ambassadors, let's remember Clark Terry's observation that heads of state could learn something from jazz musicians. In early 2002, in the wake of the terrorist attacks on the World Trade Center and the Pentagon, responsibility for cultural affairs was moved back to the State Department. While it may be premature to pass judgment, the government's recent efforts—the hiring of corporate advertisers to craft images of contented Arab Americans, the attempt to capitalize on the popularity of Britney Spears in Iran to build support for American foreign policy—suggest, at the very least, a lack of awareness about the history of culture and foreign policy.

For decades, Louis Armstrong, Dizzy Gillespie, Duke Ellington, Dave Brubeck, Phil Woods, and other jazz musicians represented America for people around the world. The jazz ambassadors projected the opposite of the arrogance and belligerence that many in the world had come to associate with U.S. foreign policy since the Vietnam War. Audiences throughout the world fell in love with the jazz ambassadors for their brilliant creativity, their irreverence, and their wit, and for the all of ways in which they voiced their affinities with peoples struggling for freedom in Africa, Asia, the Middle East, the Soviet Union, and Eastern Europe. If there is anything that can be learned from the tours, it is that audiences never confused or conflated their love of jazz and American popular culture with an acceptance of American foreign policy.

Today, the American nation is represented abroad by McDonalds, *Baywatch,* Nike, Microsoft, and Britney Spears. It is impossible to translate the singular appeal of a Duke Ellington or a Louis Armstrong into the market-manufactured celebrity of the early twenty-first century. But the shift from state sponsorship of the jazz ambassadors to predominantly market-driven and corporate images is striking. The reductive logic of the market—which makes *Baywatch* the most popular American television program in the Middle East simply because the segments cost less than most other available shows—reminds us of what is lost when a potentially democratically accountable government does not assume an active role in supporting the arts and promoting its culture abroad.[12]

Moreover, the decline in government support for the arts does not mean that policymakers or their corporate counterparts in the American-dominated global political economy have given up on attempts to manage and contain the meanings of blackness. The indispensable role of Colin Powell's global tours on behalf of the Bush administration suggests that U.S. officials continue to depend on blackness to legitimate global agendas, even as they have reverted to an empty politics of racial symbolism, devoid of any relation to the vibrant egalitarian movements that animated the jazz tours of the 1960s. In the 1950s and 1960s tours, the unprecedented global scope of the government sponsorship of the arts enabled the musicians to travel, perform, and collaborate independent of the competitive logic of commodity capitalism and even state control. If cultural exchange was a strange commodity, what happens when "blackness" becomes a commodity in and of itself, abstracted from movements for justice or the creative endeavors and negotiations of actual black people? In the State Department jazz tours, artists moved in a liminal space, overlapping with but not bounded or defined by the market or the state. As musicians struggled over representations of blackness, they redefined the nation and illuminated the creative possibilities of transnational subjectivities. By the late twentieth century, blackness was circulating as a global commodity, via the bodies of athletes and other celebrities who not only were selling their images to multinational corporations for fees unimaginable to even the most commercially successful jazz artists, but were allowing their very lives to be scripted by such global conglomerates.[13]

Funding of the arts during the Cold War was always contested, often bitterly. Large segments of American society never accepted the idea that government should support culture in any form, and there was particular objection to African American and modernist content. But out of the conflicting agendas and political exigencies of Cold War America, artists, State Department personnel, and supporters of the arts crafted programs that related to the world through a wide cross-section of America, including its most creative artists. The jazz ambassadors represented hope and possibility, not a smug claim to a perfected democracy. They articulated their connection to the world as artists and humans, not a sense of uniqueness or superiority. While a jazz combo may not have been a model for a government, it did symbolize the qualities of a vibrant democracy. The jazz artists expressed individual excellence within a profound dependence on and accountability to a collective. Their improvisatory techniques and openness to new musics celebrated the unexpected, and hence the possibilities of democracy and global citizenship rather than the scripted power of empire. As representatives of a nation, they did not simply sing its praises or soberly acknowledge its faults. They criticized its inequities, laughed at its foibles, and made fun of its pretensions. They spoke to the world through their instruments and with their voices in the language of connection and equality. The jazz ambassadors, many of whom were black Americans born during the consolidation of Jim Crow segregation, were not simply handed roles as international statesmen. Faced with daunting structures of power, they saw contradictions and new possibilities, just as they bent notes and altered melodies to create new sounds. Invited onto the margins of diplomacy, they refused to stay on the fringes as sidemen. They slipped into the cracks and looked around. They found modernity where official narratives said it couldn't exist—in places ranging from the cafés of Kabul and Baghdad to the clubs of Accra and Kinshasa.

Citizens of the twenty-first century cannot afford to ignore the example of the jazz ambassadors. We may no longer have the option of voting for the late John Birks Gillespie for president, but we can recognize the importance of the creativity of musicians, poets, and artists in crafting humane and just relationships to the world. We can remember Dave Brubeck's observation that sending a jazz combo abroad costs a great deal less than the tip of a fighter plane's wing. We can demand democratic accountability, the way Louis Armstrong demanded that Eisenhower enforce the law in Little Rock. Following the musicians, we can demand a jazz approach to foreign policy. They were the Real Ambassadors.

Notes

Acknowledgments

Index

Notes

1. Ike Gets Dizzy

1. The Gillespie tour was approved by the Inter-Agency Committee (after submission by the International Cultural Exchange Service, a branch of the American National Theatre and Academy, or ANTA) on December 15, 1955, with funding of $92,500. Memo to International Educational Exchange Service from Robert C. Schnitzer (ANTA), "Progress Report No. 22" (January 10, 1956). Series 1, General and Historical Files, Box 1, Bureau of Educational and Cultural Affairs Historical Collection, J. William Fulbright Papers, University of Arkansas at Fayetteville. Hereafter cited as Bureau Historical Collection. The main records of the individual tours are filed under Series 2, Performing Arts, Subseries 1, Performers, by the name of the performer or group, and in Series 5, Committees and Panels for the Performing Arts. Box 9 contains the Final Evaluation Reports and the Performance Records.

2. Whitney Balliett, *Dinosaurs in the Morning* (London: Phoenix House, 1962), 21; quoted in Alyn Shipton, *Groovin' High: The Life of Dizzy Gillespie* (New York: Oxford University Press, 1999), 145.

3. Thomas Borstelmann, *The Cold War and the Color Line: American Race Relations in the Global Arena* (Cambridge, Mass.: Harvard University Press, 2001), 86.

4. Ibid., 87–88.

5. On the political context and contours of these propaganda efforts, see Penny M. Von Eschen, *Race against Empire: Black Americans and Anticolonialism, 1937–1957* (Ithaca: Cornell University Press, 1997). On the context for the jazz tours, see 177–181. For an early essay on this project, see Penny M. Von Eschen, "Satchmo Blows Up the World: Jazz, Race, and Empire during the Cold War," in Reinhold Wagnleitner and Elaine Tyler May, eds., *Here, There, and Everywhere: The Foreign Politics of American Popular Culture* (Hanover, N.H.: University Press of New England, 2000), 163–178. Mary L.

Dudziak explores related issues in "Josephine Baker, Racial Protest, and the Cold War," *Journal of American History* (September 1994), 543–570; and idem, *Cold War Civil Rights: Race and the Image of American Democracy* (Princeton: Princeton University Press, 2000). See also Ingrid Monson, *Freedom Sounds: Jazz, Civil Rights, and Africa* (New York: Oxford University Press, forthcoming).

6. President Dwight D. Eisenhower to the President of the Senate, Estimate No. 82, 83rd Congress, 2nd Session (July 27, 1954). Bureau Historical Collection.

7. Quoted in Frank Ninkovich, "U.S. Information Policy and Cultural Diplomacy," *Foreign Policy Association: Headline Series,* 308 (1996), 24.

8. Marie Ellen Noonan, "Porgy and Bess and the American Racial Imaginary, 1925–1985," Ph.D. dissertation, Department of History, New York University (2002), 178–249.

9. Borstelmann, *The Cold War and the Color Line,* ch. 3.

10. President Dwight Eisenhower to Secretary of State John Foster Dulles, August 18, 1954, Department of State, 511.0018-1854.

11. Richard Immerman, ed., *John Foster Dulles and the Diplomacy of the Cold War* (Princeton: Princeton University Press, 1990); Derek Leebaert, *The Fifty-Year Wound: The True Price of America's Cold War Victory* (Boston: Little, Brown, 2002).

12. This was Public Law 860. Department of State Instruction 663, No. CA-265, July 9, 1959: Memo to All Diplomatic and Consular Posts, on the subject "Cultural Presentations: President's Programs—Program Guide," Series 1, General and Historical Files, Box 1, Bureau Historical Collection. See also Anonymous, "U.S. Helps Out: Bill Passed to Make Cultural Tours a Branch of Our Foreign Policy," *New York Times* (August 5, 1956), 7.

13. See Advisory Committee on the Arts, Department of State, Washington, D.C., Minutes of Meeting, May 10, 1963, attachment, Department of State, Bureau of Educational and Cultural Affairs, "Jazz in the Cultural Programs," Series 5, Box 7, Folder 4.

14. Anonymous, "Remote Lands to Hear Old Democracy Boogie," *New York Times* (November 18, 1955), 16.

15. Ibid. On Powell at Bandung, see Von Eschen, *Race against Empire,* 170–171.

16. Paul Gordon Lauren, *Power and Prejudice: The Politics and Diplomacy of Racial Discrimination* (Boulder, Colo.: Westview, 1988); Thomas Borstelmann, *Apartheid's Reluctant Uncle: The United States and Southern Africa in the Early Cold War* (New York: Oxford University Press, 1993); Brenda Gayle Plummer, *Rising Wind: Black Americans and U.S. Foreign Affairs, 1935–1960* (Chapel Hill: University of North Carolina Press, 1996); Von Eschen, *Race against Empire;* Borstelmann, *The Cold War and the Color Line.*

17. See Borstelmann, *The Cold War and the Color Line,* 101–102, for a succinct discussion of the Eisenhower administration's pragmatic approach to non-alignment. For discussions which challenge a bipolar reading of the Cold War, see also Chris Appy, ed., *Cold War Constructions: The Political Culture of United States Imperialism, 1945–1966* (Amherst: University of Massachusetts Press, 2000); Irene L. Gendzier, "Play It Again, Sam: The Practice and Apology of Development," in Christopher Simpson ed., *Universities and Empire: Money and Politics in the Social Sciences during the Cold War* (New York: New Press, 1998); Bruce Cummings, *Parallax Visions: Making Sense of American–East Asian Relations at the End of the Century* (Durham: Duke University Press, 1999.)

18. Penny M. Von Eschen, "Challenging Cold War Habits: African Americans, Race, and Foreign Policy," *Diplomatic History,* 20, no. 4 (Fall 1996), 628–629; Borstelmann, *The Cold War and the Color Line;* Lauren, *Power and Prejudice.*

19. Nikhil Pal Singh, *Black Is a Country: Race and the Unfinished Struggle for Democracy* (Cambridge, Mass.: Harvard University Press, 2004) 000.

20. Brent Edwards has argued that developments in Paris cannot be understood as a parallel to or a version of the Harlem Renaissance; rather, they provided an alternative site that affected developments in Harlem in turn. Brent Hayes Edwards, *The Practice of Diaspora: Literature, Translation, and the Rise of Black Internationalism* (Cambridge, Mass.: Harvard University Press, 2003); William A. Shack, *Harlem in Montmartre: A Paris Jazz Story between the Great Wars* (Berkeley: University of California Press, 2001), xvi–xvii

21. There is a rapidly growing body of work on the cultural exchanges of that period. See Frank Ninkovich, *The Diplomacy of Ideas: U.S. Foreign Policy and Cultural Relations, 1938–1950* (Cambridge: Cambridge University Press, 1981). On the export of American culture abroad, see Robert A. Haddow, *Pavilions of Plenty: Exhibiting American Culture Abroad in the 1950s* (Washington, D.C.: Smithsonian Institution Press, 1997); Walter Hixson, *Parting the Curtain: Propaganda, Culture, and the Cold War, 1945–1961* (New York: St. Martin's, 1997); Frances Stonor Saunders, *The Cultural Cold War: The CIA and the World of Arts and Letters* (New York: New Press, 1999); David Caute, *The Dancer Defects: The Struggle for Cultural Supremacy during the Cold War* (Oxford: Oxford University Press, 2003); Eric J. Sandeen, *Picturing an Exhibition: The Family of Man and 1950s America* (Albuquerque: University of New Mexico Press, 1995). For an excellent exploration of U.S. Cold War cultural programs in a European context, see Reinhold Wagnleitner, *Coca-Colonization and the Cold War: The Cultural Mission of the United States in Austria after the Second World War* (Chapel Hill: University of North Carolina Press, 1994); on jazz, see 201–215. See also Reinhold Wagnleitner, "The Empire of Fun, or Talkin' Soviet Union Blues: The Sound of Freedom and

U.S. Cultural Hegemony in Europe," *Diplomatic History,* 23, no. 3 (Summer 1999), 499–524; Elizabeth Vihlen, "Jammin on the Champs-Elysées: Jazz, France, and the 1950s," in Wagnleitner and May, *Here, There and Everywhere,* 149–162.

22. Leonard Feather, *The Jazz Years: Eyewitness to an Era* (New York: Da Capo Press, 1987), 6–7.

23. Catherine Benamou, *It's All True: Orson Welles at Work in Latin America* (Berkeley: University of California Press, forthcoming), 193, manuscript. See also Michael Zwerin, *La Tristesse de Saint Louis: Jazz under the Nazis* (New York: William Morrow, 1985).

24. Feather, *The Jazz Years,* 10.

25. Ibid., 8.

26. Anonymous, "This Trumpet Madness," *Newsweek* (December 19, 1955).

27. Felix Belair, *New York Times* (November 6, 1955), 1.

28. Ibid.

29. Anonymous, "This Trumpet Madness."

30. Ingrid Monson, "The Problem with White Hipness: Race, Gender, and Cultural Conceptions in Jazz Discourse," *Journal of the American Musicological Society,* 48, no. 3 (Fall 1995), 396–422. See also Eric Porter, *What Is This Thing Called Jazz? African American Musicians as Artists, Critics, and Activists* (Berkeley: University of California Press, 2002), 91–93.

31. Anonymous, "This Trumpet Madness."

32. Arvell Shaw, interview with Penny Von Eschen and Kevin Gaines, New Orleans (August 4, 2001).

33. Ibid.

34. Ironically, Armstrong was often too busy and too expensive for the State Department to book. With the important exception of his 1960–1961 tour through the African continent Armstrong did not tour officially for the U.S. Department of State. See Chapter 3 on his African visits and on his other unofficial trips as ambassador. See Chapter 4 on government and press discussions about sending Armstrong to the Soviet Union.

35. Robert G. O'Meally discusses how to read the paradoxes in jazz and its relationship to the nation. See O'Meally, ed., *The Jazz Cadence of American Culture* (New York: Columbia University Press, 1998), 177–199 (introduction to Part 2).

36. Robert McC. Thomas Jr., "Willis Conover, 75, Voice of America Disc Jockey," *New York Times* (May 19, 1996), 35.

37. Anonymous, "Jazz around the World," *Time* (June 25, 1956); Anonymous, "Big Jazz behind the Iron Curtain," *Look,* 26 (November 20, 1962); Anonymous, "U.S. Disk Jockey a World-Wide Hit: Voice Broadcaster Ends a Visit to Some of His 30 Million Fans Abroad," *New York Times* (Sunday, June 26, 1960).

38. Anonymous, "Big Jazz behind the Iron Curtain."

39. Anonymous, "World Jazz Fans Rocked by Voice," *New York Times* (Sunday, November 13, 1955).

40. Anonymous, "Jazz around the World."

41. On radio distribution, see USIA, Office of Research and Special Reports, 1953–63, RG306.

42. "Jazz around the World," 52; Hixson, *Parting the Curtain,* 227; June Bundy, "Jazz Jargon to Cats behind Iron Curtain," *Billboard* (March 23, 1957), 1–3.

43. William F. Ryan, "Willis Conover: Nightspots of Washington and the World—The Seismic Jazz Underground," *Virginia Country,* 14, no. 1 (1989), 68. See also Lawrence Elliot, "The World's Favorite American," *Readers Digest* (July 1985), 94.

44. Anonymous, "Who Is Conover? Only We Ask," *New York Times Magazine* (September 13, 1959). For a fascinating contemporary discussion of the relationship between jazz and democracy, see Stanley Crouch, "Blues To Be Constitutional: A Long Look at the Wild Wherefores of Our Democratic Lives as Symbolized in the Making of Rhythm and Tune," 154–165, in O'Meally, *The Jazz Cadence of American Culture.* See also ibid., 117–119 (O'Meally's introduction to Part 2).

45. Serge Guilbaut, *How New York Stole the Idea of Modern Art: Abstract Expressionism, Freedom, and the Cold War* (Chicago: University of Chicago Press, 1983).

46. Saunders, *The Cultural Cold War,* 256–257.

47. Ibid.

48. Burt Korall, "Jazz Speaks Many Tongues, Vaults National Barriers: Wider Jazz Market a By-Product of American Diplomatic Policy," *Billboard* (August 19, 1957), 1.

49. The scholar Townsend Ludington has noted that the definition of "modernism" has become an industry over the past several decades. The story of the jazz tours illuminates the shifting debates and investments in the term among multiple actors in Cold War America and is especially relevant for exploring the racial constructions and international contours of the debates about modernism in this period. See Townsend Ludington, ed., *A Modern Mosaic: Art and Modernism in the United States* (Chapel Hill: University of North Carolina Press, 2000), 1–11.

50. U.S. House of Representatives, Hearings before the Subcommittee on Appropriations, Supplemental Appropriations Bill, President's Special International Program, 84th Congress, 2nd Session, Part 2 (Washington, D.C.: GPO, 1957), 747. Thompson coauthor with Senator Hubert Humphrey of the legislation (Public Law 860, 84th Congress) that made what began as the President's Emergency Fund into a permanent program.

51. Along with their sharp distinction between art and entertainment, critics

on the selection committees rejected any association with United Service Organization (USO) tours, which functioned to entertain the U.S. Armed Forces. On swing and USO tours during World War II, see Sherrie Tucker, *Swing Shift: All-Girl Bands of the 1940s* (Durham: Duke University Press, 2000), 227–258; and David W. Stowe, *Swing Changes: Big-Band Jazz in New Deal America* (Cambridge, Mass.: Harvard University Press, 1994), 148–150, 157, 159.

52. See Singh, *Black Is a Country,* 54–57, for a related discussion.

53. Paul Gilroy, *The Black Atlantic: Modernity and Double Consciousness* (Cambridge, Mass.: Harvard University Press, 1993). My thinking on the practices of the black diaspora has also been especially influenced by Robin D. G. Kelley in a great many works; see, most recently, Kelley, *Freedom Dreams: The Black Radical Imagination* (Boston: Beacon Press, 2002. See also Edwards, *The Practice of Diaspora;* Samuel A. Floyd, Jr., *The Power of Black Music: Interpreting Its History from Africa to the United States* (Oxford: Oxford University Press, 1995); Earl Lewis, "To Turn on a Pivot: Writing African Americans into a History of Overlapping Diasporas," in Darlene Clark Hine and Jacqueline McLeod, eds., *Crossing Boundaries: Comparative History of Black People in Diaspora* (Bloomington: Indiana University Press, 1999), 3–32.

54. Certainly, all these variations of the term "modern" mean very different things and refer to radically different processes. Yet I would suggest that modernity was the ideology of the U.S. government's post-1945 hegemonic project and argue that the project worked precisely through the slippages in the meanings and uses of these terms. My attempts to read the post-1945 period through a lens that challenges modernist dichotomies between culture and political economy have been influenced by Lisa Lowe and David Lloyd, "Introduction," in Lowe and Lloyd, eds., *The Politics of Culture in the Shadow of Capital* (Durham: Duke University Press, 1997), 1–32.

55. On this last point, see Kevin Gaines, "Duke Ellington: Black, Brown, and Beige and Cultural Politics during the 1940s," in Ronald Radano, ed., *Music and the Racial Imagination* (Chicago: University of Chicago Press, 2001).

56. "Cultural Presentations: List of Attractions—Newport Jazz Artists," October 24–November 11, 1975, Bureau Historical Collection.

57. Valerie Wilmer, *As Serious as Your Life: The Story of the New Jazz* (Westport, Conn.: L. Hill, 1977), 205; Porter, *What Is This Thing Called Jazz?* 82.

58. Dan Morgenstern, liner notes to Mary Lou Williams' *Trio Zodiac Suite,* LP, no. FTS-32844 (Folkways Record and Service Corp., 1975).

59. Music Advisory Panel (1958), Series 5, Box 12, Folders 10–11, Bureau Historical Collection.

60. James C. Hall, "Jazz, Gender, and the Cold War: Mary Lou Williams' Cultural Critique," paper presented at the annual meeting of the American Studies Association, Kansas City, 1996. Hall has emphasized the double standard at work in the critics' treatment of Williams.

61. Naima Prevots, *Dance for Export: Cultural Diplomacy and the Cold War* (Hanover, N.H.: University Press of New England, 1998), 102–104.

62. Ninkovich, *The Diplomacy of Ideas,* discusses the strong opposition to the involvement of government and culture. See also the excellent introduction to Haddow, *Pavilions of Plenty,* 1–17. For related discussions of the politics of modernism in this era, see Randy Martin, "Modern Dance and the American Century," and Casey Nelson Blake, "Between Civics and Politics: The Modernist Moment in Federal Public Art," both in Ludington, ed., *A Modern Mosaic.*

63. Wagnleitner, *Coca-Colonization,* 4–5.

64. Michael Denning, *The Cultural Front* (London: Verso, 1997); Ellen Graff, *Stepping Left: Dance and Politics in New York City, 1928–1942* (Durham: Duke University Press, 1997); and Benamou, *It's All True.*

65. Saunders, *The Cultural Cold War,* 256–257.

66. Ibid., 257, 268. David Caute has recently argued that Frances Stonor Saunders and other scholars have "exaggerated" the role of abstract expressionism "as an instrument of Pax Americana" (Caute, *The Dancer Defects,* 539–551). According to Caute, scholars have been misled by the excessive attention given to the pronouncements of critics, and the relative lack of attention to what got hung on the walls in the itinerant exhibitions. Without venturing into the dispute about the specific relationship between the CIA and the Museum of Modern Art (MOMA), I would note that both works resonate most closely with this study of the jazz tours when they emphasize the highly contested nature of government support of the arts. Frances Stonor Saunders believes that support of the arts went underground precisely because it met with so much opposition from members of Congress and the American public. And there is no disputing the array of purportedly independent and private cultural projects that were funded (which is not to suggest controlled) by the CIA. At the same time, Caute's emphasis on MOMA's 1950s exports as a mixed bag resulting from "political nervousness, compromise, and continual vigilante howling" illuminates dynamics very similar to those shaping jazz and other cultural-presentations tours. Both David Caute and Frances Stonor Saunders, however, remain focused on Europe, whereas the story of the jazz tours takes us into the heart of the U.S. post-1945 confrontation with Middle Eastern, African, and Asian nations emerging from decades of colonialism—regions in which, I would

suggest, the shifting relationships of race, nation, and modernity were most dynamic.

67. Graff, *Stepping Left.*

68. Von Eschen, *Race against Empire,* 104.

69. Ralph Ellison, *Invisible Man,* 2nd international ed. (New York: Vintage, 1995), 8.

70. For an astute critique of the ideology of development, see Gendzier, "Play It Again, Sam."

71. Anonymous, "White Council vs. Rock and Roll," *Newsweek* (April 23, 1956). On Southern resistance to rock and roll, see Brian Ward, *Just My Soul Responding: Rhythm and Blues, Black Consciousness, and Race Relations* (Berkeley: University of California Press, 1998).

72. Though Eisenhower certainly adapted to the new world far better than other Southerners, such as his segregationist ally Senator Allen J. Ellender of Louisiana, it was not a change he had sought or welcomed. See U.S. House of Representatives, Hearings before the Subcommittee on Appropriations, Supplemental Appropriations Bill, President's Special International Program, 84th Congress, 2nd Session, Part 2 (Washington, D.C.: GPO, 1957), 675–762. For a related discussion of congressional and conservative opposition to State Department support of abstract expressionism, see Jane De Hart Matthews, "Art and Politics in Cold War America," *American Historical Review,* 81 (1976), 762–787. See also Guilbaut, *How New York Stole the Idea of Modern Art.*

2. Swinging into Action

1. See Christina Klein's elegant discussion of what she calls the "global imaginary of integration." Klein, *Cold War Orientalism: Asia in the Middlebrow Imagination, 1945–1961* (Berkeley: University of California Press, 2003), 19–60.

2. Klein, *Cold War Orientalism;* Nikhil Pal Singh, *Black Is a Country: Race and the Unfinished Struggle for Democracy* (Cambridge, Mass.: Harvard University Press, 2004).

3. Melanie McAlister, *Epic Encounters: Culture, Media and U.S. Interests in the Middle East, 1945–2000* ((Berkeley: University of California Press, 2001), 43–55.

4. See Bruce Cumings, "The Wicked Witch of the West Is Dead: Long Live the Wicked Witch of the East," in Michael J. Hogan, ed., *The End of the Cold War: Its Meanings and Implications* (New York: Cambridge University Press, 1992), 87–101; and Walter LaFeber, "An End to Which Cold War?" also in Hogan, *The End of the Cold War,* 13–19.

5. Quoted in Derek Leebaert, *The Fifty-Year Wound: The True Price of America's Cold War Victory* (Boston: Little, Brown, 2002), 206. While I disagree with many of the political assumptions and analytic perspectives presented by Leebaert, his meticulous study on the cost of America's extensive Cold War engagements is an important contribution.

6. Ibid. See also Audrey R. Kahin and George McT. Kahin, *Subversion as Foreign Policy: The Secret Eisenhower and Dulles Debacle in Indonesia* (New York: New Press, 1995); Robert J. McMahon, *Colonialism and the Cold War: The United States and the Struggle for Indonesian Independence, 1945–1949* (Ithaca, N.Y.: Cornell University Press, 1981).

7. Thomas Borstelmann, *The Cold War and the Color Line: American Race Relations in the Global Arena* (Cambridge, Mass.: Harvard University Press, 2001); Michael H. Hunt, *Ideology and U.S. Foreign Policy* (New Haven: Yale University Press, 1987).

8. Sherrie Tucker, *Swing Shift: "All-Girl" Bands of the 1940s* (Durham: Duke University Press), 2000; Ingrid Monson, *Freedom Sounds: Jazz, Civil Rights, and Africa* (New York: Oxford University Press, forthcoming).

9. Van Gosse has examined the ways in which a masculine culture of adventurism helped to shape oppositional culture and movements, as well as mainstream America; see Gosse, *Where the Boys Are: Cuba, Cold War America and the Making of a New Left* (London: Verso, 1993). Numerous scholars have explored issues of gender and the Cold War. See, for example, Elaine Tyler May, *Homeward Bound: American Families in the Cold War Era* (New York: Basic Books, 1988); and Jane Sherron De Hart, "Containment at Home: Gender, Sexuality, and National Identity in Cold War America," in Peter J. Kuznick and James Gilbert, ed., *Rethinking Cold War Culture* (Washington D.C.: Smithsonian Institution Press, 2001). On another version of Cold War adventurism, see Elizabeth Hoffman, *All You Need Is Love: The Peace Corps and the Spirit of the 1960s* (Cambridge, Mass.: Harvard University Press, 1998).

10. Casey Nelson Blake, "Between Civics and Politics: The Modernist Moment in Federal Public Art," in Townsend Ludington, ed., *A Modern Mosaic: Art and Modernism in the United States* (Chapel Hill: University of North Carolina Press, 2000), 256–278. For a discussion of the political contours of modernism in this period, see Randy Martin, "Modern Dance and the American Century," in Ludington, *A Modern Mosaic,* 203–226.

11. Phil Woods, "Life in E Flat," unpublished manuscript, ch. 7, "Dizzy Atmosphere," 162, 171.

12. John Foran, "Discursive Subversions: *Time* Magazine, the CIA Overthrow of Musaddiq, and the Installation of the Shah," in Chris Appy, ed., *The Political Culture of American Imperialism, 1945–1966* (Amherst: University of Mas-

sachusetts Press, 2000); David S. Painter, *Oil and the American Century: The Political Economy of U.S. Foreign Oil Policy, 1941–1954* (Baltimore: Johns Hopkins University Press, 1986).

13. For overviews and regionally specific discussions of the Cold War, see Melvyn P. Leffler, *A Preponderance of Power* (Stanford: Stanford University Press, 1992); and Melvyn P. Leffler and David S. Painter, eds., *Origins of the Cold War: An International History* (London: Routledge, 1994).

14. Douglas Little, *American Orientalism: The United States and the Middle East since 1945* (Chapel Hill: University of North Carolina Press, 2002), 128–129.

15. Anonymous, "Dizzy to Rock India: Gillespie and Jazz Group to Tour East and Balkans," *New York Times* (February 2, 1956), 19.

16. William Roger Louis, "Dulles, Suez and the British," in Richard Immerman, ed., *John Foster Dulles and the Diplomacy of the Cold War* (Princeton: Princeton University Press, 1990), 134–135.

17. Borstelmann, *The Cold War and the Color Line,* 113.

18. Louis, "Dulles, Suez and the British," 134–135.

19. Borstelmann, *The Cold War and the Color Line,* 102.

20. On Indian criticisms of U.S. racism and the U.S. response to these critiques, see Mary L. Dudziak, *Cold War Civil Rights: Race and the Image of American Democracy* (Princeton: Princeton University Press, 2000), 33–34, 104–105.

21. Bureau Historical Collection, Series 5, Box 9, file, Performers G–P. For African American coverage of the tour, see Penny M. Von Eschen, *Race against Empire: Black Americans and Anticolonialism, 1937–1957* (Ithaca: Cornell University Press, 1997).

22. Quoted in Anonymous, "Indians Dizzy over Gillespie's Jazz," *Pittsburgh Courier* (June 9, 1956).

23. Leonard Feather, "Norman Granz: Millionaire," *Esquire* (January 1957), 100. See also Anonymous, "Dizzy Gillespie a Hit with Middle East Cats on U.S. Goodwill Tour," *Variety* (April 25, 1956), 61.

24. Anonymous, "Gillespie's Band a Hit in Beirut: American Jazz, Sponsored by State Department, Packs the Middle Eastern Halls," *New York Times* (Sunday, April 29, 1956), 124.

25. Marshall Stearns, *The Story of Jazz* (Oxford: Oxford University Press, 1956).

26. John Gennari, "Swinging in a High-Class Groove: Mainstreaming Jazz in Lenox and Newport," in Gennari, *Canonizing Jazz: An American Art and Its Critics* (Chicago: University of Chicago Press, forthcoming).

27. Quoted ibid., 5, 17.

28. Dizzy Gillespie with Ralph Ginzburg, "Jazz Is Too Good for Americans," *Esquire* (June 1957), 55. The United States Information Service (USIS) is the name for the field offices of the United States Information Agency (USIA), a Washington-based government agency.

29. Anonymous, "Dizzy Urges Ike to Back Jazz Tours," *Pittsburgh Courier* (August 4, 1956), 21.

30. Music Advisory Panel meetings (April 24, 1956; June 12, 1956). Bureau of Educational and Cultural Affairs Historical Collection, J. William Fulbright Papers, University of Arkansas at Fayetteville. Hereafter cited as Bureau Historical Collection.

31. Dizzy Gillespie with Al Fraser, *To Be or Not to Bop* (Garden City, N.Y.: Doubleday, 1979), 414.

32. Ibid., 415–418.

33. Marshall W. Stearns, "Is Jazz Good Propaganda? The Dizzy Gillespie Tour," *Saturday Review* (July 14, 1956), 30. See also the *Down Beat* account (June, 27, 1956) which quotes Gillespie: "We're here to play for the people."

34. Alyn Shipton, *Groovin' High: The Life of Dizzy Gillespie* (Oxford: Oxford University Press, 1999), 303; and Eric Porter, *What Is This Thing Called Jazz? African American Musicians as Artists, Critics, and Activists* (Berkeley: University of California Press, 2002), 98.

35. Al Grey, interview with Penny Von Eschen and Kevin Gaines, Austin, Texas (November 9, 1997).

36. Quincy Jones, *Q: The Autobiography of Quincy Jones* (New York: Doubleday, 2001), 112.

37. Ibid.

38. Ibid.

39. Ibid., 114.

40. Burt Korall, "Jazz Speaks Many Tongues, Vaults National Barriers," *Billboard* (August 19, 1957).

41. Jones, *Autobiography,* 113.

42. Marshall W. Stearns, "Dizzy's Troupe Casts Spell over Mid-East Audiences," *Down Beat* (June 13, 1956).

43. Marshall Stearns, "Turkey Resounds, Reacts to Dizzy Gillespie Band," *Down Beat* (June 26, 1956).

44. Jones, *Autobiography,* 116.

45. Stearns, "Turkey Resounds."

46. Ibid.

47. Melba Liston, quoted in Porter, *What Is This Thing Called Jazz?* 82.

48. Melba Liston, quoted in Gillespie, *To be or Not to Bop,* 415–416; Melba Liston, interview with Steven Isoardi, September 12, 1992.

49. Porter, *What Is This Thing Called Jazz?* 82.

50. Jones, *Autobiography,* 115.

51. Stearns, "Is Jazz Good Propaganda?" 28.

52. Music Advisory Panel meeting (April 24, 1957), 2. Bureau Historical Collection.

53. Stearns, "Is Jazz Good Propaganda?" 28–31.

54. President's Special International Program, Hearings House, 1957; The Supplemental Appropriations Bill, 1957; Hearings before Subcommittee on Appropriations House of Representatives Eighty-Fourth Congress Second Session Part 2, 675–762. For a related discussion of congressional and conservative opposition to State Department support of abstract expressionism, see Jane De Hart Matthews, "Art and Politics in Cold War America," *American Historical Review*, 81 (1976); 762–787. See also Serge Guilbaut, *How New York Stole the Idea of Modern Art: Abstract Expressionism, Freedom, and the Cold War* (Chicago: University of Chicago Press, 1983).

55. U.S. House of Representatives, Appropriations Committee, "Promotional Expenses for Dizzy Gillespie Tour" (Washington, D.C.: GPO, 1956), 736.

56. Reinhold Wagnleitner, *Coca-Colonization and the Cold War: The Cultural Mission of the United States in Austria after the Second World War* (Chapel Hill: University of North Carolina Press, 1994), 212.

57. Anonymous, "Biceps and Choirs: Senate Group Backs Them to Promote U.S. Abroad," *New York Times* (July 18, 1956), 54.

58. Gillespie, *To Be or Not to Bop,* 428.

59. Jones, *Autobiography,* 116.

60. Ibid., 117.

61. U.S. House of Representatives, Hearings before the Subcommittee on Appropriations, President's Special International Program, 85th Congress, 2nd Session (Washington, D.C.: GPO, 1958), 410.

62. See Anonymous, "Marking Time: Cultural Program Abroad Is Modified to Win Congressional Support," *New York Times* (Sunday, September 15, 1963); Robert Bendiner, "The Diplomacy of Culture," *Show* (April 1962), 51–54, 100. See also Anonymous, "Show Biz Pans Cultural Exchange: Pros Say Amateurs Hurt U.S. Image," *Variety* (September 18, 1963), 1.

63. Martha Graham, quoted by Stuart Hodes, interview with Penny Von Eschen (May 1999).

64. Stuart Hodes, ibid.

65. Anonymous, "Legislator Asks Censorship Following Martha Graham Dance Sent Abroad," *New York Times* (September 10, 1963); "The Trojan, No the Cold War," *New York Times,* editorial (September 11, 1963); "Mrs. Kelly Abroad: She Saw *Phaedra* and Walked Out," *New York Times* (Sunday, September 15, 1963).

66. Naima Prevots, *Dance for Export: Cultural Diplomacy and the Cold War* (Hanover, N.H.: Wesleyan University Press, 1998). See also Randy Martin, "Modern Dance and the American Century," in Townsend Ludington, ed., *A Modern Mosaic: Art and Modernism in the United States* (Chapel Hill: Uni-

versity of North Carolina Press, 2000). Through the sponsorship of artists in financially vulnerable art forms, critics exercised considerable influence over the development of the arts. Marshall Stearns and John Wilson were the jazz critics on the music committee. Dance critics are increasingly recognizing the importance of the jazz tours in shaping the world of dance. See, for example, Jennifer Dunning, *Alvin Ailey: A Life in Dance* (New York: Da Capo Press, 1998).

67. Gillespie, "Jazz Is Too Good for Americans." See also Jack Tracy, "The First Chorus," *Down Beat* (June 13, 1957), for a reaction to the article.

68. Gillespie, "Jazz Is Too Good for Americans," 140.

69. Ibid.

70. Shipton, *Groovin' High*, 320–324.

71. Anonymous, "Goodman to Tour Asia: He and His Orchestra Will Play throughout the Far East," *New York Times* (October 10, 1956), 43; Anonymous, "Buoyant Benny Back from Bangkok Bash," *Down Beat* (March 6, 1957), 23.

72. Whitney Balliett, "Our Local Correspondents S.R.O.," *New Yorker* (December 26, 1977). See also Henry Anton Steig, "Profiles: Alligators' Idol— Benny Goodman," *New Yorker* (April 17, 1937); Leonard Feather and Ira Gitler, *The Biographical Encyclopedia of Jazz* (Oxford: Oxford University Press, 1999), 263–264.

73. Hal Davis, Press release, Radio Publicity Department, Kenyon and Eckhardt (April 1, 1947), Benny Goodman Papers, Yale University Music Library.

74. Benny Goodman to Marion Glendining, (April 30, 1947), Benny Goodman Collection, Yale University Music Library. Benny Goodman, letter to the editor, *New York Times* (April 30, 1947).

75. Benny Goodman, "Jazz Comes of Age," Box 5/25, Benny Goodman Papers, Yale University Music Library.

76. Anonymous, "Buoyant Benny Back from Bangkok Bash."

77. Christina Klein, *Cold War Orientalism: Asia in the Middlebrow Imagination, 1945–1961* (Berkeley: University of California Press, 2003), 1–3, 191–197; on banning in Thailand, see 221.

78. George Herring, *America's Longest War: The United States and Vietnam, 1950– 1975,* 3rd ed. (New York: McGraw-Hill, 1996), 61–66.

79. Kahin and Kahin, *Subversion as Foreign Policy.*

80. Anonymous, "King of Swing Swings with King," *Down Beat* (August 18, 1960).

81. Bernard Kalb, "Kings of Swing and Thailand Jive: Benny Goodman and the Monarch in Palace Session," *New York Times* (December 7, 1956), 1. Hal

Davis, "Benny and the King of Siam," *Saturday Review* (January 12, 1957), 64–65.

82. Kalb, "Kings of Swing and Thailand Jive," 1.

83. Davis, "Benny and the King of Siam," 64–65.

84. Anonymous, "Benny Goodman Sways Thailand: Band's Visit Is Credited with Doing More for U.S. Ties Than Any Recent Mission," *New York Times* (December 23, 1956), 8.

85. Anonymous, "Buoyant Benny Back from Bangkok Bash," 23. Anonymous, "Goodman Beats Drums for Asians; King of Swing Found Them 'Hep,'" *New York Times* (January 25, 1957), 23.

86. "Buoyant Benny Back from Bangkok Bash," 23.

87. The sentence continues: "but it is doubtful whether anyone will seriously propose that Benny Goodman be our representative in the next summit conference." Overall, however, the article suggests that "artists have an important role in building a world community." *Christian Century* (January 2, 1957), 5.

88. Anonymous, "King of Swing Swings with King," 13; McCandlish Phillips, "Thai King Plays for Two Hours at Encore Jam Session: Joins Jazz Greats at Fete Here Given by Benny Goodman," *New York Times* (July 6, 1960), 12; Anonymous, "Monarch Gets in Hot Licks with a New Gift Saxophone," *New York Times* (July 6, 1960), 12.

89. For contemporary coverage of the tour, see Dave Brubeck, "The Beat Heard Round the World," *New York Times Magazine* (June 15, 1958), 14–16; Anonymous, "Warsaw Extols Brubeck Jazz," *New York Times* (March 13, 1958); Anonymous, "Pianist Most Outstanding: Brubeck Concert Captivating," *Times of India* (April 4, 1958).

90. Fred M. Hall, *It's about Time: The Dave Brubeck Story* (Fayetteville: University of Arkansas Press, 1996), 3–10, 22–27.

91. Ibid., 34–35.

92. Ibid, 57.

93. Dave Brubeck, in Ken Burns, dir., *Jazz,* documentary film (Washington, D.C.: Public Broadcasting Service and Florentine Films, 2000).

94. Hall, *It's about Time,* 72–73. See Porter, *What Is This Thing Called Jazz?* ch. 3, on Charles Mingus' questioning of Brubeck's recognition.

95. Dave Brubeck and Iola Brubeck, interview with Penny Von Eschen and Kevin Gaines, March 13, 1997, Wilton, Conn.

96. Ibid. See also Hall, *It's about Time,* 68–69.

97. Dave Brubeck Quartet, Final itinerary as reported by Iola Brubeck (June 11, 1958), Bureau Historical Collection.

98. Dave Brubeck and Iola Brubeck, interview with Von Eschen and Gaines.

Ralph Gleason, "Overseas with the Brubeck Clan: Mrs. Dave Brubeck Discusses Jazz Abroad," *Down Beat* (July 10, 1958), 14, 42–43.

99. Dave Brubeck and Iola Brubeck, interview with Von Eschen and Gaines.

100. Gleason, "Overseas with the Brubeck Clan," 42.

101. Ibid.

102. Brubeck, "The Beat Heard Round the World," 31–32.

103. Ibid.

104. Dave Brubeck and Iola Brubeck, interview with Von Eschen and Gaines.

105. For Brubeck's later reflections on his evolving style, see Malcolm Miller, "Dave Brubeck: Malcolm Miller Takes Five and a Few More with a Legend of Jazz Piano, *Jazz Journal International,* 45, no. 8 (August 1992), 6–8.

106. Liner notes, *Jazz Impressions of Eurasia,* Dave Brubeck Quartet, LP, no. CL1251 (Columbia Records, 1958).

107. Ibid.

108. Dave Brubeck and Iola Brubeck, interview with Von Eschen and Gaines.

109. Ibid.

110. Ibid. A poster in the Brubecks' possession reads: "The Iranian Oil Refinery Co. in cooperation with the U.S. Information Service presents the Dave Brubeck Quartet: Dave Brubeck, Paul Desmond, Gene Wright, Eugene Wright at the Taj Theater, Abadan, Iran, Sunday, May 4 [1958]."

111. Anonymous, "Iraq: After the Bloodbath," *Time* (August 4, 1958), 20. For a succinct discussion of the Iraqi coup and Middle East crisis of July 1958 from the U.S. perspective, see Walter LaFeber, *America, Russia, and the Cold War,* 6th ed., *1945–1990* (New York: McGraw-Hill, 1991), 201–202; and Little, *American Orientalism,* 198–206. For a detailed discussion of events leading up to the coup and of Iraqi politics from 1958 through 1980, see Marion Farouk-Sluglett and Peter Sluglett, *Iraq since 1958: From Revolution to Dictatorship* (London: KPI, 1987), 47–84. I am following Douglas Little's spelling of Qassim, which is also spelled Qasim, Kassim (the American spelling most frequently used in those years), and Qassem.

112. Dave Brubeck and Iola Brubeck, interview with Von Eschen and Gaines. LaFeber, *America, Russia, and the Cold War,* 201–202; Little, *American Orientalism,* 202.

113. Little, *American Orientalism,* 199.

114. State Department official quoted in Little, *American Orientalism,* 201.

3. The Real Ambassador

1. Music Advisory Panel (November 15, 1955), 2. Series 5, Box 12, Folder 12, Bureau of Educational and Cultural Affairs Historical Collection, J. Wil-

liam Fulbright Papers, University of Arkansas at Fayetteville. Hereafter cited as Bureau Historical Collection.

2. Ingrid Monson, *Freedom Sounds: Jazz, Civil Rights and Africa,* (London: Oxford University Press, forthcoming), ch. 3; Eric Porter, *What Is This Thing Called Jazz? African American Musicians as Artists, Critics, and Activists* (Berkeley: University of California Press, 2002), chs. 3–4.

3. Robert Raymond, *Black Star in the Wind* (London: MacGibbon and Kee, 1960), 215.

4. Ibid., 225.

5. Ibid., 225. For a discussion of the rapport between Armstrong and Nkrumah, see also Jack B. Moore, "Black Power Revisited: In Search of Richard Wright," *Mississippi Quarterly* (Spring 1988), 168.

6. "Satchmo Is a Smash on the Gold Coast," *Life* (June 11, 1956), 38–39. See also "100,000 Dig the King: Armstrong Gasses Ghanese Fans," *Pittsburgh Courier* (June 2, 1956).

7. Raymond, *Black Star in the Wind,* 238–239.

8. Ibid.

9. Raymond, *Black Star in the Wind,* 241.

10. Gary Giddins, *Satchmo* (New York: Doubleday, 1988), 159–160.

11. American Consulate General, Accra, to Department of State (June 4, 1956), RG 59, 745K.00/6-456.

12. Anonymous, "Satchmo Blows Up the World," *Drum* (August 1956), 40.

13. Raymond, *Black Star in the Wind,* 232.

14. Anonymous, "Armstrong to Tour Russia, South America," *Pittsburgh Courier* (August 10, 1957), 22.

15. On Armstrong and the Little Rock incident, see Penny Von Eschen, *Race against Empire: Black Americans and Anticolonialism, 1937–1957* (Ithaca: Cornell University Press, 1997), 179–180. See also Mary L. Dudziak, *Cold War Civil Rights: Race and the Image of American Democracy* (Princeton: Princeton University Press, 2000), which provides the best overview of the crisis and its impact on foreign policy.

16. Gary Giddins, *Satchmo* (New York: Doubleday, 1988), 160–165; Anonymous, "Louis Armstrong Barring Soviet Tour, Denounces Eisenhower and Governor Faubus," *New York Times* (September 19, 1957), 23; Anonymous, "Satchmo Tells Off U.S.," *Pittsburgh Courier* (September 28, 1957).

17. Anonymous, "Satchmo Tells Off U.S.," *Pittsburgh Courier* (September 28, 1957).

18. Anonymous, "Armstrong May Tour: U.S. Hopes He'll Visit Soviet Despite Segregation Issue," *New York Times* (September 20, 1957), 15.

19. Anonymous, "Musician Backs Move, Armstrong Lauds Eisenhower for Little Rock Action," *New York Times* (September 26, 1957), 12.

20. Giddins, *Satchmo*, 183.
21. Anonymous, "Arkansas U. Drops Armstrong's Date," *New York Times* (October 16, 1957), 27.
22. Dudziak, *Cold War Civil Rights*, 131; Walter Hixson, *Parting the Curtain: Propaganda, Culture, and the Cold War, 1945–1961* (New York: St. Martin's, 1997), 131.
23. Anonymous, "Hot Jazz Trails Hot Jets to Rio," *New York Times* (November 21, 1957), 20. On American reaction to Sputnik, see Hixson, *Parting the Curtain*, 123.
24. Ibid.
25. Ibid.
26. Ibid. See also Anonymous, "Rio Greets Armstrong: Brazilian Capital Rolls Out Carpet for Bandleader," *New York Times* (November 26, 1957), 41.
27. Anonymous, "Trumpeter, in Venezuela, Sees U.S. Negroes Better Off," *New York Times* (November 30, 1957), 22.
28. Thomas Borstelmann, *The Cold War and the Color Line: American Race Relations in the Global Arena* (Cambridge, Mass.: Harvard University Press, 2001), 115.
29. Ibid., 128–132; David N. Gibbs, *The Political Economy of Third World Intervention: Mines, Money, and U.S. Policy in the Congo Crisis* (Chicago: University of Chicago Press, 1991), 95.
30. Thomas Borstelmann, *Apartheid's Reluctant Uncle: The United States and Southern Africa in the Early Cold War* (New York: Oxford University Press, 1993), 44–46, 181, 198–199; William Minter, *King Solomon's Mines Revisited: Western Interests and the Burdened History of Southern Africa* (New York: Basic Books, 1986), 116–117.
31. Gibbs, *The Political Economy of Third World Intervention*, 84–95; Richard D. Mahoney, *JFK: Ordeal in Africa* (New York: Oxford University Press, 1983), 35–58.
32. Borstelmann, *The Cold War and the Color Line*, 128–132.
33. Anonymous, "Armstrong's Akwaaba in Ghana," *Down Beat* (November 24, 1960), 12.
34. Ibid.
35. Robert W. July, *An African Voice: The Role of the Humanities in African Independence* (Durham: Duke University Press, 1987), 4.
36. Ibid.
37. Frantz Fanon, "This Africa to Come," in Fanon, *Toward the African Revolution* (New York: Grove Press, 1967), 178.
38. Anonymous, "We Claim Jazz: Listen to Africa," *Voice of Africa* [Accra] (July 1962).
39. Paul Hofmann, "Satchmo Plays for Congo Cats: Trumpeter Arrives on

Red Throne and Crew of Bearers," New York *Times* (October 29, 1960), 8. See also Gilbert Millstein, "Africa Harks to Satch's Horn," *New York Times Magazine* (November 20, 1960), 24.

40. Millstein, "Africa Harks to Satch's Horn."

41. President's Special International Program, "Ninth Semi-Annual Report" (July 1–December 31, 1960), Bureau Historical Collection.

42. Hofmann, "Satchmo Plays for Congo Cats."

43. Anonymous, "Armstrong in Katanga: Trumpeter and U.S. Aide Go to Area on Goodwill Tour," *New York Times* (November 21, 1960); Arvell Shaw, Interview with Penny Von Eschen and Kevin Gaines, New Orleans (August 4, 2001).

44. Papers of Louis Armstrong, Area and Country Breakdown, July 1954 through March 1962, 1, Series 4, Box 1, Bureau Historical Collection; Paul Hofmann, "Satchmo Plays for Congo Cats"; Mahoney, *JFK*, 69–74; Ludo De Witte, *The Assassination of Lumumba* (London: Verso, 2001); Madeleine G. Kalb, *The Congo Cables: The Cold War in America, from Eisenhower to* Kennedy (New York: Macmillan, 1982); William Blum, *Killing Hope: U.S. Military and CIA Interventions since World War* II (Monroe, Maine: Common Courage Press, 1995), 156–162. While it is not clear that U.S. agents were present at the assassination of Lumumba, it is clear that President Eisenhower approved the assassination.

45. President's Special International Program, "Ninth Semi-Annual Report" (July 1–December 31, 1960), 8–9, Bureau Historical Collection.

46. Ibid.

47. Anonymous, "Soviets Scores Visit," *New York Times* (October 29, 1960), 8; President's Special International Program, "Tenth Semi-Annual Report" (January 1–June 30, 1961), Bureau Historical Collection.

48. President's Special International Program, "Ninth Semi-Annual Report" (July 1–December 31, 1960), 9, Bureau Historical Collection.

49. Anonymous, "Africa Hears Satchmo's Horn, but in Kenya They Behaved Like Squares—They Just Didn't Dig!" *Drum* (December 1960), 21–23.

50. President's Special International Program, "Ninth Semi-Annual Report" (July 1–December 31, 1960), 9, Bureau Historical Collection.

51. Leonard Ingalls, "Armstrong Horn Wins Nairobi, Too," *New York Times* (November 7, 1960), 5.

52. Armstrong's stunning range of expression through his voluminous writings and collages has only recently been explored by scholars. See Thomas Brothers, ed., *Louis Armstrong in His Own Words: Selected Writings* (New York: Oxford University Press, 1999); and Brent Edwards, "Louis Armstrong and the Syntax of Scat," paper presented at "Rhythm-a-Ning: A Symposium on Jazz Culture," Columbia University (May 2000).

53. Louis Armstrong, "Daddy, How the Country Has Changed," *Ebony* (May 1961), 84.

54. Ibid., 88.

55. Anonymous, "Africa Hears Satchmo's Horn," 21.

56. Anonymous, "Satchmo Goes to Paris: Arrives after Tour of Africa Suffering from Fatigue," *New York Times* (December 6, 1960), 53.

57. Arvell Shaw, Interview with Penny Von Eschen and Kevin Gaines, New Orleans (August 4, 2001).

58. Anonymous, "King Hears Armstrong: Thai Royalty Attends Show in Switzerland by Trumpeter," *New York Times* (January, 9, 1961), 30.

59. President's Special International Program, "Tenth Semi-Annual Report" (January 1–June 30, 1961), 40–43, Bureau Historical Collection.

60. Kevin Gaines, *Black Expatriates in Nkrumah's Ghana* (Chapel Hill: University of North Carolina Press, forthcoming), ch. 3; Brenda Gayle Plummer, *A Rising Wind: Black Americans and U.S. Foreign Affairs, 1935–1960* (Chapel Hill: University of North Carolina Press, 1996), 303–304; Nikhil Pal Singh, *Black Is a Country: Race and the Unfinished Struggle for Democracy* (Cambridge, Mass.: Harvard University Press, 2004), 186–187.

61. Quoted in Dudziak, *Cold War Civil Rights,* 157–159.

62. Ibid., 157.

63. Anonymous, "Louis Armstrong: The Reluctant Millionaire," *Ebony* (November 1964), 136–146.

64. Brent Edwards has brilliantly theorized a "parallel between the forms of Armstrong's performance, from trumpet, to singing, to writing" (Edwards, "Louis Armstrong and the Syntax of Scat"). See also Brothers, *Louis Armstrong in His Own Words,* 203; and Porter, *What Is This Thing Called Jazz?* 43, 344, note 93.

65. Porter, *What Is This Thing Called Jazz?* 43–44, 72.

66. Farah Jasmine Griffin, *In Search of Billie Holiday: If You Can't Be Free, Be a Mystery* (New York: Ballantine Books, 2001), 124–125.

67. Edwards, "Louis Armstrong and the Syntax of Scat."

68. The Norfolk-based group "began broadcasting from a Columbia, South Carolina, radio station in 1936 and recording for Bluebird in 1937." See Michael Denning, *The Culture Front* (London: Verso, 1997), 353–357.

69. Project summation and itinerary, "Golden Gate Quartet" (October 12, 1958–April 7, 1959), Bureau Historical Collection.

70. Memo from American Embassy Brazzaville to the Department of State, Washington, D.C. (March 19, 1962) on "Educational and Cultural Exchange: Cultural Presentations—Golden Gate Quartet, W. Wendell Blancke," Bureau Historical Collection.

71. Ibid., 5.

72. See Yevette Richards, *Maida Springer: Pan-Africanist and International Labor Leader* (Pittsburgh: University of Pittsburgh Press, 2000).

73. Memo from American Embassy Brazzaville to the Department of State, 6.

74. Trip itinerary and summation, "Golden Gate Quartet: African Tour 1962," Bureau Historical Collection.

75. Ibid.

76. From: USIS-Accra to USIS Washington, "Program Highlights" (January– February 1963; March 1, 1963), Bureau Historical Collection.

77. Iola Brubeck, liner notes to *The Real Ambassadors,* Columbia LP (1962). *The Real Ambassadors,* book by Iola Brubeck, music by Dave Brubeck, lyrics by Iola and Dave Brubeck, premiered on September 23, 1962, at the Monterey Jazz Festival in Monterey, California, with the following cast: Louis Armstrong, Dave Brubeck, Carmen McRae, Iola Brubeck, Trummy Young, Dave Lambert, Jon Hendricks, Yolande Bavan, Joe Morello, Eugene Wright, Joe Darensburg, Billy Kyle, Willy Kronk, and Danny Barcelona. Howard Brubeck was the Musical Coordinator. A folio of fifteen songs and related narration from *The Real Ambassadors* was printed in 1963 and published by Hansen Publications. That folio is no longer available. Twenty songs from *The Real Ambassadors* were recorded in September and December 1961 by Louis Armstrong, Dave Brubeck, Carmen McRae, Dave Lambert, Jon Hendricks, Annie Ross, and additional musicians, most of whom later performed at the 1962 premiere. Fifteen of those recorded songs were released by Columbia Records in 1962 on an LP entitled *The Real Ambassadors* (COL CL 5850). That LP is no longer available. In 1994 all twenty recorded songs were released by Sony Music Entertainment on the Columbia/Legacy label on a CD entitled *The Real Ambassadors* (CK 57663).

78. Dave and Iola Brubeck, Interview with Penny Von Eschen and Kevin Gaines (March 13, 1997), Wilton, Conn. The Bureau Historical Collection contains scant records of those early tours but has an itinerary for Brubeck's trip. For more on Brubeck's tours, see the materials in the Dave Brubeck Collection, University of the Pacific, Stockton, California; and Ralph J. Gleason, "Overseas with the Brubeck Clan: Mrs. Dave Brubeck Discusses Jazz Abroad," *Downbeat* (July 10, 1958). The itinerary for Armstrong's 1960– 1961 tour is held in the Papers of Louis Armstrong, Queens College, Queens, New York, Scrapbook 58. See also Scrapbooks 22 and 36 and Photo Box 30. See also Anonymous, "Armstrong's Akwaaba in Ghana," *Down Beat* (November 24, 1960), 12; Anonymous, "Africa Hears Satchmo's Horn," *Drum* (December 1960), 21–23; Leonard Ingalls, "Armstrong Horn Wins Nairobi, Too," *New York Times* (November 7, 1960), 5; Anonymous, "South Africa Bars Armstrong," *New York Times* (September 26, 1960), 2;

Paul Hoffman, "Satchmo Plays for Congo's Cats," *New York Times* (October 29, 1960), 8.

79. Leonard Feather, syndicated column *Life with Feather,* reprinted with the published score for *The Real Ambassadors,* along with reviews from *Down Beat,* which gave it a five-star rating. See also Anonymous, "Recordings Reports: Jazz LPs," *Saturday Review* (October 13, 1962), 42; and Ralph Gleason, "Brubeck's Ambassador Wow'em as Monterey Jazz Festival Pulls 87½ G," *Variety* (September 26, 1962), 49, 52.

80. Ibid. See especially the reviews by Feather, *Down Beat,* and Ralph Gleason.

81. Dave and Iola Brubeck, Interview with Von Eschen and Gaines.

82. Ibid. *The Real Ambassadors,* Libretto, 2 (in possession of author).

83. Seeking a distinctly American alternative to Soviet and European dominance in the arts, the program committees became venues for debating what was considered "modern" and "uniquely American" in dance, art, and music.

84. Dave and Iola Brubeck, Interview with Von Eschen and Gaines; Von Eschen, *Race against Empire,* 179–180.

85. See Anonymous, "Dave Brubeck's Band Won't Play in Georgia," *New York Post* (February 24, 1959); "22 Colleges Bar Quartet, Bias Charged," *New York Herald Tribune* (January 13, 1960); Ralph Gleason, "Brubeck's Dixie Dilemma," *Pittsburgh Sun-Telegram* (February 6, 1960); Ralph Gleason, "Racial Issue 'Kills' Brubeck Jazz Tour of the South," *San Francisco Chronicle* (February 1959); George E. Pitts, "Give Brubeck Credit for a Slap at Bias," *Pittsburgh Courier* (February 13, 1960). Brubeck expressed disappointment that critics have represented his contribution as bringing jazz to white audiences. Understandably uncomfortable with this reductive view of his legacy, he was proud to have topped popularity polls in black newspapers, such as the *Pittsburgh Courier.*

86. *The Real Ambassadors,* Libretto, 3–4.

87. Ibid., 4.

88. Dave and Iola Brubeck, Interview with Von Eschen and Gaines.

89. Clark Terry, Interview with Penny Von Eschen, Chapel Hill, N.C. (February 28, 1997). See also Series 2, Performers, Box 28, Bureau Historical Collection.

90. *The Real Ambassadors,* Libretto, 6.

91. Ibid.

92. Anonymous, "Armstrong's Akwaaba in Ghana," 12.

93. Dave and Iola Brubeck, Interview with Von Eschen and Gaines; Liner notes to Columbia CD; Fred M. Hall, *It's about Time: The Dave Brubeck Story* (Fayetteville: University of Arkansas Press, 1996), 86.

94. Millstein, "Africa Harks to Satch's Horn," 24.

95. *The Real Ambassadors*, Libretto, 7–9.

96. In the liner notes for the original LP, Iola Brubeck wrote: "Obviously, no vocal group but Lambert-Hendricks-Ross could manage to sound like a crowd or a full chorus on demand."

97. Chip Stern, liner notes to 1993 Columbia reissue of *The Real Ambassadors*.

98. Several songs were performed by Brubeck at Monterey forty years later, in 2002, in remembrance of Armstrong and the original production.

99. Dave and Iola Brubeck, Interview with Von Eschen and Gaines.

100. From the finale, "Swing Bells / Blow Satchmo."

4. Getting the Soviets to Swing

1. Thomas Borstelmann, *The Cold War and the Color Line* (Cambridge, Mass.: Harvard University Press, 2001), 112, 142; Walter L. Hixson, *Parting the Curtain: Propaganda, Culture, and the Cold War, 1945–1961* (New York: St. Martin's, 1997).

2. For a discussion of views of free jazz, see, Eric Porter, *What Is This Thing Called Jazz? African American Musicians as Artists, Critics, and Activists* (Berkeley: University of California Press, 2002), 191–239; John Gennari, *Canonizing Jazz: An American Art and Its Critics* (Chicago: University of Chicago Press, forthcoming).

3. On jazz and dissent within the Soviet Union, see Michael May, "Swingin' under Stalin: Russian Jazz during the Cold War and Beyond," in Reinhold Wagnleitner and Elaine Tyler May, eds., *Here, There, and Everywhere: The Foreign Politics of American Popular Culture* (Hanover, N.H.: University Press of New England, 2000), 179–191. For a discussion of Soviet dissent in this period, in the context of global rebellions, see Jeremi Suri, *Power and Protest: Global Revolution and the Rise of Détente* (Cambridge, Mass.: Harvard University Press, 2003), 105–114.

4. Nathaniel Mackey, "Other: From Noun to Verb," in Krin Gabbard, ed., *Jazz among the Discourses* (Durham: Duke University Press, 1995), 86. Amiri Baraka, *Blues People: Negro Music in White America* (New York: Morrow, 1963). Porter, *What Is this Thing Called Jazz?* ch. 2.

5. Phil Woods, "Life in E Flat," unpublished manuscript, ch. 7, "Dizzy Atmosphere."

6. Mary L. Dudziak, *Cold War Civil Rights: Race and the Image of American Democracy* (Princeton: Princeton University Press, 2000), 158–159.

7. Here, the State Department was building on Voice of America radio broadcasts by Leonard Feather *(Jazz Club USA)* and Willis Conover *(Music*

USA), and a history of jazz in the Soviet Union. On the early VOA music programs and Leonard Feather's program *Jazz Club USA*, see Leonard Feather, "Music is Combating Communism: Voice of America Shows Bring Universal Harmony," *Down Beat* (October 8, 1952), 1, 19.

8. S. Frederick Starr, *Red and Hot: The Fate of Jazz in the Soviet Union, 1917–1980* (New York: Oxford University Press, 1983); Walter Hixson, *Parting the Iron Curtain: Propaganda, Culture, and the Cold War* (New York: St. Martin's, 1997); Michael May, "Swingin' under Stalin: Russian Jazz during the Cold War and Beyond," in Wagnleitner and May, *Here, There, and Everywhere,* 179–191; Uta G. Poiger, *Jazz Rock and Rebels: Cold War Politics and American Culture in a Divided Germany* (Berkeley: University of California Press, 2000), 20–21, 151. For a contemporary discussion of the history of jazz in the Soviet Union and the Eastern bloc see, Eric Bourne, "Jazz in the Soviet Sphere," *Christian Science Monitor* (April 3, 1962). For a contemporary report on the exchange, see Anonymous, "Intercontinental Culture: Swapping Benny Goodman and the Bolshoi Ballet," *National Observer* (Sunday, March 11, 1962).

9. Hixson, *Parting the Iron Curtain,* 115.

10. See "Text of the Joint Communiqué of U.S. and Soviets," special to the *New York Times* (January 28, 1958), 8; and Anonymous, "U.S., Soviet Widen Exchange in Arts and Other Fields," *New York Times* (January 28, 1958), 1. The latter piece reported, for example, that in the initial agreement the United States had "failed to persuade the Soviet Union to stop jamming new broadcasts" or "to permit uncensored explanations of U.S. policy over the Soviet television and radio." The Soviets had failed to persuade the United States to "send large numbers of industrial technicians to the Soviet Union, or to work out an . . . agreement on direct plane travel between the two countries."

11. Max Frankel, "West Denounced on Culture Issue," *New York Times* (November 1, 1959), 20.

12. Osgood Caruthers, "A Top Soviet Orchestra Leader Tells Russians: 'We Need Jazz,'" *New York Times* (February 27, 1961), 1.

13. Anonymous, "The Reds and Dr. Stearns," *Down Beat* (July 9, 1959), 9.

14. Ibid.

15. Ibid.

16. Poiger, *Jazz Rock and Rebels,* 21–22, 151.

17. Soviet views of race were further complicated by the fact that a great many African expatriate students were attending Soviet universities. Students said they encountered racism, but also enjoyed enormous opportunities for training they would otherwise not have had. See Edward T. Wilson, *Russia*

and Black Africa before World War II (New York: Holmes and Meier, 1974), 280–301. See also Poiger, *Jazz Rock and Rebels,* 42–43, for a fascinating discussion of parallel issues in Weimar and Third Reich Germany.

18. Anonymous, "The Reds and Dr. Stearns," 9.
19. Ibid.
20. Ibid.
21. Max Frankel, "West Denounced on Culture Issue: Russia Says It Tries to Use 'Trojan Horse'—Bars Any Easing of Soviet Control," *New York Times* (November 1, 1959), 20.
22. Ibid.
23. Ibid. See also Dana Adams Schmidt, "Plea for Politeness Notes Coming Camp David Talk," *New York Times* (September 22, 1959), 1; "Soviet Performers Seen Getting the Better of Cultural Exchange," *New York Times* (December 15, 1959).
24. Max Frankel, "U.S.-Soviet Accord in Cultural Field Extended Two Years," *New York Times* (November 22, 1959), 1, 27; E. W. Kenworthy, "Capital Pleased on Soviet Accord" (November 22, 1959), 26; Howard Taubman, "Experiment in Goodwill," *New York Times* (January 24, 1960), 9.
25. Anonymous, "Big Jazz behind the Iron Curtain," *Look* (November 20, 1962).
26. Anonymous, "The Reds and Dr. Stearns," 9.
27. Caruthers, "A Top Soviet Orchestra Leader Tells Russians: 'We Need Jazz,'" 1.
28. Ibid.
29. Suri, *Power and Protest,* 109.
30. Anonymous, "Soviet Changes Its Tune and Urges Jazz Clubs," *New York Times* (April 7, 1961), 5.
31. Ibid.
32. Anonymous, "Soviet Changes Its Tune."
33. John Tynan, "Russian Cultural Workers Meet Western Jazzmen," *Down Beat* (August 17, 1961), 18–19.
34. Anonymous, "Goodman Scolds Soviet Scholars: Tells Musicologists He Has Been Put Off in Attempts to Play in Their Country," *New York Times* (March 18, 1961), 16.
35. Ibid.
36. Ibid.
37. E. W. Kenworthy, "U.S. and Soviet to Expand Their Cultural Exchange: Benny Goodman to Tour," *New York Times* (March 9, 1962), 1.
38. Anonymous, "Cultural Exchange for Kremlin Cats," *Newsweek* (March 19, 1962), 34.

39. Anonymous, "The King of Swing: Benjamin David Goodman," *New York Times* (March 9, 1962), 2; Alan Rich, "Benny Goodman to Tour in Soviet," *New York Times* (March 9, 1962), 2.

40. Rich, "Benny Goodman to Tour in Soviet," 2.

41. Anonymous, "Goodman Russian Tour Stirs Mild Dissent," *Down Beat* (April 26, 1962), 13.

42. Ibid.

43. Seymour Topping, "Goodman's Tour May Be Expanded: Soviet Said to Yield to U.S. on Including 8 or 9 Cities," *New York Times* (April 12, 1962), 4.

44. "Soviet, Out of Step with Twist, Finds Sedate Jazz Is Tolerable" (headline for two articles): Seymour Topping, "Moiseyev Scorns Rock n' Roll as 'Disgusting Dynamism'—Calls for Russian Works"; and Theodore Shabad, "Benny Goodman's Band, Due in May, Will Find Dixieland Being Played in Moscow," *New York Times* (April 29, 1962), 4.

45. *Melody Maker* magazine ran a story claiming that the Soviets had entertained the idea of having Louis Armstrong tour the previous year (1961); Armstrong reportedly turned down the tour because it wouldn't have paid enough. Anonymous, "Russians want Satchmo for 30-City Autumn Tour," *Melody Maker* (May 20, 1961), 1. On Armstrong's turning down the tour, see Bill Cross, "Benny Goodman: On the First Steppe," *Down Beat* (May 24, 1962), 16–17.

46. Anonymous, "The Goodman Tour and the Teapot Tempest," *Down Beat* (May 24, 1962), 14.

47. Rich, "Benny Goodman to Tour in Soviet."

48. Cross, "Benny Goodman: On the First Steppe," 17.

49. Ibid.

50. Ibid.

51. Milton Bracker, "Goodman Signs 12 for Russian Tour," *New York Times* (April 10, 1962), 47.

52. Ibid.

53. Theodore Shabad, "Russians Greet Benny Goodman," *New York Times* (May 29, 1962), 20; Leonard Feather, "Report from Russia: Moscow Diary," *Down Beat* (July 19, 1962), 19. The initial *Times* story on the signing listed Oliver Nelson (tenor sax) and Jimmy Rainey (guitar); ultimately, neither made the tour.

54. Ibid. On the tour negotiations, see also Theodore Shabad, "Russians Extend Goodman's Tour: Agree to 8 Weeks, but U.S. Can Arrange for Only 5," *New York Times* (April 18, 1962), 29; Topping, "Goodman's Tour May Be Expanded"; and Memo of conversation between Sidney Kaye, lawyer for

Benny Goodman, and Alfred V. Boerner, director, Bureau of Educational and Cultural Affairs, Department of State (April 12, 1962), Bureau of Educational and Cultural Affairs Historical Collection, J. William Fulbright Papers, University of Arkansas, Fayetteville. Hereafter cited as Bureau Historical Collection.

55. Anonymous, "Benny Goodman's Band Leaves on Soviet Tour," *New York Times* (May 28, 1962), 25.

56. Ibid. See also Anonymous, "Swingsville, *Newsweek* (June 11, 1962), 38; and Feather, "Report from Russia," 17.

57. Shabad, "Russians Greet Benny Goodman," 20.

58. Terrence F. Catherman (cultural attaché, American Embassy, Moscow), Memo to Department of State on "Benny Goodman and His Band in the Soviet Union" (July 10, 1962), 1–2 of 19. Series 5, Box 9, Bureau Historical Collection.

59. Ibid., 2.

60. Ibid.

61. The First Deputy Ministers were Anastas I. Mikoyan, Frol R. Kozlov, and Alcksel N. Kosygi (ibid., 3).

62. Anonymous, "Benny Goodman's Moscow Concert Pleases but Puzzles Khrushchev," *New York Times* (May 31, 1962), 1; Feather, "Report from Russia," 19. The display of portraits of jazz greats as Goodman "indulged in musical reminiscences" of Louis Armstrong, Duke Ellington, Glen Miller, Dave Brubeck, and Count Basie would later elicit substantial criticism.

63. Anonymous, "Benny Goodman's Moscow Concert Pleases but Puzzles Khrushchev," 1, 21; Feather, "Report from Russia," 17–19, 59–60.

64. Anonymous, "Benny Goodman's Moscow Concert Pleases but Puzzles Khrushchev, 21.

65. Ibid.; Catherman, Memo to Department of State, 3.

66. Catherman, Memo to Department of State, 3.

67. "Benny Goodman's Concert in Moscow Pleases but Puzzles Khrushchev," 21.

68. Ibid.

69. Ibid.

70. Catherman, Memo to Department of State, 3–4; "Benny Goodman's Concert in Moscow Pleases but Puzzles Khrushchev," 21.

71. Anonymous, "One-Man Session by Goodman Attracts a Crowd in Red Square," *New York Times* (June 2, 1962), 8.

72. Catherman, Memo to Department of State, 5.

73. Ibid.

74. Phil Woods, "Life in E Flat," unpublished manuscript, ch. 12, "The King and I," 348–349.

75. Ibid.
76. Catherman, Memo to Department of State, 5.
77. Ibid.
78. Ibid., 6.
79. Ibid.
80. Ibid., 6–7.
81. Anonymous, "Soviet Police Curb Goodman Jazz Band," *New York Times* (June 5, 1962), 38; Anonymous, "Goodman Discounts Snags," *New York Times* (June 6, 1962), 35; Catherman, Memo to Department of State, 8.
82. Catherman, Memo to Department of State, 6; Anonymous, "Russian Youth Is Arrested in Goodman Band Incident," *New York Times,* (June 7, 1962), 31.
83. Catherman, Memo to Department of State, 6.
84. Ibid., 6.
85. Quoted in, Woods, "Life in E Flat," 352. See Woods's version of the incident, in which he recounts stronger language used to characterize Goodman than that reported by Catherman.
86. Catherman, Memo to Department of State, 6.
87. Ibid., 9.
88. Anonymous, "Goodman Told 'Acoustics' Caused Uproar over Song," *New York Times* (June 11, 1962), 11; Catherman, Memo to Department of State, 10.
89. Ibid.
90. Ibid.
91. Ibid., 12.
92. Anonymous, "Leningrad Hails Benny Goodman: Orchestra Wildly Applauded in Biggest Success of Tour," *New York Times* (June 21, 1962), 25; Catherman, Memo to Department of State, 12.
93. Theodore Shabad, "Leningrad Hails Goodman, Janis," *New York Times* (June 22, 1962), 2.
94. Catherman, Memo to Department of State, 12.
95. Ibid.
96. Ibid.
97. Ibid., 13.
98. Ibid., 14.
99. Anonymous, "Goodman's Choice of Music in Soviet Dissatisfies Band," *New York Times* (July 1, 1962), 8.
100. Anonymous, "Stompin It Up at the Savoy-Marx," *Life* (July 6, 1962), 17–19, 21, 26.
101. Joya Sherrill, Interview with Penny Von Eschen and Kevin Gaines, Austin Texas, November 1998.

102. Catherman, Memo to Department of State, 14.

103. Ibid.

104. The quote is from Suri, *Power and Protest,* 113.

105. Anonymous, "Premier Voices Good Wishes," *New York Times* (July 5, 1962), 34.

106. Catherman, Memo to Department of State, 16–17.

107. Ibid., 16.

108. John S. Wilson, "Goodman Basks in Success of Soviet Jazz Tour: Band Members' Complaints Are Called Unjustified," *New York Times* (July 20, 1962), 15; Anonymous, "Goodman Returns after Soviet Tour," *New York Times* (July 19, 1962).

109. Anonymous, "Goodman Tells President about trip to Soviet Union," *New York Times* (July 25, 1962), 25.

110. Anonymous, "Goodman Basks in Success of Soviet Jazz Tour."

111. Anonymous, "Goodman Men Sound Off About Soviet Tour," *Down Beat* (August 30, 1962), 13, 36; Anonymous, "Goodman's Band Assesses Its Trip," *New York Times* (July 10, 1962), 30; John S. Wilson, "Rectifying the Rumor Mills," *New York Times* (October 28, 1962), 16; Leonard Feather, "Feather Replies," *Down Beat* (October 11, 1962), 11.

112. Porter, *What Is This Thing Called Jazz?* chs. 3–4; Gennari, *Canonizing Jazz.*

113. Catherman, Memo to Department of State, 16.

114. S. Frederick Starr, *Red and Hot: The Fate of Jazz in the Soviet Union, 1917–1980* (New York: Oxford University Press, 1983); Hixson, *Parting the Curtain,* 229.

115. Max Frankel, "New Spirit in the Soviet Union: Jazz, Lipstick, and Freer Expression Mark Period of 'Post-Repressionism,'" *New York Times* (August 17, 1963), 3.

116. Anonymous, "Contradictions Seen in Soviet Arts Line," *New York Times* (December 18, 1963), 39.

117. Frankel, "New Spirit in the Soviet Union," 3. For an assessment of jazz and the cultural tours during this period, see Don De Micheal, "Jazz in Government," *Down Beat* (January 17, 1963), 15–17, 45; and idem, "Jazz in Government, Part II," *Down Beat* (January 31, 1963), 19–20.

5. Duke's Diplomacy

1. "The Duke Ellington Orchestra, September 6–November 28, 1963," Sixteen weeks, Synopsis, Series 2, Box 9. Bureau of Educational and Cultural Affairs Historical Collection, J. William Fulbright Papers, University of Arkansas at Fayetteville. Hereafter cited as Bureau Historical Collection.

2. Anonymous, "Busy Duke Likes It That Way: Jazz Leader Seems to Be Picking Up Steam at 64," *New York Times* (August 9, 1963). Ingrid Monson, "Duke Ellington and Civil Rights," paper presented at the Duke Ellington Centenary Conference, University of North Carolina Jazz Symposium, Chapel Hill (February 25–27, 1999).

3. Duke Ellington, *Music Is My* Mistress (Garden City, N.Y.: Doubleday, 1973), 197–199. Monson, "Duke Ellington and Civil Rights."

4. Mary L. Dudziak, *Cold War Civil Rights: Race and the Image of American Democracy* (Princeton: Princeton University Press, 2000), 169–175; Thomas Borstelmann, *The Cold War and the Color Line: American Race Relations in the Global Arena* (Cambridge, Mass.: Harvard University Press, 2001), 160–161.

5. Dudziak, *Cold War Civil Rights,* 178; Borstelmann, *The Cold War and the Color Line,* 161.

6. For a discussion of the idea that Ellington's orchestra was his instrument and of the dynamics within the band, see Wynton Marsalis and Robert G. O'Meally, "Duke Ellington: Music Like a Big Hot Pot of Good Gumbo," in Robert G. O'Meally, ed., *The Jazz Cadence of American Culture* (New York: Columbia University Press, 1998), 147–150.

7. Thomas W. Simons Jr., "General Report on the Ellington Tour," Introduction, 1. Series 5, Box 9; see also Series 2, Box 9, Bureau Historical Collection.

8. For a related discussion of black worldliness, see Nikhil Pal Singh, *Black Is a Country: Race and the Unfinished Struggle for Democracy* (Cambridge, Mass.: Harvard University Press, 2004), 125.

9. On the U.S. invasion and occupation of Haiti, see Mary Renda, *Taking Haiti: Military Occupation and the Culture of U.S. Imperialism, 1915–1940* (Chapel Hill: University of North Carolina Press, 2001).

10. Duke Ellington, "The Race for Space," in Mark Tucker, ed., *The Duke Ellington Reader* (New York: Oxford University Press, 1993), 295.

11. Ibid., 294.

12. I am indebted to Paul Gilroy for a discussion about Ellington and modernity.

13. Ellington, "The Race for Space," 296.

14. Duke Ellington, "The Duke Steps Out," in Tucker, *The Duke Ellington Reader,* 46–50. Mark Tucker, *Ellington: The Early Years* (Urbana: University of Illinois Press, 1991), 3–15, 111–117, 121–122; Janet Mabie, "Ellington's 'Mood Indigo': Harlem's Duke Seeks to Express His Race," in Tucker, *The Duke Ellington Reader,* 41–43; Graham Lock, *Blutopia: Visions of the Future and Revisions of the Past in the Work of Sun Ra, Duke Ellington, and Anthony Braxton* (Durham: Duke University Press, 1999), 77–78.

15. Anonymous, "Duke to Play in Russia," *Evening Star* (August 30, 1971).

16. Quoted ibid. On this last point, see Kevin Gaines, "Duke Ellington: Black, Brown, and Beige and Cultural Politics During the 1940s," in Ronald Radano and Philip V. Bohlman, eds., *Music and the Racial Imagination* (Chicago: University of Chicago Press, 2000). See also Eric Porter, *What Is This Thing Called Jazz? African American Musicians as Artists, Critics, and Activists* (Berkeley: University of California Press, 2002), 37–39.

17. Ellington, *Music Is My Mistress,* 301; Complete itinerary of Ellington's 1963 Mideast tour, Series 2, Box 9, Bureau Historical Collection.

18. Thomas W. Simons Jr. went on to a highly successful career in the State Department. His posts included ambassador to Poland (1990–1993) and ambassador to Pakistan (1996–1998), before his retirement in 1998.

19. Ellington, *Music Is My Mistress,* 302.

20. Simons, "General Report on the Ellington Tour," Part 2, "The Role of the Escort Officer," 15.

21. The best overall discussion of U.S.–Middle Eastern relations is Douglas Little, *American Orientalism: The United States and the Middle East since 1945* (Chapel Hill: University of North Carolina Press, 2002). For a discussion of some of the specific tensions in 1963 related to the Saudi-Egyptian proxy war in southwest Arabia, see ibid., 184–185; 238–239.

22. Malcolm H. Kerr, *The Arab Cold War: Gamal 'Abd al-Nasir and His Rivals, 1958–1970* (London: Oxford University Press, 1971), 4–5.

23. Complete itinerary of Ellington's 1963 Mideast tour, "Post Comments," 7.

24. Kerr, *The Arab Cold War.* Tariq Ali, *The Clash of Fundamentalisms: Crusades, Jihads and Modernity* (London: Verso, 2002), 110–113.

25. Simons, "General Report on the Ellington Tour," 4. See also Anonymous, "Ellington in Syria, Has Fever Day after Successful Debut," *New York Times* (September 11, 1963), 46.

26. "The Duke Ellington Orchestra," Synopsis, 5.

27. Simons, "General Report on the Ellington Tour," 5.

28. Ibid.

29. Memo from Thomas W. Simons Jr., American Embassy, Amman, Jordan, to Glenn Wolfe, Office of Cultural Presentations, Department of State, Washington D.C. (September 17, 1963). Series 2, Box 9, Bureau Historical Collection.

30. Ibid.

31. Ibid.

32. Complete itinerary of Ellington's 1963 Mideast tour, "Post Comments," 8.

33. Ibid., 9.

34. Simons, "General Report on the Ellington Tour," 23.

35. Thomas Simons Jr., Interview with Penny Von Eschen (June 17, 2003).

36. Ibid.

37. Ibid.

38. Simons, "General Report on the Ellington Tour," 6.

39. Complete itinerary of Ellington's 1963 Mideast tour, "Post Comments," 10. On Ellington's health, see Simons, "General Report on the Ellington Tour," 39.

40. Complete itinerary of Ellington's 1963 Mideast tour, "Post Comments," 9.

41. Ibid., 10–11.

42. Ibid., 10.

43. Ibid., 12.

44. Ibid., 13–14.

45. Ali, *The Clash of Fundamentalisms,* 110–113; Con Coughlin, *Saddam: King of Terror* (New York: Ecco, HarperCollins, 2002), 39.

46. Little, *American Orientalism,* 205.

47. Ibid., 205–206.

48. Memo from anonymous U.S. official, Baghdad, to United States Information Service, Washington, D.C. (November 11, 1963). Bureau Historical Collection.

49. Ibid.

50. Memo from anonymous U.S. official, Baghdad, to United States Information Service, Washington, D.C. (November 14, 1963). Bureau Historical Collection.

51. Simons, "General Report on the Ellington Tour," 20; Memo from U.S. official to United States Information Service (November 14, 1963).

52. Memo from U.S. official to United States Information Service (November 14, 1963). See also Anonymous, "Baghdad Was Swinging, Says Ellington of Coup, *New York Times* (November 16, 1963), 9.

53. Complete itinerary of Ellington's 1963 Mideast tour, "Post-Comments," 14.

54. Anonymous, "Army Said to Oust Baathists in Iraq: President Reported to Lead Revolt—Communications from Baghdad Cut," *New York Times* (November 18, 1963), 1.

55. Little, *American Orientalism,* 206.

56. Recent scholars have wisely emphasized the limits to U.S. power and control in the Middle East. Yet the enormous scope of political and military involvement, not to mention the sheer number of CIA-backed coups d'état, should serve as a reminder that the United States is deeply implicated in this history. For an excellent discussion of U.S entanglement in this history, see Michael H. Hunt, "In the Wake of September 11: The Clash of What?"

Journal of American History, 89, no. 2 (2000), 416–425. For a delineation of CIA-backed coups from a conservative perspective, see Derek Leebaert, *The Fifty-Year Wound: The True Price of America's Cold War Victory* (Boston: Little, Brown, 2002).

57. Ellington, *Music Is My Mistress*, 314.

58. Anonymous, "Jazz Seemed a Discord, Ellington Tour Ended," *New York Herald Tribune* (November 29, 1963).

59. Simons, Interview with Von Eschen (June 17, 2003); Ellington, *Music Is My Mistress*, 308.

60. Ellington, *Music Is My Mistress*, 302.

61. Ibid., 309. There were actually four girls killed in the bombing.

62. Alyn Shipton, *Groovin' High: The Life of Dizzy Gillespie* (Oxford: Oxford University Press, 1999), 322–324; Dizzy Gillespie with Al Fraser, *To Be or Not to Bop* (Garden City, N.Y.: Doubleday, 1979), 452–461.

63. Gillespie, *To Be or Not to Bop*, 452–461.

64. Stanley Dance, *The World of Duke Ellington* (New York: Scribner's, 1970), 21.

65. Ibid.

66. Simons, "General Report on the Ellington Tour," 6.

67. Ibid., 8.

68. Ibid., 13.

69. Ibid., 15.

70. Simons, Interview with Von Eschen (June 17, 2003).

71. Thomas W. Simons, Jr., "Effectiveness Report: Ellington Tour, 1963," 15–17. Series 2, Box 9, Bureau Historical Collection.

72. Ibid.

73. Ibid.

74. Ibid.

75. Simons, "General Report on the Ellington Tour," 17.

76. Discussion, Duke Ellington Centenary Conference, University of North Carolina Jazz Symposium, Chapel Hill (February 25–27, 1999).

77. Ellington, *Music Is my Mistress*, 318. In Delhi, the band members were invited to the university, where they were given demonstrations of indigenous Indian instruments and introduced to several forms of dance (ibid., 312).

78. Simons, "General Report on the Ellington Tour," 39–40.

79. Ellington, *Music Is My Mistress*, 302.

80. Ibid., 312.

81. Simons, "General Report on the Ellington Tour," 18.

82. Ibid., 14–15.

83. Simons, Interview with Von Eschen (June 17, 2003).

84. Simons, "General Report on the Ellington Tour," 14–15.

85. Ibid., 19.

86. Ibid.

87. Ibid., 20.

88. Ibid., 40.

89. Simons, "The Role of the Escort Officer," 14.

90. Ibid., 16.

91. Simons, "General Report on the Ellington Tour," 24.

92. Ibid., 23–34, 31–33.

93. Ibid., 33–34.

94. Ibid., 41.

95. Ibid., 41–42.

96. Ibid., 43.

97. Ibid., 44.

98. Ibid.

99. Ibid., 44–45.

100. Ibid., 45.

101. David Hajdu, *Lush Life: A Biography of Billy Strayhorn* (New York: Farrar Straus Giroux, 1996), 230–231.

102. Ellington, *Music Is My Mistress,* 330. Ellington's close friend Marian Logan recalled that he was "beside being beside himself. The whole tour was already strange, and now the president went and died on him" (Hajdu, *Lush Life,* 230–231). On the tour's early end, see Anonymous, "Tour Curtailed," *Washington Daily News* (November 29, 1963); and Anonymous, "Jazz Seemed a Discord, Ellington Tour Ended," *New York Herald Tribune* (November 29, 1963), Series 5, Box 11, Bureau Historical Collection.

103. Complete itinerary of Ellington's 1963 Mideast tour, 16.

104. Ibid.

105. Simons, Interview with Von Eschen (June 17, 2003).

106. Complete itinerary of Ellington's 1963 Mideast tour, "Ellington Reaction to Cancellation of the Tour," 16–17.

107. Duke Ellington with Sally Hammond, *Washington Post* (December 6, 1963), in Complete itinerary of Ellington's 1963 Mideast tour, 17.

108. Ibid.

109. Travis A. Jackson, "Tourist Point of View: Ellington's Musical Souvenirs," paper presented at Columbia University, Jazz Studies Group (November 30, 1999).

110. Ellington, "The Duke Steps Out," in Tucker, *The Duke Ellington Reader,* 49.

111. Randy Martin has astutely argued that the modernist appropriation of the

art of "the other" rested on a denial of labor, positing art as pure expression (of the nation) rather than something technical and produced through labor. Randy Martin, "Modern Dance and the American Century," in Townsend Ludington, ed., *A Modern Mosaic: Art and Modernism in the United States* (Chapel Hill: University of North Carolina Press, 2000), 203–226.

112. I am indebted to conversation with Brent Edwards in elaborating this point. For a brilliant reading of Ellington's writing and use of language, see Brent Hayes Edwards, "The Literary Ellington," *Representations,* 77, no. 1 (Winter 2002), 1–29.

113. Jackson, "Tourist Point of View." Practices of appropriation of such pop musicians as Paul Simon and David Byrne have been trenchantly critiqued by George Lipsitz in *Dangerous Crossroads: Popular Music, Postmodernism and the Poetics of Place* (London: Verso, 1994), 56–63.

114. Jackson, "Tourist Point of View."

115. Penny M. Von Eschen, "Satchmo Blows Up the World: Jazz, Race, and Empire during the Cold War," in Reinhold Wagnleitner and Elaine Tyler May, eds., *Here, There, and Everywhere: The Foreign Politics of American Popular Culture* (Hanover, N.H.: University Press of New England, 2000), 163–178.

116. Ellington, *Music Is My Mistress,* p. 436.

117. Dizzy Gillespie, "Morning of the Carnival," *Dizzy for President,* LP, no. ADC1 (Douglas Music).

6. Jazz, Gospel, and R&B

1. George Herring, *America's Longest War: The United States and Vietnam, 1950–1975,* 2nd ed. (New York: Knopf, 1979), 100, 102, 105–106; Jeremi Suri, *Power and Protest: Global Revolution and the Rise of Détente* (Cambridge, Mass:: Harvard University Press, 2003), 144–145.

2. Robin D. G. Kelley, *Freedom Dreams: The Black Radical Imagination* (Boston: Beacon Press, 2002), 60–63.

3. Ibid.

4. Eric Porter, *What Is This Thing Called Jazz? African American Musicians as Artists, Critics, and Activists* (Berkeley: University of California Press, 2002), 210 and all of ch. 5. Ronald Radano, *New Musical Figurations: Anthony Braxton's Cultural Critique,* (Chicago: University of Chicago Press, 1993).

5. Craig Werner, *A Change Is Gonna Come: Music, Race and the Soul of America* (New York: Plume, 1999); Suzanne E. Smith, *Dancing in the Street: Motown and the Cultural Politics of Detroit* (Cambridge, Mass.: Harvard University Press, 1999).

6. On artists' ties to Africa and the importance of the continent in the radical black imagination, see Kelley, *Freedom Dreams,* 13–35.

7. *Foreign Relations of the United States, 1964–1968,* Vol. 24: *Africa,* ed. Nina Davis Howland (Washington, D.C.: GPO, 1999), 300, Document 197: Memo from Ulric Haynes, National Security Council Staff, to McGeorge Bundy, President's Special Assistant for National Security Affairs (June 5, 1965). On African concerns about U.S. policy after the assassination of Kennedy, see Mary L. Dudziak, *Cold War Civil Rights: Race and the Image of American Democracy* (Princeton: Princeton University Press, 2000), 206–207.

8. Thomas Borstelmann, *The Cold War and the Color Line: American Race Relations in the Global Arena* (Cambridge, Mass.: Harvard University Press, 2001), 195–199.

9. David N. Gibbs, *The Political Economy of Third World Intervention: Mines, Money, and U.S. Policy in the Congo Crisis* (Chicago: University of Chicago Press, 1991), 163; Borstelmann, *The Cold War and the Color Line,* 183; Richard D. Mahoney, *JFK: Ordeal in Africa* (New York: Oxford University Press, 1983). Mahoney documents the State Department's embarrassment at the exposure of extensive CIA support for Ghanaian opposition to Nkrumah.

10. *Foreign Relations of the United States, 1964–1968,* 310–312, Document 201: Memo from Secretary of State Rusk to President Johnson (October 14, 1965).

11. Memo to USIS, Department of State, from American Embassy, Dakar, "US Image Bright: Russians Scrambling," Festival Status Report (April 11, 1966); and Memo to Miss Pouplain, White House, from Clive Chandler, on "Dakar Festival," Box 9, Folder 7, Box 33, Folder 25. Bureau of Educational and Cultural Affairs Historical Collection, J. William Fulbright Papers, University of Arkansas at Fayetteville. Hereafter cited as Bureau Historical Collection.

12. Alvin Ailey, Interview with Jane Stott, National Radio of Senegal (April 1966), tape in possession of the author.

13. Ibid.

14. Virginia Inness-Brown, "A Brief Documentary Report on United States Participation in the First World Festival of Negro Arts," Series 2, Box 33, Folder 25, Bureau Historical Collection. "American Artists Winning Prizes at Festival," enclosure to Ambassador McIlvaine from J. Roland Jacobs (August 5, 1966) with proposal that President Senghor present awards to American prize-winners at Dakar festival, Series 2, Box 33, Folder 25, Bureau Historical Collection.

15. Duke Ellington, *Music Is My Mistress* (Garden City, N.Y.: Doubleday, 1973), 337.

16. Duke Ellington, liner notes to *Soul Call,* CD (Verve, 1999).

17. Ellington, *Music Is My Mistress,* 199.

18. Seymour Hersh, "CIA Said to Have Aided Plotters Who Overthrew

Nkrumah," *New York Times* (May 9, 1978), 6; Kevin K. Gaines, *Black Expatriates in Nkrumah's Ghana* (Chapel Hill: University of North Carolina Press, 2005).

19. Bruce Oudes, "Senghor's Arts Festival Held Cultural Imperialism," *Sunday Star* (May 8, 1966); Lloyd Garrison, "The Duke and Those Fabulous Dancers," *New York Times* (April 24, 1966). On Rhodesia and the U.S. response, see Borstelmann, *The Cold War and the Color Line*, 195–201.

20. Lloyd Garrison, "Debate on 'Negritude' Splits Festival in Dakar," *New York Times* (April 24, 1966).

21. Kelley, *Freedom Dreams*, 166.

22. Ibid., 176.

23. On Negritude in a Francophone context, see Brent Hayes Edwards, *The Practice of Diaspora: Literature, Translation, and the Rise of Black Internationalism* (Cambridge, Mass.: Harvard University Press), 24, 120–121, 156, 178–179.

24. Barry Farrell, "Within the Show's Excitement, the Deeper Issue of Négritude," Clipping file, Dakar Festival, Schomburg Center for Research in Black Culture, New York City.

25. Garrison, "Debate on 'Negritude' Splits Festival in Dakar."

26. Ailey, interview with Stott (April 1966).

27. Ibid. See Judith Jamison with Howard Kaplan, *Dancing Spirit: An Autobiography* (New York: Doubleday, 1993), for a discussion of the Ailey Company's "obligation" to make their dance accessible.

28. Garrison, "Debate on 'Negritude' Splits Festival in Dakar."

29. For a recap of the NEA's first years, see "National Endowment Puts Government into Role of Major Patron of the Arts," *New York Times* (August 12, 1973).

30. Richard F. Shepard, "10 Painters Quit Negro Arts Fete," *New York Times* (March 10, 1966); Leslie Carpenter, "Negro Artists Ask 'Rental,'" *Washington Star* (March 13, 1966).

31. Clive Barnes, "Dance: Hoping for a $130,000 Miracle," *New York Times* (March 17, 1966); Donald H. Louchheim, "U.S. Artists Impressive at Dakar, but Organizational Effort Is Rapped," *Washington Post* (April 8, 1966).

32. Lloyd Garrison, "A Gentle Cold-War Wind Wafts through Senegal's Festival of Negro Arts," *New York Times* (Tuesday April 19, 1966).

33. Frank Kofsky, *Black Nationalism and the Revolution in Music* (New York: Pathfinder Press, 1970), 109–111, 119–121.

34. This discussion is in "Recapitulation," Buddy Guy Band, Tour of Africa (April 22–June 16, 1969), 1. Bureau Historical Collection.

35. Memo to Department of State from the U.S. Embassy in on "Educational and Cultural Exchange, Marion Williams Trio Performances in the UAR."

(November [mislabeled October] 28, 1966), Box 32, Folders 1–4. Bureau Historical Collection.

36. Ibid., enclosure 4, page 2.

37. Memo to USIA, Department of State, from American Embassy Lomé on "Cultural Presentation: Marion Williams Trio" (January 6, 1967). Bureau Historical Collection.

38. Memo to Department of State from American Embassy, Cairo, on "Marion Williams Trio Performance in the UAR" (December 14, 1966). Bureau Historical Collection.

39. Ibid.

40. Jennifer Dunning, *Alvin Ailey: A Life in Dance* (New York: Da Capo Press, 1998), 225, 258; Naima Prevots, *Dance for Export: Cultural Diplomacy and the Cold War* (Hanover, N.H.: University Press of New England, 1998).

41. "Recapitulation," Alvin Ailey American Dance Theater, Tour of North Africa (June 29–August 2, 1970), Series 2, Box 1, Folder 12, Bureau Historical Collection. See also Series 5, Box 9, Bureau Historical Collection; Dunning, *Alvin Ailey*, 255, 258.

42. Dunning, *Alvin Ailey*, 224.

43. Ibid.

44. "Itinerary," Alvin Ailey American Dance Theater, Tour of Africa (September 13–November 6, 1967), Bureau Historical Collection.

45. Dunning, *Alvin Ailey*, 224.

46. Jamison, *Dancing Spirit*, 98.

47. Ibid.

48. Ibid., 99.

49. Ibid.

50. "Recapitulation," Alvin Ailey American Dance Theater, Tour of North Africa, 1. Dunning, in contrast to the State Department reports and Jamison's autobiography, emphasizes the difficulty of the tour, from the State Department's failure to provide adequate accommodations to initially cool receptions at each stop (Dunning, *Alvin Ailey*, 225).

51. Jamison, *Dancing Spirit*, 198.

52. Dunning, *Alvin Ailey*, 224.

53. "Recapitulation," Alvin Ailey American Dance Theater, Tour of North Africa, 1.

54. Ibid., 4.

55. Gibbs, The *Political Economy of Third World Intervention*, 163. For U.S. response to and involvement in events in the years preceding the coup, see Borstelmann, *The Cold War and the Color Line*, 183–186.

56. Jamison, *Dancing Spirit*, 100.

57. Borstelmann, *The Cold War and the Color Line,* 183–184.

58. Jamison, *Dancing Spirit,* 100.

59. "Recapitulation," Alvin Ailey American Dance Theater, Tour of North Africa, 1.

60. Ibid.

61. Catherine M. Cole, *Ghana's Concert Party Theatre* (Bloomington: Indiana University Press, 2001); Laura Fair, *Pastimes and Politics: Culture, Community, and Identity in Post-Abolition Urban Zanzibar, 1890–1945* (Athens: Ohio University Press, 2001).

62. Jamison, *Dancing Spirit,* 100–101.

63. Ibid., 100.

64. Minutes, Meeting of the Subcommittee on Jazz (August 30, 1967), 3. Series 5, Box 13, Folder 13, Bureau Historical Collection.

65. Ibid.

66. Memo to Department of State from Arthur T. Tienken, American Consul, Elisabethville (Republic of the Congo), on "Visit of Woody Herman Band" (May 3, 1966).

67. Ibid.

68. Memo to Department of State from Charles M. Ellison on "AP Story on Woody Herman" (May 10, 1966). Series 2, Box 14, Folder 7, Bureau Historical Collection.

69. Randy Weston, Interview with Ingrid Monson, Washington University, St. Louis, Missouri (March 1998). Valerie Wilmer, "Randy Weston: The Beat Is Universal," *Down Beat* (September 4, 1969), 16–17, 30. The following section draws on Monson's interview, as well as on the research she generously shared with me from her book *Freedom Sounds: Jazz, Civil Rights and Africa* (New York: Oxford University Press, forthcoming).

70. On the *Freedom Now Suite* and the evocation of Africa in jazz, see Monson, *Freedom Sounds;* and Eric Porter, *What Is This Thing Called Jazz? African American Musicians as Artists, Critics, and Activists* (Berkeley: University of California Press, 2002), 195–196.

71. Harry Hirsch to Charles M. Ellison, Director, Office of Cultural Presentations, Department of State, Washington, D.C. (January 22, 1967), Box 31, Folders 23–27, Bureau Historical Collection.

72. Randy Weston, "Background Material on Compositions To Be Used in Regular Concerts" (December 6, 1966). Series 2, Box 31, Bureau Historical Collection.

73. Ibid.

74. Ibid.

75. Georgia Griggs, "With Randy Weston in Africa," *Down Beat* (July 13, 1967), 16–17, 38–39.

76. Anonymous, "Randy Weston in Algiers," *El Moudjahid* [Algiers] (April 4, 1967), original and English translation in Bureau Historical Collection.

77. Anonymous, "Return to Origins," *An Nasr* [Algiers] (April 4, 1967), Bureau Historical Collection.

78. Randy Weston to Thomas Huff, Office of Cultural Presentations, Department of State (April 28, 1967); and Randy Weston, "Report on State Department Tour of West and North Africa" (January 16–April 11, 1967). Series 5, Box 9, and Series 2, Box 31, Bureau Historical Collection. Hirsch insisted that Griggs wrote the report, but Weston's authorship and his sharing of these views with Griggs were corroborated by Weston, Interview with Penny Von Eschen and Kevin Gaines, Austin, Texas (October 1998).

79. Harry Hirsch to Charles M. Ellison, Director, Office of Cultural Presentations, Department of State, Washington, D.C. (November 25, 1966; emphasis added), Box 31, Folders 23–27, Bureau Historical Collection.

80. Randy Weston, Interview with Von Eschen and Gaines (October 1998).

81. Porter, *What Is This Thing Called Jazz?* 205–206.

82. Ibid.

83. Griggs, "With Randy Weston in Africa," 17.

84. Ibid.

85. Ibid., 38.

86. Harry Hirsch to Charles M. Ellison, Director, Office of Cultural Presentations, Department of State, Washington, D.C. (February 7, 1967), Box 31, Folders 23–27, Bureau Historical Collection.

87. Airgram to Department of State from American Embassy, Algiers, on "The Randy Weston Sextet in Algiers" (April 13, 1967), 2. Series 2, Box 31, Bureau Historical Collection.

88. Ibid.

89. "Recapitulation," Randy Weston Jazz Sextet, Tour of Africa (January 17–April 10, 1967), 7.

90. Wilmer, "Randy Weston: The Beat Is Universal," 16–17, 30.

91. "Recapitulation," Charlie Byrd Quintet, Tour of Africa (June 29–August 23, 1969).

92. In addition to the 1969 tour of East and Central Africa, Buddy Guy and his band would return to the continent as the Guy-Wells Blues Band in 1975 for a fourteen-country tour.

93. Manthia Diawara, *In Search of Africa* (Cambridge, Mass.: Harvard University Press, 1998), 102.

94. Through the vagaries of memory, Diawara notes the year as 1965 rather than 1968 for the Wells concert. Several of the songs he remembers Wells playing had not yet been written in 1965.

95. Manthia Diawara, "The 1960s in Bamako: Malik Sidibé and James Brown,"

Paper Series on the Arts, Culture, and Society, Andy Warhol Foundation for the Visual Arts, Paper 11 (2001), 11–20.

96. Memo to Department of State from American Embassy, Dar es Salaam, on "Visit of Buddy Guy and His Band" (May 7, 1969). Series 2, Box 13, Folders 9–12, Bureau Historical Collection.

97. Anonymous, "Buddy Goes but Leaves His 'Soul' Behind," *Sunday News* [Dar es Salaam] (May 11, 1969), Bureau Historical Collection.

98. Anonymous article, *Sunday News* [Dar es Salaam] (May 4, 1969), Bureau Historical Collection.

99. Memo to Department of State from American Embassy, Dar es Salaam on "Visit of Buddy Guy and His Band" (May 7, 1969).

100. Andrew M. Ivaska, "Negotiating 'Culture' in a Cosmopolitan Capital: Urban Syle and the Tanzanian State in Colonial and Postcolonial Dar es Salaam," Ph.D. dissertation, University of Michigan, Ann Arbor (2003).

101. Ibid.

102. Memo to Department of State from American Embassy, Nairobi, on "Buddy Guy Band, Nairobi" (June 1–8, 1969; June 18, 1969), Bureau Historical Collection.

103. Memo to Department of State from American Embassy, Dar es Salaam on "Visit of Buddy Guy and His Band" (May 7, 1969), 7–8.

104. On ties between African American and Indian freedom movements, see Penny M. Von Eschen, *Race against Empire: Black Americans and Anticolonialism, 1937–1957* (Ithaca: Cornell University Press, 1997), 28–32, 83–95, 162–163; and Brenda Gayle Plummer, *Rising Wind: Black Americans and U.S. Foreign Affairs, 1935–1960* (Chapel Hill: University of North Carolina Press, 1996), 218–222.

105. Memo to Department of State from American Embassy, New Delhi, India, on "Educational and Cultural Exchange: Cultural Presentations—Mahalia Jackson" (June 17, 1971), Box 15, Folders 1–3, Bureau Historical Collection.

106. Quoted in H. W. Brands, *India and the United States: The Cold Peace* (Boston: Twayne, 1990), 130. See also Andrew Jon Rotter, *Comrades at Odds: The United States and India, 1947–1964* (Ithaca: Cornell University Press, 2000).

107. Tariq Ali, *The Clash of Fundamentalisms: Crusades, Jihads and Modernity* (London: Verso, 2003), 186–188.

108. U.S. consul in Dacca, quoted in Brands, *India and the United States,* 130.

109. Memo to Department of State from American Embassy, New Delhi, India, on "Educational and Cultural Exchange: Cultural Presentations—Mahalia Jackson" (June 17, 1971).

110. Ibid., 3.

111. Shanta Serjeet Singh, "A Spell-Binder Who Overcame," *Economic Times* [Bombay] (May 10, 1971), Bureau Historical Collection.

112. Anonymous, "Godward on Wings of Song," *Times of India* (May 3, 1971), Bureau Historical Collection.

7. Improvising Détente

1. The best discussion of the Nixon administration's policies on race, both domestically and internationally, is in Thomas Borstelmann, *The Cold War and the Color Line: American Race Relations in the Global Arena* (Cambridge, Mass.: Harvard University Press, 2001), 223–242.

2. Ibid., 227–228.

3. Jeremi Suri, *Power and Protest: Global Revolution and the Rise of Détente* (Cambridge, Mass.: Harvard University Press, 2003), 246.

4. George Herring, *America's Longest War: The United States and Vietnam,* 2nd ed. (New York: Knopf, 1979), 241–244. See also Maurice Isserman and Michael Kazin, *America Divided: The Civil War of the 1960s* (New York: Oxford University Press, 2000).

5. Geoff Eley, *Forging Democracy: The History of the Left in Europe, 1850–2000* (Oxford: Oxford University Press, 2002), 356–357.

6. Suri, *Power and Protest,* 200.

7. Eley, *Forging Democracy,* 357–360.

8. Suri, *Power and Protest,* 204–205, 246.

9. Ibid., 206.

10. Phil Woods, "Life in E Flat," unpublished manuscript, 196–197.

11. George Wein and Bob Jones, Interview with Penny Von Eschen and Kevin Gaines, May 15, 2001, New York City; George Wein with Nate Chinen, *Myself among Others: A Life in Music* (New York: Da Capo Press, 2003), 182–186.

12. Transcript of Proceedings, Sub-Panel on Folk Music and Jazz (May 27, 1970). Series 5, Box 13, Folder 13, Bureau of Educational and Cultural Affairs Historical Collection, J. William Fulbright Papers, University of Arkansas at Fayetteville. Hereafter cited as Bureau Historical Collection.

13. Eric Porter, *What Is This Thing Called Jazz? African American Musicians as Artists, Critics, and Activists* (Berkeley: University of California Press, 2002), 134–135.

14. Ibid., 195–196.

15. Ibid.

16. Ibid., 271.

17. Suri, *Power and Protest,* 164–212.

18. See, for example, the State Department discussion of this relationship in "Recapitulation," Dave Brubeck–Gerry Mulligan and Trio and Earl "Fatha" Hines, Eastern Europe (1970), Bureau Historical Collection. Also George Wein and Bob Jones, Interview with Von Eschen and Gaines, May 15, 2001.

19. George Wein and Bob Jones, Interview with Von Eschen and Gaines, May 15, 2001.

20. "Recapitulation," Dave Brubeck–Gerry Mulligan and Trio and Earl "Fatha" Hines.

21. Memo to Department of State, Washington, D.C., from Stoessel, American Embassy, Warsaw, on "Concert by Dave Brubeck and Trio with Gerry Mulligan at 1970 Warsaw Jazz Jamboree," 1. Bureau Historical Collection.

22. Ibid. The average monthly income for an adult employed Pole in 1969 was 2,422 złotys (*Rocznik Statystyczny 1970* [Warsaw: Główny Urząd Statystyczny, 1970], 522). Six thousand złotys in 1970 was the rough equivalent of $60. The average price of one dollar on the black market (the only way to obtain dollars at the time) fluctuated between 80 and 120 złotys. I thank my colleagues Brian Porter and Magdalena Zaborowska for their assistance on this point.

23. Memo to Department of State, Washington, D.C., from American Embassy, Bucharest (December 28, 1970), 4, Bureau Historical Collection.

24. "Recapitulation," Dave Brubeck–Gerry Mulligan and Trio and Earl "Fatha" Hines.

25. Memo to Department of State from American Embassy, Bucharest (December 28, 1970), 3.

26. "Recapitulation," Dave Brubeck–Gerry Mulligan and Trio and Earl "Fatha" Hines.

27. Ibid., 2–3.

28. Leonard Feather and Ira Gitler, *The Biographical Encyclopedia of Jazz* (Oxford: Oxford University Press, 1999), 446–447.

29. Transcript of proceedings, Panel on Folk Music and Jazz (May 30, 1972), 36–37. Bureau Historical Collection.

30. Memo to Department of State, Washington, D.C., from American Embassy, Belgrade, on "Newport Jazz in Belgrade: Wrap-Up Report" (December 10, 1970), 1–2.

31. Memo to Department of State from American Embassy, Bucharest (December 28, 1970), 4–6.

32. "Recapitulation," Dave Brubeck–Gerry Mulligan and Trio and Earl "Fatha" Hines.

33. Ibid.

34. Memo to Department of State from American Embassy, Bucharest (December 28, 1970), 6.

35. Brian Ward, *Just My Soul Responding: Rhythm and Blues, Black Consciousness, and Race Relations* (Berkeley: University of California Press, 1998); Uta G. Poiger, *Jazz Rock and Rebels: Cold War Politics and American Culture in a Divided Germany* (Berkeley: University of California Press, 2000).

36. "Recapitulation," Blood, Sweat, and Tears, Tour of Yugoslavia, Romania, Poland (June 13–July 8, 1970). Series 2, Box 5, Bureau Historical Collection.

37. Ibid., 2.

38. Ibid.

39. Memo to President Nixon from William P. Rogers on "Lionel Hampton in Eastern Europe" (April 12, 1971), Series 2, Box 14, Folder 2, Bureau Historical Collection. On the policies of Rogers, see Borstelmann, *The Cold War and the Color Line,* 227–228.

40. Memo to President Nixon from William P. Rogers on "Lionel Hampton in Eastern Europe" (April 12, 1971), Attachments.

41. Memo from Howard Meyers to Thomas D. Huff on "Meeting on Duke Ellington Tour" (June 3, 1969). Bureau Historical Collection.

42. Ibid., 3. See also "Recapitulation," American Jazz Week in Eastern Europe: Czechoslovakia, Poland, Yugoslavia, Hungary, Romania (October 29–November 4, 1971) and Sweden (November 9–10, 1971), Bureau Historical Collection.

43. "Recapitulation," American Jazz Week in Eastern Europe and Sweden, 1.

44. Ibid., 2–3.

45. Dejan Patakovic, "The Newport '72 Festival, November 7–10: Belgrade Jazz Days," *Politika Ekspres* [Belgrade] (February 14, 1972), Bureau Historical Collection.

46. Memo to State Department, Washington, D.C., from the American Embassy, Moscow, on "Cultural Exchange: The Earl Hines Band in the Soviet Union" (September 6, 1966), 2. Series 2, Box 14, Folder 11, Bureau Historical Collection.

47. Ibid.

48. Ibid., 4, 9.

49. Ibid.

50. Ibid., 10.

51. Ibid., 11.

52. Ibid., 1–3.

53. Ibid., 1, 3.

54. Ibid., 13.

55. "Recapitulation," Alvin Ailey American Dance Theater, Tour of USSR, France, and England, 1–2. Bureau Historical Collection.

56. Ibid., 2.

57. Judith Jamison with Howard Kaplan, *Dancing Spirit: An Autobiography* (New York: Doubleday, 1993).

58. Telegram to American Embassy, Moscow, from the Secretary of State, Washington, D.C., on "Exchanges, Incident at Soviet Exhibit" (March 1970), Series 1, Box 4, Bureau Historical Collection.

59. Memo of Conversation, Department of State, Washington, D.C., on "Disruption of Moiseyev Dance Ensemble Performance" (August 27, 1970), Bureau Historical Collection; and Telegram to American Embassy, Moscow, from Secretary of State, Washington, D.C. (August 1970), Series 1, Box 4, Bureau Historical Collection.

60. Memo of Conversation, Department of State, Washington, D.C., on "Disruption of Moiseyev Dance Ensemble Performance" (August 27, 1970), Bureau Historical Collection.

61. Memo to Secretary of State, Washington, D.C., from American Embassy, Moscow, on "Another JDL Denunciation" (December 1970), Series 1, Box 4, Bureau Historical Collection. Memo to American Embassy, Moscow, from Secretary of State, Washington, D.C., on "Exchanges: Cancellation of Bolshoi Opera and Ballet" (December 1970), Bureau Historical Collection.

62. Memo to Secretary of State, Washington, D.C., from American Embassy, Moscow, on "Cancellation of Bolshoi Engagements" (December 1970), Series 1, Box 4, Bureau Historical Collection.

63. Ibid. See also Memo to American Embassy, Moscow, from Secretary of State, on "Exchanges: Cancellation of Bolshoi Opera and Ballet." See also David Caute, *The Dancer Defects: The Struggle for Cultural Supremacy during the Cold War* (Oxford: Oxford University Press, 2003), 468–505.

64. Memo to Secretary of State from American Embassy, Moscow, on "Cancellation of Bolshoi Engagements."

65. Murrey Marder, "U.S. Boycotts Soviet Festival: Films Protested," *Washington Post* (May 1, 1971).

66. Robert D. Schulzinger, *American Diplomacy in the Twentieth Century* (New York: Oxford University Press, 1994), 299. Herbert S. Parmet, *Richard Nixon and His America* (Boston: Little Brown, 1990); Joan Hoff, *Nixon Reconsidered* (New York: Basic Books, 1994); Tom Wicker, *One of Us: Richard Nixon and the American Dream* (New York: Random House, 1991).

67. Schulzinger, *American Diplomacy in the Twentieth Century,* 299–300.

68. John Edward Hasse, *Beyond Category: The Life and Genius of Duke Ellington* (New York: Simon and Schuster, 1993), 373.

69. Ibid.
70. For accounts of Ellington at the White House, see Duke Ellington, *Music Is My Mistress* (Garden City, N.Y.: Doubleday, 1973), 424–433; Hasse, *Beyond Category*, 373–375; Stanley Dance, *The World of Duke Ellington* (New York: Scribner's, 1970), 283–289.
71. Memo from Howard Meyers to Thomas D. Huff on "Meeting on Duke Ellington Tour" (June 3, 1969), 4.
72. Joseph A. Presel (escort officer), "Duke Ellington in the USSR, September–October 1971" (Trip Report), 5. Series 5, Box 9, Bureau Historical Collection.
73. Ellington, *Music Is My Mistress*, 364. For Ellington's reflections on the tour, see 364–380.
74. "Recapitulation," Duke Ellington Orchestra, Tour of Soviet Union (September 10–October 3, 1971), Bureau Historical Collection.
75. Memo to Department of State, Washington, D.C., from B. H. Klosson, American Embassy, Moscow, on "Duke Ellington in the USSR" (December 10, 1971), 2. Bureau Historical Collection.
76. Memo to President Nixon from William P. Rogers (October 20, 1971), 2. Bureau Historical Collection.
77. Presel, "Duke Ellington in the USSR," 2.
78. Hasse, *Beyond Category*, 380.
79. Leonard Feather, "Ellington Concert a Diplomatic Coup" (October 24, 1971), Series 2, Box 9, Bureau Historical Collection.
80. Hendrick Smith, "Leningrad Goes Wild over the Duke," *New York Times* (September 14, 1971).
81. Ibid.
82. Ibid.
83. Feather, "Ellington Concert a Diplomatic Coup."
84. Memo to Department of State, Washington, D.C., from B. H. Klosson, American Embassy, Moscow, on "Duke Ellington in the USSR" (December 10, 1971), 4, 6–8. Bureau Historical Collection.
85. Presel, "Duke Ellington in the USSR," 8–9.
86. Memo to Department of State, Washington, D.C., from department official Beam, American Embassy, Moscow, on "Some Notes on the 1971 Leningrad Jazz Scene" (October 22, 1971), 1. Bureau Historical Collection.
87. Memo to Department of State from B. H. Klosson (December 10, 1971), 4.
88. Memo to Department of State from B. H. Klosson (December 10, 1971), 1.
89. Presel, "Duke Ellington in the USSR," 12.
90. "Recapitulation," Duke Ellington Orchestra, Tour of Soviet Union (September 10–October 3, 1971), 2.

91. Memo to Department of State from department official Beam,(October 22, 1971), 1–2.
92. Ibid., 3.
93. Ibid.
94. Presel, "Duke Ellington in the USSR," 5.
95. Ibid., 6, 11.
96. Memo to Department of State from B. H. Klosson (December 10, 1971), 8.
97. Presel, "Duke Ellington in the USSR," 7–8.
98. Ibid.
99. Ibid., 8.
100. Memo from U.S. Internal Revenue Service to Department of State (September 21, 1971), Bureau Historical Collection.
101. Memo of Conversation, Department of State, on "Duke Ellington Tax Indebtedness" (September 22, 1971), Bureau Historical Collection.
102. Memo to Department of State from B. H. Klosson (December 10, 1971), 9.
103. Presel, "Duke Ellington in the USSR," 11; Memo to Department of State from B. H. Klosson (December 10, 1971), 3.
104. Quoted in Stanley Dance, "The Long Road Home: Mercer Ellington Talks to Stanley Dance," *Down Beat,* 39, no. 7 (April 13, 1972).
105. Robert G. O'Meally, "Duke Ellington Plays the Audience," paper presented at the Duke Ellington Centenary Conference, University of North Carolina Jazz Symposium, Chapel Hill (February 25–27, 1999).
106. Presel, "Duke Ellington in the USSR," 5. Apparently, the escort officer's report was becoming something of a literary genre in its own right. Presel's often witty and blunt twelve-page report poked fun at the earnest restraint of the approximately seventy-page report by escort officer Thomas W. Simons Jr., composed after Ellington's 1963 Middle Eastern tour. "Since it seems inconceivable to me that more than five people will ever read this paper," wrote Presel, "and since they all know who the escort officer was, I propose to eschew the third person so beloved of authors of similar efforts" (ibid., 1).
107. Memo to Department of State from B. H. Klosson (December 10, 1971), 9.
108. Ibid.
109. Feather, "Ellington Concert a Diplomatic Coup." Ellington notes the acknowledgment of Pravda in *Music Is My Mistress,* 374.
110. Presel, "Duke Ellington in the USSR," 4.
111. Feather, "Ellington Concert a Diplomatic Coup."
112. Memo to Department of State from B. H. Klosson (December 10, 1971), 7.
113. Ibid.
114. Presel, "Duke Ellington in the USSR," 2.

115. Feather, "Ellington Concert a Diplomatic Coup."

116. Mary Campbell, "Duke to Play in Russia," *Evening Star* (August, 30, 1971).

117. Grant Agreement, letter to George Wein, Festival Productions, from Mark Lewis, Department of State (May 20, 1971). Bureau Historical Collection.

118. Memo to U.S. Information Agency, Department of State, from American Embassy, San José, on "Cultural Presentations: Duke Ellington Acclaimed in San José Concert" (December 17, 1971). Bureau Historical Collection.

119. Memo to Department of State, Washington, D.C., from Turner Shelton, American Embassy, Managua, on "Duke Ellington Orchestra Concerts" (December 16, 1971), 1–2. Bureau Historical Collection.

120. Memo to L. Dayton Coe II from Martin C. Carroll Jr. on "ARA Tour by Duke Ellington and Orchestra" (April 8, 1971). Bureau Historical Collection.

121. Memo to American embassies in Bogotá, Buenos Aires, Caracas, Lima, Managua, Mexico, Montevideo, Panama, Quito, Rio de Janeiro, San José, and Santiago from Department of State, Washington, D.C., on "Cultural Presentations: Duke Ellington and Orchestra" (November 4, 1971). Bureau Historical Collection.

122. Quoted in Dance, "The Long Road Home: Mercer Ellington Talks to Stanley Dance."

123. Iola Brubeck, Interview with Penny Von Eschen, Ann Arbor, Michigan (December 2002).

124. Quoted in Dance, "The Long Road Home: Mercer Ellington Talks to Stanley Dance," 14.

125. Ibid.

126. Dave Brubeck and Iola Brubeck, Interview with Penny Von Eschen and Kevin Gaines (March 13, 1997), Wilton, Conn.

127. "Recapitulation," Duke Ellington Orchestra, Rangoon, Burma (January 31–February 1, 1970), 1–2.

128. T. D. Allman, "Ellington's Music Part of a Stream Fed from Many Sources," *Bangkok Post* (February 1, 1970).

129. Ibid.

130. Wein, *Myself among Others,* 301–302.

131. Robert J. McMahon, *Limits of Empire: The United States and Southeast Asia since World War II* (New York: Columbia University Press, 1999), 150–170, and especially 164–165 on the United States and Laos.

132. Bob Jones, Interview with Penny Von Eschen and Kevin Gaines (May 15, 2001), New York City.

133. Ellington, *Music Is My Mistress,* 381–389; Bob Jones, Interview with Von Eschen and Gaines (May 2001); George Wein and Bob Jones, Interview

with Von Eschen and Gaines (May 15, 2001); Memo to Department of State from American Embassy, Manila, on "Cultural Presentations, Duke Ellington" (February 26, 1971); Memo to Department of State from American Embassy, Rangoon, on "End-of-the-Month Round-Up: Duke Ellington Visits Mandalay" (January 31, 1972); Memo to Department of State from American Embassy, Colombo, on "Educational and Cultural Exchange: Duke Ellington" (February 9, 1972). All memos in Bureau Historical Collection.

134. Memo to Secretary of State, Washington, D.C., from American Embassy, Saigon, no subject heading (December 1971). Bureau Historical Collection.

135. American Embassy, Saigon, "Educational and Cultural Exchange: Annual Report" (July 16, 1968). Country Files, Bureau Historical Collection.

136. Memo to U.S. Information Agency, Washington, D.C., from U.S. Information Service, Saigon, on "Martha Graham Dance Company in Saigon" (October 21, 1974), 9. Boxes 12–13, Bureau Historical Collection.

137. On this point, see Bruce Cumings, "The Wicked Witch of the West Is Dead: Long Live the Wicked Witch of the East," in Michael J. Hogan, ed., *The End of the Cold War: Its Meaning and Implications* (New York: Cambridge University Press, 1992), 87–101; and Walter LaFeber, "An End to Which Cold War?" also in Hogan, *The End of the Cold War,* 13–19.

138. Reinhold Wagnleitner, "The Empire of Fun, or Talkin' Soviet Blues: The Sound of Freedom and U.S. Cultural Hegemony in Europe," *Diplomatic History,* 23, no. 3 (Summer 1999).

8. Playing the International Changes

1. Meher Pestonji, "Jazz Yatra '78," *Eve's Weekly* (March 18–24, 1978), Bureau Historical Collection; Leonard Feather and Ira Gitler, *The Biographical Encyclopedia of Jazz* (Oxford: Oxford University Press, 1999), 567–568.

2. Pestonji, "Jazz Yatra '78," 8.

3. Jeremi Suri, *Power and Protest: Global Revolution and the Rise of Détente* (Cambridge, Mass.: Harvard University Press, 2003), 215.

4. Thomas C. Holt, *The Problem of Race in the Twenty-First Century* (Cambridge, Mass.: Harvard University Press, 2000); Robin D. G. Kelley, *Yo' Mamma's Disfunktional! Fighting the Culture Wars in Urban America* (Boston: Beacon Press, 1997), 4–9.

5. Kelley, *Yo' Mamma's Disfunktional!* 7.

6. Gil Scott-Heron, "Bicentennial Blues" (1976), Gil Scott-Heron and Brian Jackson, *It's Your World* (5001, Arista).

7. Department of State, Press Release, "Department-Sponsored Tour by Fifth Dimension" (February 2, 1973). Bureau of Educational and Cultural Affairs Historical Collection, J. William Fulbright Papers, University of Arkansas at Fayetteville. Hereafter cited as Bureau Historical Collection.

8. Marilyn McCoo, Radio interview, broadcast on WMJC FM, Austin, Texas, January 1998.

9. Rogers, Cowan, and Brenner, Inc., Public relations release, "The Fifth Dimension, by Marilyn McCoo," Bureau Historical Collection. See also Memo to Department of State, Washington, D.C., from American Embassy, Ankara, on "The Visit of the Fifth Dimension to Turkey" (April 24, 1973), Bureau Historical Collection.

10. Public relations release, "The Fifth Dimension, by Lamonte McLemore." Bureau Historical Collection.

11. Memo to Secretary of State, Washington, D.C., from U.S. Information Service, Istanbul, on "Fifth Dimension Concert in Turkey" (April 1973). Bureau Historical Collection.

12. Memo to Department of State, Washington, D.C., from American Embassy, Warsaw, on "Fifth Dimension in Poland" (April 17–25, 1973). Bureau Historical Collection.

13. The Fifth Dimension, Interview with Ted Koppel, *ABC's Issues and Answers* (May 13, 1973). Transcript, Bureau Historical Collection.

14. Memo to Department of State, Washington, D.C, from American Embassy, Belgrade, on "Newport Jazz Festival in Belgrade" (December 28, 1973). Bureau Historical Collection.

15. Anonymous, "Four Days of Jazz," *Borba* [Belgrade] (November 9, 1973), 15–16.

16. Anonymous, "Two Famous Legends," *Politika* [Belgrade] (November 7, 1973), 7.

17. Anonymous, "Jazz Will Exist as Long as There Are Young People," *Vecernje Novosti* [Belgrade] (November 6, 1973), 4.

18. Anonymous, "Four Days of Jazz," 16.

19. Vojislav Simic, "The Birth of New Sound," *Politika* [Belgrade] (November 9, 1973), 18.

20. Ibid.

21. Anonymous, "Four Days of Jazz," 15–16.

22. Igor Antic, "Is Duke Tired of Everything?" *Delo* [Belgrade] (November 9, 1973), 14; John Edward Hasse, *Beyond Category: The Life and Genius of Duke Ellington* (New York: Simon and Schuster, 1993), 384.

23. George Wein to L. Dayton Coe II, Office of Cultural Presentations (August 6, 1973). Bureau Historical Collection.

24. Memo to Department of State, Washington, D.C., from American Embassy, Addis Ababa, on "Duke Ellington and Orchestra Visit to Ethiopia" (December 14, 1973). Bureau Historical Collection.

25. Ibid., 3.

26. Ibid., 4.

27. Ibid., 3.

28. Memo to Department of State from American Embassy, Addis Ababa (December 14, 1973), 5.

29. The biographical information on Astatqé is from the liner notes of *Ethiopiques: Golden Years of Ethiopian Music* (Amha Eshete / Amha Records).

30. Memo to Department of State from American Embassy, Addis Ababa (December 14, 1973), 5.

31. News release, U.S. Information Service, Addis Ababa and Asmara (November 21, 1973). Bureau Historical Collection.

32. Memo to Mark Lewis, Director of Cultural Presentations, Department of State, Washington, D.C., from Arthur W. Lewis, Public Affairs Officer, U.S. Foreign Service, Lusaka, Zambia (August 23, 1973). Bureau Historical Collection.

33. Memo to Department of State, Washington, D.C., from American Embassy, Lusaka, Zambia (December 18, 1973), 1–2. Bureau Historical Collection.

34. Ibid., 1–5.

35. Ibid., 2–3.

36. Anonymous article, *Zambia Daily Mail* [Lusaka] (November 24, 1973), 5.

37. Valerie Wilmer, "Jazz: Africa Makes the People Dance," *Zambia Daily Mail* [Lusaka] (November 24, 1973).

38. Michael E. Veal, *Fela: The Life and Times of an African Musical Icon* (Philadelphia: Temple University Press, 2000), 69–71; George Lipsitz, *Dangerous Crossroads: Popular Music, Postmodernism, and the Poetics of Place* (Verso: London, 1994), 39–40.

39. Veal, *Fela,* 72, 80.

40. Ibid., 70.

41. Ibid., 88–89.

42. Memo to Department of State, Washington, D.C., from American Embassy, Lagos, Nigeria, on "B. B. King: Final Report—Nigerian Stopover, November 23–26." Box 15, Folders 19–20, Bureau Historical Collection.

43. Memo to Department of State, Washington, D.C., from American Embassy, Accra, Ghana, on "B. B. King in Accra" (December 4, 1973), Bureau Historical Collection. On black expatriates in Ghana, see Kevin K. Gaines,

Black Expatriates in Nkrumah's Ghana (Chapel Hill: University of North Carolina Press, 2005).

44. Memo to Department of State from American Embassy, Accra, on "B. B. King in Accra" (December 4, 1973).

45. Memo to Department of State from American Embassy, Lagos, on "B. B. King: Final Report," 2–3.

46. Les Ledbetter, "B. B. King Refreshed by First Africa Tour," *New York Times* (December 7, 1973), 37.

47. Memo to Secretary of State, Washington, D.C., from American Embassy, Nairobi, on "Kenyan Tenth Anniversary Celebration" (July 1973). Box 12, Folder 10, Bureau Historical Collection.

48. Ibid. Memo to American Embassy, Nairobi, from Department of State, on "Kenya Anniversary Celebration" (September 1973). Memo to George Wein from Department of State, on "Contract Made through Festival Productions: Grant Agreement SCC-1069-477011" (December 3, 1973), 1–3. All in Bureau Historical Collection.

49. "Recapitulation: Cultural Presentations—List of Attractions," 6, "Jazz: Kenya Independence Anniversary and Tanzania—Dizzy Gillespie Quartet" (December 9–15, 1973). Bureau Historical Collection.

50. Anonymous, "Dizzy Praises Kenyans," *Daily Nation* [Nairobi] (December 7, 1973), 16; Anonymous, "The Dizzy Heights," *Daily Nation* (December 13, 1973), 17. See also Anonymous, "U.S. Musicians for Our Celebrations," *Sunday Post* [Nairobi] (December 2, 1973), 1.

51. Leonard Feather, "African Debut for Ambassador Diz," *Los Angeles Times* (January 6, 1975).

52. Olinga Fernandez, "Gillespie May Be Back—to Play with the People," *Daily Nation* [Nairobi] (December 19, 1973), 15.

53. Feather, "African Debut for Ambassador Diz."

54. Ibid.

55. Ibid.

56. Memo to Secretary of State from American Embassy, Nairobi, on "The Dizzy Gillespie Quartet's Visit to Kenya, December 10–12, 1973" (December 28, 1973), 2.

57. Fernandez, "Gillespie May Be Back."

58. Ibid.

59. Ibid.

60. Memo to Department of State, Washington, D.C., from American Embassy, Nairobi, on "The Dizzy Gillespie Quartet's Visit to Kenya" (December 10–12, 1973). Bureau Historical Collection.

61. "Recapitulation: Cultural Presentations—List of Attractions" (December 9–15, 1973), 1–2.
62. Memo to Secretary of State, Washington, D.C., from American Embassy, Dar es Salaam, on "Dizzy Gillespie Visit" (December 1973). Bureau Historical Collection.
63. Memo to U.S. Information Agency, Washington, D.C., from U.S. Information Service, Dar es Salaam, on "Dizzy Gillespie Quartet in Tanzania" (December 20, 1973), 2. Bureau Historical Collection.
64. "Dizzy Gillespie in East Africa (Kenya and Tanzania)," Cultural Presentations Weekly Report (January 31, 1974), Box 12, Folder 10, Bureau Historical Collection.
65. Memo to Department of State from American Embassy, Nairobi, on "The Dizzy Gillespie Quartet's Visit to Kenya, December 10–12, 1973" (December 28, 1973), 3.
66. See John Collins, *West African Pop Roots* (Philadelphia: Temple University Press, 1992).
67. Memo to American Embassy, Athens, from Henry Kissinger, Department of State (November 1973). Bureau Historical Collection.
68. Hasse, *Beyond Category,* 384.
69. Script and correspondence, Festival Production archives, personal papers of George Wein. Memo to U.S. Information Agency, Washington, D.C., from American Embassy, Warsaw, on "1975 Jazz Jamboree" (October 29, 1975), Bureau Historical Collection.
70. Memo to U.S. Information Agency from American Embassy, Warsaw, on "1975 Jazz Jamboree" (October 29, 1975). George Wein and Bob Jones, Interview with Penny Von Eschen and Kevin Gaines (May 15, 2001), New York City.
71. Thomas Borstelmann, *The Cold War and the Color Line: American Race Relations in the Global Arena* (Cambridge, Mass.: Harvard University Press, 2001), 239.
72. Ibid., 150.
73. Ibid., 238.
74. Scott-Heron, "Bicentennial Blues."
75. Borstelmann, *The Cold War and the Color Line,* 240.
76. Memo to U.S. Information Agency, Washington, D.C., from U.S. Information Service, Accra, Ghana, on "December Highlights" (January 19, 1976). Bureau Historical Collection.
77. Ibid.
78. Borstelmann, *The Cold War and the Color Line.*

79. Memo to Guy E. Coriden from Randolph Marcus on "Escort Report: The Guy-Wells Blues Band" (February 6, 1976). Box 13, Folders 14–17, Bureau Historical Collection.

80. Memo to U.S. Information Agency from U.S. Information Service, Accra, on "December Highlights" (January 19, 1976).

81. Memo to U.S. Information Agency from U.S. Information Service, N'Djamena, Chad, on "Junior Wells–Buddy Guy Blues Band" (December 16, 1975). Bureau Historical Collection.

82. Ibid.

83. Ibid., 1.

84. Memo to U.S. Information Agency from U.S. Information Service, N'Djamena, on "Junior Wells–Buddy Guy Blues Band" (December 16, 1975). Memo to U.S. Information Agency from U.S. Information Service, Accra, on "December Highlights" (January 19, 1976).

85. Memo to U.S. Information Agency from U.S. Information Service, Accra, on "December Highlights" (January 19, 1976), 2.

86. Memo to U.S. Information Agency from U.S. Information Service, N'Djamena, on "Junior Wells–Buddy Guy Blues Band" (December 16, 1975), 1–2.

87. Memo to Department of State, Washington, D.C., from American Embassy, Kinshasa, Zaïre (February 4, 1976). Bureau Historical Collection.

88. Memo to Department of State, Washington, D.C., from American Embassy, Dakar, Senegal, on "Guy-Wells Blues Band" (January 23, 1976). Bureau Historical Collection.

89. Memo to U.S. Information Agency from U.S. Information Service, N'Djamena, on "Junior Wells–Buddy Guy Blues Band" (December 16, 1975), 2.

90. "Cultural Presentations: List of Attractions—Newport Jazz Artists" (October 23–November 16, 1974). Bureau Historical Collection.

91. Memo to Department of State, Washington, D.C., from American Embassy, Bucharest, on "Cultural Presentations: Visit of George Wein" (May 30, 1975). Bureau Historical Collection.

92. Ibid.

93. Ibid.

94. "Cultural Presentations: List of Attractions—Newport Jazz Artists" (October 24–November 11, 1975). Bureau Historical Collection.

95. "Cultural Presentations: List of Attractions—Newport Jazz Group" (October 20–November 4, 1976). Bureau Historical Collection.

96. Wein and Jones, Interview with Von Eschen and Gaines (May 15, 2001).

97. Rachel R. Birtha, "Jolly Giants Expected to Make Big Imprint in Pakistan," PR release (February 6, 1978). Series 2, Box 28, Bureau Historical Collection.

98. Ibid.

99. Memo to American Embassies in Ankara, Cairo, Islamabad, Kabul, New Delhi, Bombay, Calcutta, Istanbul, Karachi, Lahore, Madras, Peshawar, Teheran, from Department of State, on "Clark Terry and His Jolly Giants" (January 18, 1978). Bureau Historical Collection.

100. Clark Terry, Interview with Penny Von Eschen, Chapel Hill, N.C. (February 1997).

101. Ibid. See also Clark Terry, "C.T.'s Diary," *Jazz Journal International* (May 1978), 7–8.

102. Memo to Secretary of State, Washington, D.C., from American Embassy, Islamabad, on "Clark Terry and His Jolly Giants" (March 15, 1976), Bureau Historical Collection. Terry, "Diary." Anonymous, Exciting Trip to Jazz World for Lahorites," *Pakistan Times* (February 9, 1978).

103. Terry, "C.T.'s Diary."

104. Pestonji, "Jazz Yatra '78."

105. M. Saeed Malik, "The Three Generations of Jazz," *Pakistan Times* (February 3, 1978).

106. Alyn Morgan, "Clark Terry—Jazz: A Profile," *Jazz Journal International* (May 1978), 6; and Terry, "C.T.'s Diary," 6–8.

107. The new agency combined the reduced functions of the USIA and the Department of State's Bureau of Educational and Cultural Affairs. Milton C. Cummings Jr., "Cultural Diplomacy and the United States Government: A Survey," Center for Arts and Culture, Washington, D.C. (2002), 10. An abbreviated cultural-presentations program was administered by the Office of Citizen Exchanges–Cultural Programs (Arts America) from 1978 until it was abolished in 1997. According to Juliet Antunes Sablosky, its "program included a limited performing arts touring program, tours of fine arts exhibitions, speakers on the arts and literature, and cultural specialists." See Juliet Antunes Sablosky, "Recent Trends in Department of State Support for Cultural Diplomacy, 1993–2002," Center for Arts and Culture (2003), 10.

9. Epilogue

1. Frantz Fanon, "This Africa to Come," in Fanon, *Toward the African Revolution* (New York: Grove, 1967), 178; Catherine Gunther Kodat, "Conversing with Ourselves: Canon, Freedom, Jazz," *American Quarterly,* 55, no. 1 (March 2003), 13.

2. For a related discussion of reading the paradoxes in jazz and its relationship to the nation, see Robert G. O'Meally, *The Jazz Cadence of American Culture* (New York: Columbia University Press, 1998), 177–199. See also Eric Porter, *What Is This Thing Called Jazz? African American Musicians as Artists, Critics, and Activists* (Berkeley: University of California Press, 2002), 308.

3. Earl Lewis, "To Turn as on a Pivot: Writing African Americans into a History of Overlapping Diasporas," in Darlene Clark Hine and Jacqueline McLeod, eds., *Crossing Boundaries: Comparative History of Black People in Diaspora* (Bloomington: Indiana University Press, 1999), 3–32.

4. I am indebted to Dizzy Gillespie's friend Maxine Gordon for talking with me about the meaning and implications of this meeting. On Gillespie's United Nations Orchestra, see Alyn Shipton, *Groovin' High: The Life of Dizzy Gillespie* (New York: Oxford University Press, 1999), 356–360, 361–363.

5. For a short summation of the agencies handling cultural presentations after 1978, see Milton C. Cummings Jr., "Cultural Diplomacy and the United States Government: A Survey," Center for Arts and Culture (2003), 10–12.

6. Juliet Antunes Sablosky, "Recent Trends in Department of State Support for Cultural Diplomacy, 1993–2002," Center for Arts and Culture (2003); Frank Ninkovich, "U.S. Information Policy and Cultural Diplomacy," Foreign Policy Association, Washington, D.C., Headline Series, no. 308 (1996), 34.

7. Robert McG. Thomas Jr., "Willis Conover, 75, Voice of America Disc Jockey," *New York Times* (May 19, 1996), 35. Walter Hixson, in his nuanced discussion of U.S.-Soviet cultural exchange in his book *Parting the Curtain,* rejects what he terms "the crude and parochial triumphalist perspective on the end of the Cold War." Yet, in his view, the role of culture remains decisive. For Hixson, it was not militarism but the modern version of old-fashioned idealist diplomacy, with its belief in the inevitability of "the nation serving as a model of material success and democratic values," that "ultimately proved more effective in combating the Soviet Empire." Walter L. Hixson, *Parting the Curtain: Propaganda, Culture, and the Cold War, 1945–1961* (New York, St. Martin's, 1997), 231–232.

8. Michael H. Hunt, "In the Wake of September 11: The Clash of What?" *Journal of American History,* 89, no. 2 (2000), 416–425. In the depiction of the United States as a Janus-faced power, I am drawing on Perry Anderson, "Internationalism: A Breviary," *New Left Review,* 14 (March–April 2002), 23; and on Nikhil Pal Singh, *Black Is a Country: Race and the Unfinished Struggle for Democracy* (Cambridge, Mass.: Harvard University Press, 2004), 136.

9. Irene L. Gendzier, "Play It Again, Sam: The Practice and Apology of Devel-

opment," in Christopher Simpson, ed., *Universities and Empire: Money and Politics in the Social Sciences during the Cold War* (New York: New Press, 1998), 57–95.

10. My characterization of this period draws on the work of Lisa Lowe and David Lloyd. See their introduction to Lisa Lowe and David Lloyd, eds., *The Politics of Culture in the Shadow of Capital* (Durham: Duke University Press, 1997).

11. Reinhold Wagnleitner, "The Empire of Fun, or Talkin' Soviet Union Blues: The Sound of Freedom and U.S. Cultural Hegemony in Europe," *Diplomatic History,* 23, no. 3 (Summer 1999), 499–524.

12. John Romano, paper presented at "Arts and Minds" conference, School of Journalism, Columbia University (April 15, 2003).

13. Thomas C. Holt, *The Problem of Race in the Twenty-First Century* (Cambridge, Mass.: Harvard University Press, 2000), 108–113; Walter LaFeber, *Michael Jordan and the New Global Capitalism* (New York: W. W. Norton, 1999).

Acknowledgments

I am extremely fortunate to have had the chance to talk with some of the extraordinary jazz musicians who toured for the State Department and to experience first-hand their generosity, brilliance, and critical wit. It is impossible to describe my debt to those who have shared their time and their stories. Clark Terry, Dave and Iola Brubeck, Al Grey, Jon Hendricks, Arvell Shaw, Joya Sherrill, Randy Weston, and Phil Woods shared their stories and helped me to think through the meaning of the tours and interpret the gaps and silences in the official records. Dave and Iola Brubeck opened their home and their archives when I first began this project, and have been encouraging and patient throughout the years it took shape. Clark Terry and Al Grey took time from gigs to revisit their tours as well as reflect on the meaning of the tours for the jazz world. Randy Weston demonstrated his warmth, humor, and ambassadorial skills by generously talking with students as he sorted through tour archives. Joya Sherrill, Jon Hendricks, and Arvell Shaw generously gave of their time and have been indispensable in my attempts to understand the tours. George Wein and Robert Jones were supportive collaborators, pulling insights out of the welter of recollections and trying to remember what George "was doing in the Seventies." Gail Minault and Bob Stout, colleagues at the University of Texas, shared sources and experiences from their involvement in the tours as USIS employees. Stuart Hodes's memories of dancing for Martha Graham on tour have helped shape my sense of the period and the relationship between the tours and the arts. Thomas Simons was most generous in sharing his memories of his first State Department assignment on tour with Duke Ellington. He served a dual role as historical informant and mentor, directing me to relevant scholarship and helping me to see the tours from various perspectives.

Many archivists and scholars guided me through sources and helped me to locate documents. State Department records of the tours are housed with the William Fulbright Papers at the University of Arkansas at Fayetteville; scholars concerned with these cultural programs are enormously fortunate that the records are under the stewardship of Betty Austin. Thanks also to archivists at the National

Archives in College Park, Maryland; Suzanne Engleston Lovejoy for assistance with the Benny Goodman papers at the Yale University Music Library; Michael Cogswell and Peggy Alexander, at the Louis Armstrong Archives in Queens, New York; Kay Peterson at the Smithsonian Institution in Washington; Joseph Peterson at the Institute for Jazz Studies, Rutgers University; and Don Walker, curator of the Dave Brubeck papers at the University of the Pacific, Stockton, California. I also thank Susan Cannon for assisting me with research in Austin, Texas.

Early in this project, Ingrid Monson and Paul Berliner not only taught me to listen to jazz as conversation, but, along with the late Mark Tucker, invited me to join a lively conversation of jazz scholars who have enriched the work immeasurably. I am grateful to Mark for his enthusiastic response to the "new Ellington material" and his generosity in guiding a historian and African American studies scholar without formal training in musicology or jazz studies. He and Jim Ketch invited me to participate in the University of North Carolina's jazz symposium, and introduced me to Robert O'Meally and other members of the Columbia Institute for Jazz Studies. Over the past several years, my work has benefited from dialogue and critical engagement with the Columbia jazz studies group, especially Robert O'Meally, Ingrid Monson, Farah Griffin, Robin D. G. Kelley, Diedre Harris-Kelley, Brent Edwards, Krin Gabbard, John Gennari, Maxine Gordon, Sherrie Tucker, Garnette Cadogan, and Travis Jackson. Robin Kelley supported my venture from the very beginning and facilitated my first meetings with jazz scholars in Chapel Hill and Durham, North Carolina. His exacting criticism and warm encouragement have been invaluable. I thank Brent Edwards for his brilliant readings and insights, which at various points have pushed me to think more deeply and differently about the tours and the artists. His scholarship has provided challenge and inspiration.

I knew that I had found the right editor when I first talked with Joyce Seltzer at Harvard University Press. She has brilliantly guided me in turning what was at times an unwieldy project into a book. And thanks to Maria Ascher at the Press for her expert editorial stewardship. Eric Foner, George Lipsitz, and Tim Borstelmann have all provided essential support and critical readings. I am deeply grateful to Eric Foner for his encouragement and indispensable insights. Portions of the work were presented at workshops and seminars, including the African American Workshop at Yale University, the Atlantic Studies Seminar at Rutgers University, and the Black Atlantic Conference at Purdue University. Thanks to Hazel Carby, Paul Gilroy, Michael Veal, Jonathan Holloway, Michael Hogan, William Chafe, Nell Painter, Winston James, David Hajdu, Phil Schaap, Reinhold Wagnleitner, Elaine Tyler May, Ruth Feldstein, Robert Vitalis, Chris Brown, Michael Z. Wise, Lynn Garafola, Manisha Sinha, Martha Biondi, Martha Hodes, and Barbara

Ransby. Special thanks to Nikhil Singh and Judith Jackson Fossett for enlightening conversations, inspiring wisdom, and humor.

I thank the Rockefeller Foundation for a grant that enabled me to work at the National Humanities Center in Research Triangle Park, North Carolina. Thanks to Kent Mulliken and the staff at the center for providing a year of foundational research and thinking about the book, and to T. J. Anderson, George Chauncey, and Jacqueline Hall for their warm collegiality. The research was supported in large part by three great public institutions. My first exploratory funding came from the University of Iowa; I thank my colleagues Jeff Cox, Shel Stromquist, Ken Cmiel, Colin Gordon, and Linda Kerber for their assistance. The University of Texas at Austin provided generous supplemental assistance for my year in North Carolina, as well as summer research funding. Thanks to Carolyn Boyd, Judith Coffin, Mauricio Tenorio, Neil Foley, Gunther Peck, and Kevin Kenny. More recently, the University of Michigan provided funding for writing time and research. I especially thank Vice Provost Lester Monts for facilitating that support and for his enthusiasm about Louis Armstrong and jazz. I am also grateful to my fellow participants in the Global Ethnic Literatures Seminar at the University of Michigan, especially Ann Stoler, Frieda Ekotto, Paul Anderson, and Andy Ivaska.

At the University of Michigan, I found a stimulating intellectual environment with Earl Lewis, Mamadou Diouf, Julius Scott, Arlene Keizer, Michele Mitchell, Martha Jones, Matthew Countryman, Tiya Miles, Rebecca Scott, Catherine Benamou, Magdalena Zaborowska, Sandra Gunning, David Cohen, Fred Cooper, Jane Burbank, Carol Karlsen, Robert Maclean, Jonathan Freedman, Sara Blair, Gina Morantz-Sanchez, Geoff Eley, Nancy Hunt, Brian Porter, Catherine Burns, Maria Montoya, James Cook, James Jackson, Alan Wald, Xiamara Santamarina, Phil Pochoda, Phil Deloria, Peggy Burns, Hubert Rast, and Gunter Rose. Thanks to Sonya Rose and Carroll Smith-Rosenberg for feedback on parts of the manuscript and—along with Kathleen Canning, Mary Kelley, Julia Adams, and Susan Douglas—for their friendship, their intellectual rigor, and their professional and personal integrity. Thanks especially to Magdalena Zaborowska for assistance with Polish and Russian translations, and to Phil Deloria, Mamadou Diouf, and Keith Breckenridge for reading the manuscript in its entirety.

Family members and a group of gifted educators made it possible for me to devote attention to the book and provided support, joy, and peace of mind by sharing my son Maceo's early life. Thanks above all to "Nana" Marilyn Gaines, and to Polly Cuthbert, Elaine Neelands, Kyle Krause, Maggie Mariano, Sigrid Bower, and Susan Carpenter.

This book is dedicated to my beloved family, Kevin and Maceo Gaines, who have provided endless stories, robots, comics, slow food, and music, along with unceasingly cheerful engagement with the book. Maceo has lived with the book for his entire life, singing along with "Such Sweet Thunder" and "Summer Song" and later becoming a six-year-old interrogator on everything from the book's title to the relationship between art and war. Kevin's passion for jazz and his proliferating music archive have been treasures. From his infectious enthusiasm as the project was launched, to his constant companionship in research as our parallel projects brought us to many of the same cities and archives, he has been a greater presence as critic, collaborator, and partner than I could ever acknowledge. He collaborated with me on nearly all of the interviews with musicians and other participants in the tours. His erudition, insights, and wit enlivened those conversations, as they have enriched the pages of the book and so much more. Thank you.

Index